Happy Toddler Mealtimes

Judy More

For UK order enquiries: please contact Bookpoint Ltd,
130 Milton Park, Abingdon, Oxon OX14 4SB.
Telephone: +44 (0) 1235 827720. Fax: +44 (0) 1235 400454.
Lines are open 09.00–17.00, Monday to Saturday, with a 24-hour
message answering service. Details about our titles and how to
order are available at www.teachyourself.com

Long renowned as the authoritative source for self-guided learning –
with more than 50 million copies sold worldwide – the **Teach Yourself**
series includes over 500 titles in the fields of languages, crafts, hobbies,
business, computing and education.

British Library Cataloguing in Publication Data: a catalogue record
for this title is available from the British Library.

First published in UK 2008 by Hodder Education, part of Hachette
Livre UK, 338 Euston Road, London NW1 3BH.

This edition published 2010.

Previously published as *Teach Yourself Feeding Your Toddler*.

The **Teach Yourself** name is a registered trade mark of Hodder Headline.

Typeset by MPS Limited, a Macmillan Company.

Printed in Great Britain for Hodder Education, an Hachette UK
Company, 338 Euston Road, London NW1 3BH, by CPI Cox &
Wyman, Reading, Berkshire, RG1 8EX.

The publisher has used its best endeavours to ensure that the URLs
for external websites referred to in this book are correct and active
at the time of going to press. However, the publisher and the
author have no responsibility for the websites and can make no
guarantee that a site will remain live or that the content will remain
relevant, decent or appropriate.

Hachette UK's policy is to use papers that are natural, renewable
and recyclable products and made from wood grown in sustainable
forests. The logging and manufacturing processes are expected to
conform to the environmental regulations of the country of origin.

Impression number   10 9 8 7 6 5 4 3 2 1
Year   2014 2013 2012 2011 2010

For my father, Tom Williams

....

Acknowledgements

Throughout my career I have worked with many parents, children and healthcare professionals who have influenced my understanding of childhood nutrition and how best to feed babies. I am particularly grateful to have worked with Dr Gillian Harris at the University of Birmingham whose work on fussy, faddy eating is well known and some of which is included in this book. Other health professionals whose work and collaboration has particularly influenced the content of this book are my colleagues on the expert panel of the Infant and Toddler Forum: Professor Lawrence Weaver, Dr Carina Venter, Dr Atul Singhal, Dr Robert Coombs and health visitors Carolyn Taylor and Dipti Aistrop. Dr Gillian Harris is also on this panel. I am grateful for permission to reproduce material from the factsheets that are available on the website www.infantandtoddlerforum.org.

Image credits

Front cover: © Foodcollection/Getty Images

Back cover: © Jakub Semeniuk/iStockphoto.com, © Royalty-Free/Corbis, © agencyby/iStockphoto.com, © Andy Cook/iStockphoto.com, © Christopher Ewing/iStockphoto.com, © zebicho – Fotolia.com, © Geoffrey Holman/iStockphoto.com, © Photodisc/Getty Images, © James C. Pruitt/iStockphoto.com, © Mohamed Saber – Fotolia.com

Contents

Meet the author

I have loved being a nutritionist and dietician ever since I
graduated from university having studied nutrition and dietetics.
Food quality, food choices and the health implications of what
we choose to eat is a fascinating subject. I specialized in children
about 20 years ago and worked as a paediatric dietician in
teaching hospitals and in the community. Learning through
working with psychologists, speech and language therapists,
health visitors, doctors and midwives in multidisciplinary clinics
has given me a wider view on feeding than just nutrition. Advice
on feeding toddlers needs to take account of psychology, the
way toddlers develop and parents' attitudes to food in addition
to the nutritional needs of the toddler. Feeding my own two
children and their friends and talking to hundreds of parents
about feeding their children has given me an inside view on
how different each child and family can be. I set up the Child
Nutrition consultancy (www.child-nutrition.co.uk) about ten
years ago to provide the best advice on feeding children and
dealing with today's challenges of poor diets and rising rates
of rickets and obesity. I keep abreast of the latest research on
feeding babies and children; advise food companies, nurseries,
schools and government agencies; teach students; train
healthcare professionals and write about feeding children in
addition to seeing children with their parents in a weekly clinic.

Judy More

Only got a minute?

Toddlers need very nutritious food as they are growing rapidly but have small stomachs. Feeding toddlers is not always easy as they are going through the normal stage of development called food neophobia when they are wary of eating new foods or foods they are not familiar with. Some parents find this very frustrating and may resort to cajoling, coercing and force-feeding to get their toddler to eat more food. This isn't necessary as toddlers eat well at some meals and on some days and eat less well at other times. Make it your responsibility to offer only nutritious food but always allow your toddler to choose what and how much he eats. Make mealtimes happy social occasions and take away uneaten food without comment and without showing you are upset. Over time, any fussy, faddy eating will dissipate as long as you manage mealtimes well.

For a nutritious diet offer food from each food group each day:

Food group	How much?
Bread, rice, potatoes, pasta/other starchy foods	Include at each meal, and some snacks
Fruit and vegetables	Include at each meal, and some snacks
Milk, cheese and yoghurt	Three servings per day where one serving of milk is 3–4 oz/100–120 ml
Meat, fish, eggs, nuts and pulses	Two to three servings per day
Foods high in fat and foods high in sugar	Very small amounts with meals. Limit sweet foods to four times per day
Drinks	Six to eight per day or one with each meal and snack

In addition give a daily vitamin supplement containing Vitamins A and D as most toddlers do not get enough of these vitamins from their food. The common disorders in toddlers who do not eat well are iron deficiency anaemia, dental caries, obesity and constipation. Most toddlers who have a food allergy or intolerance will grow out of it by about four years old.

Introduction

Feeding toddlers is challenging but can be fun and rewarding. Your behaviour as a parent can largely determine which way it goes. In this book I have tried to steer you towards enjoying feeding your toddler and being confident that you are feeding him/her well.

For some parents, the responsibility of feeding their toddler to make sure he/she survives and grows can seem overwhelming. You may receive lots of well-intentioned advice but some of it may be conflicting. There may be days when you despair and think you may never get it right. Just remember, there isn't only one right way to feed your toddler – you, your toddler and your lifestyle will determine what suits you both best.

I have attempted to explain the important factors in successful feeding. If you understand how your toddler learns to like and enjoy the food and meals you give him/her, then working together you should be able to find a way to achieve this.

I have included sample routines, menu plans and recipes. These are not to be followed rigidly but are there as a guide to what your toddler needs and what has worked for many other families.

There is so much more to feeding than just providing your toddler with nutrients: there is the joy of watching your toddler learn, develop and progress and the love and trust that you give and receive at each feeding experience. Try to make each meal a pleasant time, something that you both enjoy and look forward to. Always smile and praise your toddler for eating well but remember to let him/her decide how much he/she eats or drinks – your toddler knows much better than you do how much he/she needs at each meal.

For easy reading I have used 'he' and 'him' throughout this book rather than 'he/she' and 'him/her' repeatedly. However, this book applies to girls just as much as boys.

Enjoy feeding your toddler.

1

Becoming fussy about food

In this chapter you will learn:
- *how your toddler will grow and develop*
- *why toddlers can become fussy eaters*
- *why fussy eating will resolve with time*
- *how to create an environment to encourage toddlers to eat well.*

Your growing toddler

At the toddler stage, children still grow rapidly but their average weight gain is lower than that of babies under 12 months of age. Your toddler will only gain about 2 kg (4.5 lb) each year, compared with the 6.6 kg (14.5 lb) he gained during his first year. Similarly, the increase in his height will be less than the rapid increases during his first year.

Average weight and height gain (0–4 years)

Age	Weight gain (kg/year)	Height increase (cm/year)
0–12 months	6.6	25
1–2 years	2.4	12
2–3 years	2	8
3–4 years	2	7

Some parents expect the rapid growth and weight gain of the first year of life to continue. This can cause unnecessary worry that their toddler is not gaining enough weight. In fact, during the toddler years your toddler should slim down and appear thinner – this is quite normal. Toddlers continue to get slimmer and slimmer until they are about 4–5 years old. Those who do not slim down during the toddler years are at risk of becoming overweight and obese as children.

HOW OFTEN SHOULD YOU MEASURE YOUR TODDLER'S GROWTH?

Your toddler should have been weighed when he had his immunizations. After this, if all is well, he will not be measured again until he is ready to begin school. However, if you have any concerns, or if you just want some reassurance that he is growing as expected, ask your health visitor to weigh and measure him and plot the measurements on the growth charts in his Personal Child Health Record (PCHR) or 'red book'. It is important that the measurements are taken on accurate, calibrated scales, so it is best to have him measured at a health clinic by healthcare professionals.

Do not have him weighed or measured more frequently than every three months, as any changes in weight and height are very small. Toddlers can easily lose a little weight if they have been ill and they will put it back on quite quickly when they have recovered.

IS YOUR TODDLER GROWING NORMALLY?

Your toddler will be growing normally if his height and weight increase at the same rate as the centile lines on the height and weight charts in his PCHR.

In the UK, the growth charts show centile lines and centile spaces between the centile lines. The lines are marked with the number of the centile: 0.4th, 2nd, 9th, 25th, 50th, 75th, 91st, 98th or 99.6th. Sample height and weight centile charts for boys are shown in the Appendix on page 290. The height and weight of an average-sized toddler will be around the 50th centile line, but any weight or height between the 2nd and 98th centile lines is considered normal. If your toddler measures anywhere above the 98th centile, or below the 2nd centile, your health visitor may ask you to return in three months to re-check his measurements.

The height growth of a toddler is largely determined by the genes which they have inherited from their parents. Toddlers with tall parents will be taller and on a higher centile line for height than other toddlers of the same age. Likewise, toddlers with short parents will tend to be shorter and on a lower centile line for height. Normally toddlers remain on the same height centile throughout their early childhood.

Insight

Many parents worry that their toddler's adult height will be affected if he does not eat enough. But toddlers will just become very slim if they do not eat enough. Their adult height is unlikely to be affected as by this age their increase in height is under the control of growth hormones.

Your toddler will not necessarily be on the same centile line or channel for his height and weight. If your toddler is tall and slim, his weight may be on a lower centile than his height. If he is a little chubby, his weight centile may be higher than his height centile.

Remember that toddlers can grow in spurts – increases in height and weight will not always be steady and regular. There may be times when they do not gain any weight or height followed by a short period of relatively quick growth. These growth patterns can affect the size of their appetite, making it less some weeks and greater other weeks.

Case study

'I used to take Tom to be weighed almost every week when he was a baby. I found the increases in his weight very reassuring.

(Contd)

I continued this after he was one but I began to worry when some weeks he only gained a few ounces or nothing at all. Even though the health visitor said there was nothing to worry about I thought he wasn't having enough to eat. I would sit for hours with him trying to encourage him to eat more. Eventually I asked the GP if anything was wrong. He explained the charts in the back of his red book and reassured me that he was gaining weight normally even though it was less than I expected.'

Lesley

Your developing toddler

You will be amazed by your toddler's development, as he masters talking and asking questions, feeding himself and increasing his physical agility. Always encourage his progress by praising him as he masters new skills.

GAINING INDEPENDENCE

Toddlers increasingly start to assert themselves, often saying 'no' to requests and enjoying doing so. Parents tend to become more anxious when a toddler refuses food than when he refuses to wear his hat or socks. But to the toddler it is all just part of the same game – testing your reaction to his actions and exerting some control over his life.

MANAGING DIFFERENT FOOD TEXTURES

Toddlers, like babies, will only learn to manage new textures of food if given the opportunity to try them. Your young toddler should have been able to manage chopped and minced food by his first birthday. He should now be adept at biting into foods such as sandwiches and breadsticks. Offer him all the different food textures you eat as a family – although you may still need to cut up very hard foods into bite-sized pieces. As he gets older and his teeth come through, encourage him to bite into hard, whole foods such as apples and carrots.

Toddlers are different and will each have their own individual likes and dislikes in terms of flavour and texture of foods. Some toddlers like their food smothered in sauces while others prefer it dry. Some like every food kept separate from others on the plate. Many do not like stringy meat or foods that are difficult to chew. Bear this in mind and don't insist your toddler eats something he is not enjoying – this will only serve to create a negative association with that food. With time his tastes and preferences may change, so it is important to keep offering him all the foods that you and your family are eating. Make sure there is always at least one food at each meal that he enjoys eating.

Insight

Learning to manage different textures is quite a skill and most toddlers will master this quite quickly. However, some take longer and if your toddler is still spitting out lumps then it means he needs more practice at eating them. Do not stop giving the textures he can't manage but give most of his food in the textures he has already mastered.

LEARNING ABOUT FOOD THROUGH PLAY

Toddlers learn all the time through play. Your toddler will learn about foods if you allow him to play with his food. He will happily eat finger foods with his fingers but he may also like to put his hands into runny foods like yoghurt and milk puddings. This will be messy – which some parents may find hard to cope with – but it is an important learning process for your toddler.

When dropping things your toddler will notice that they fall to the floor, thus learning about the law of gravity. Sitting in a highchair is an ideal opportunity to watch objects, including his food, fall to the ground. Attempt to see it through his eyes – he is investigating and learning and not deliberately trying to make a mess for you to clear up. Try not to scold severely, even though it is obviously an activity you will need to discourage. Always make mealtimes pleasant and not a time when you are excessively scolding; smile and praise behaviour you want to encourage and ignore behaviour you don't want him to repeat.

Figure 1.1 Dropping food is a learning process!

Insight

I have noticed that toddlers who are always fed on their own usually display very poor eating behaviours such as throwing food on the floor. Toddlers need to be included in family meals with their parents and siblings to learn that other people do not throw food around when they are eating.

SELF-FEEDING AND CUTLERY

As a baby, your toddler should have learnt to feed himself with finger foods. By around 15 months he should be able to hold a spoon well – although he may not be able to hold it level and steady between the plate and his mouth (and the food may fall off!).

You will need to help your young toddler feed himself as he may not be able to eat as quickly as he would like, especially when he is very hungry. But at the same time make sure he is involved in feeding himself so that he will continue to learn and acquire new skills; always give him some finger foods at each meal but also give him a spoon or fork so that he can learn to feed himself the non-finger foods that are soft or semi-liquid.

Developing your toddler's feeding skills

▶ *At around 15 months he should be able to hold and use a spoon.*
▶ *By 18 months he should be able to suck from a straw.*
▶ *At around three years he should be able to use a knife to cut soft foods.*
▶ *At around four years he should be able to use a knife and fork to feed himself. Toddlers in traditional Asian families should have mastered chopsticks at this age.*

Becoming fussy about food

Sometime during his second year you will begin to notice that your toddler is becoming quite choosy about what he will eat and will not eat. It may be most noticeable around the time he is about 18 months old, but can begin any time in this second year. Your toddler may:

▶ *eat less than you expect him to*
▶ *refuse to taste new foods you offer*
▶ *refuse to eat certain foods, including some he has previously eaten well.*

There are many reasons why toddlers refuse foods – or even a whole meal – and anxious parents may worry unnecessarily about this. Toddlers are very good at eating as much as they need and you should always allow him to decide how much to eat. Coercing him to eat more – or force-feeding – are negative ways to treat your toddler. Ideally each meal should be an enjoyable occasion for all of you, no matter how much he eats.

WHY MOST YOUNG TODDLERS BECOME FUSSY EATERS

Young toddlers become fussy because they are entering a normal stage in their development where they become wary of trying new foods. It is called a neophobic response to food; neophobia means 'fear of new'.

This stage of food neophobia develops soon after toddlers start to walk. They become more adept at getting about and can roam further to investigate their environment. This fear of new foods is probably a survival mechanism to prevent mobile young toddlers from harming themselves through eating anything and everything; if they were to taste any interesting-looking berry on a bush they could poison themselves.

Once the neophobic stage begins, your toddler is likely to refuse to try tasting a new food he is not familiar with. He will take much longer to learn to like and eat new foods than he did as a baby.

▶ *He may need to watch others eating a food that is new to him several times before he becomes confident to try it himself.*
▶ *He may take much longer to learn to like a new food, tasting just a little each time you include it in a meal. It is the number of times he tastes the new food – and not the amount he eats – that will determine the length of time it takes for him to learn to like the food.*

HOW COMMON IS FUSSY EATING?

As a recognized and specific part of development, all young toddlers will go through this stage – however, it will be more evident in some than others. If your toddler was happily eating a wide range of most of your family meals by the start of his second year, you will continue to offer foods that he is already familiar with and you may not notice this stage. Fussy eating will be more evident in toddlers who have only been offered a narrow range of foods before this phase of food neophobia begins. This will include toddlers who, as babies, were mainly fed on commercial baby foods and who did not eat many family foods during weaning. These young toddlers may restrict themselves to a very small range of foods. Parents of very fussy toddlers may become quite exasperated and worry that their toddler is not eating enough and not getting enough nutrients to grow and develop.

Older toddlers, from around three years, may refuse foods for other reasons, for example:

▶ *Toddlers are beginning to associate things that look similar, so he may associate a food with an inanimate object that he finds disgusting. He may think noodles look like worms or sausages look like dog poo. He will be unable to bring himself to eat a food that reminds him of something unpalatable.*
▶ *The food looks slightly different from the food he is familiar with:*
  ▷ *a piece of apple has a mark on the skin*
  ▷ *a yoghurt is a different colour or in a different carton*
  ▷ *a biscuit is broken, not whole.*
▶ *A food he likes may be contaminated with a food he dislikes, or is wary of. If a food he dislikes is touching – or just on the same plate as – food he usually eats, he may be reluctant to eat any of the food (including the food that he likes).*

FUSSY AND FADDY EATING NORMALLY RESOLVES WITH TIME

Over time almost all toddlers will grow out of this neophobic phase. Toddlers learn by copying their parents, siblings and peers. When eating with you and others, your toddler will notice which foods you are eating and he will learn that these foods are safe to eat. With time – and seeing you eating them a few times – he will become confident to taste those foods. He may want to try foods from your plate rather than his own. He needs to taste new foods several times to reassure himself that he likes them. Some toddlers need to be offered a new food ten or more times before they learn to like it.

By the same learning process, if he sees a sibling or parent refusing certain foods he may also refuse those foods.

Figure 1.2 Your toddler will copy your eating habits and tastes.

ENCOURAGING YOUR TODDLER TO LIKE NEW FOODS

Toddlers learn by:

▶ *watching adults and other children*
▶ *receiving praise and encouragement for desired behaviour*
▶ *being ignored when their behaviour is undesirable*
▶ *their parents being firm and consistent*
▶ *their parents setting boundaries and sticking to them.*

To help your toddler through this stage of food neophobia, eat together as a family as often as possible so that he will learn to eat the foods you are eating. If he is looked after by a nanny or an au pair for long periods then ask this carer to eat with him, eating the same foods that he is being offered.

Top tips

▶ *Set a good example yourself – eat the foods you would like your toddler to eat and make only positive comments about them.*

▶ *Allow him plenty of time to become familiar with new foods – do not force him to try new foods before he is ready. If he will not even try the new food, then wait and offer it again when you are next eating it.*

▶ *When he is happy to taste new or unfamiliar foods, let him have as little as he chooses to. He will learn to like new foods by having small tastes each time you or others are eating them. He does not need to eat large quantities of them.*

▶ *Praise him when he tries a food he hasn't eaten before.*

▶ *Do not show that you are upset or disappointed when he does not taste or eat a food you have offered him.*

Chapters 6 and 7 discuss how to cope with fussy, faddy eating when it becomes a problem.

Other reasons for refusing to eat

Not all food refusal will be due to this phase of food neophobia. Young toddlers may also be reluctant to eat well for other reasons. As your toddler cannot explain to you why he doesn't want to eat, you will have to determine the reason yourself. He will signal to you quite clearly when he has had enough.

Your toddler is saying he does not want more food when he:

▶ *refuses to eat*
▶ *says 'no' when you encourage him to eat*

(Contd)

- ▶ *keeps his mouth shut when food is offered*
- ▶ *turns his head away from the food being offered*
- ▶ *puts his hand in front of his mouth*
- ▶ *pushes away a spoon, bowl or plate containing food*
- ▶ *holds food in his mouth and refuses to swallow it*
- ▶ *spits out food repeatedly*
- ▶ *cries, shouts or screams when you try to feed him*
- ▶ *tries to climb out of his high chair*
- ▶ *gags or retches when given food.*

There are several possible reasons why your toddler does not want any more food.

HE IS NO LONGER HUNGRY

- ▶ *He may have already eaten enough to satisfy his hunger at that meal. Many parents overestimate how much food their toddler needs and expect him to eat more than he needs. A toddler's appetite may also vary from day to day depending on how active he has been and on how he is feeling at the time. Appetite will also vary due to growth spurts; his energy needs vary from time to time and there will be periods when he eats more or eats less than his usual amount.*
- ▶ *If he grazes on food between meals because there is no set meal pattern, he may not be very hungry at mealtimes. Make sure there is a set meal and snack routine so that he is not eating or drinking too close to a mealtime.*
- ▶ *If he takes a lot of calories from drinks, such as too much milk or large volumes of juices and squashes, he will be less hungry at meals times. Some toddlers prefer to do this as they find drinking easier than the effort involved in eating. If this is the case you will need to cut back on such drinks and encourage water as a drink instead. If he is still waking and drinking milk during the night you will need to phase out these milk drinks.*

Insight
Parents often tell me that they believe they should decide how much their toddler eats. They find it very difficult to accept that their toddler knows better than them how much he needs to eat.

HE DOESN'T LIKE THE TASTE OF THAT FOOD

Each toddler has his own taste preferences. Taste buds are very sensitive and change with time as he learns to like new foods. However, there will always be certain flavours of a few foods that your toddler may never learn to like.

HE MAY BE BORED WITH THE MEAL OR THAT COURSE BECAUSE HIS ATTENTION SPAN IS SHORT

A toddler's attention span is fairly short and he may become bored if the meal goes on too long for him. This does not necessarily mean he has had enough to eat, and he may be happy to try a second course of different foods which will be more interesting for him. Always offer two courses: a savoury course followed by a pudding. It gives two chances for calories and nutrients to be eaten. Make sure puddings are delicious and nutritious, by choosing those based on some fruit and containing other nutritious ingredients such as flour, milk, eggs and ground or chepped nuts.

HE MAY BE BORED IF HE IS NOT INVOLVED IN FEEDING HIMSELF

A toddler needs to be involved in touching the food and learning to feed himself. If he is expected to sit still and be fed by an adult, he will quickly lose interest in the meal. Allow him to touch his food, feed himself finger foods and give him his own spoon so that he can join in and feed himself.

HE IS DISTRACTED BY TOYS, GAMES, TV OR A NEW ENVIRONMENT

A toddler can only concentrate on one thing at a time and, if something else distracts him, he will stop eating. If you are out he may be more curious about his new environment, or the people there, than the meal. One lost meal won't matter – he will probably eat more at the next meal or snack that you offer on familiar ground.

HE IS TOO TIRED TO EAT

If you offer meals just before a daytime sleep or just before bedtime, your toddler may be too tired to summon the effort to eat. After a very busy time or a day full of new experiences he may be just too exhausted to eat well in the evening. In general, try and avoid meals too close to bedtime or a daytime sleep. When this is unavoidable, offer a quick snack and a drink of milk and give a more substantial meal later, when he has had a sleep and is wide-awake and alert.

If he goes to bed having had very little for his last meal of the day, he may make up for this by having a larger-than-normal breakfast the next day.

Insight

I remember battling with my first child to encourage her to eat my lovingly prepared meal just before her afternoon sleep. It always ended with me feeling frustrated and it took me a while to realize a change of timing was all that was needed for us to remain friends.

HE IS TOO MISERABLE BECAUSE HE HAS BECOME OVER-HUNGRY

Toddlers do not realize why they are miserable. If your toddler has gone too long since his last meal he will just know that he is miserable – he will not be aware that by eating he would begin to feel better. Having a set routine of regular mealtimes will avoid this – however, life does not always go to plan.

HE IS FEELING UNWELL

Your toddler may have a sore throat, be getting a cold or fighting an infection but doesn't yet have the symptoms of a temperature or runny nose for you to be aware that he is feeling unwell. Appetite is usually reduced when a child has a temperature. Painful gums during teething will also reduce his appetite. You will know the feeling of not being hungry a day or so before getting a heavy cold or flu – just remember, your toddler is not able to explain this to you. If you insist that he tries to eat, you will be making him more miserable. You also run the risk of putting him off the food, as in the future he may associate that food with feeling miserable.

HE IS CONSTIPATED

This situation may have developed because of poor eating and drinking but there may also be a physical reason why he is constipated. You will probably be aware that your toddler is constipated because he will strain a lot when passing a stool and may also cry with the pain. Constipation reduces appetite and coercing a constipated toddler to eat more will be a lost cause. Inadequate fluid and/or inadequate fibre are common causes. You may need to ask your doctor to treat the constipation first before you can encourage him to eat better. See Chapter 9, page 185, for more on preventing and treating constipation.

HE HAS IRON DEFICIENCY ANAEMIA

Toddlers who are not eating enough iron-rich foods and become anaemic usually have a poor appetite. You may also notice that your toddler is tired and often miserable, picking up colds and other infections frequently. If necessary, your GP can arrange for your toddler to have a blood test for anaemia; if your toddler tests positive for anaemia, the usual treatment is an iron supplement. As he gets better, make sure you are offering iron-rich foods at each meal (see Chapter 9, page 174, for a table of iron-rich foods).

HE HAS REFLUX

Although reflux is fairly common in babies, most have grown out of it by 12 months of age. However, in some toddlers it may persist longer, continuing to cause discomfort and pain when eating, as the food mixed with stomach acid comes back up into the oesophagus. Mealtimes will become unpleasant for your toddler and his appetite will reduce. If you suspect that your toddler is suffering from reflux, talk to your GP who may refer you for simple tests at your local hospital.

HE IS ANXIOUS AT MEALTIMES

Your toddler may be anxious because he has had negative experiences at mealtimes. The negative experience may involve him having been force-fed or pressured to eat something he didn't like or was scared of. Alternatively, the negative experiences may involve others if there is a lot of tension, shouting or arguing at mealtimes. Whatever the cause of his anxiety, as mealtimes approach, he may lose his appetite.

HE IS SAD, LONELY OR INSECURE

Toddlers need to be loved and to interact and socialize with others. It is not known why neglected toddlers who are not loved and stimulated through social interaction grow less than expected, but research studies have shown that this happens.

Your toddlers will not eat well if he:

- *is not hungry*
- *is bored with the food or because he is not involved in feeding himself*
- *does not like the taste of the food*
- *is tired*
- *is distracted by toys, games, TV or a new environment*
- *is anxious, sad, lonely or insecure*
- *is feeling unwell*
- *has a medical problem such as constipation, anaemia or gastro-oesophageal reflux.*

Creating a positive feeding environment for your toddler

- *Make sure you toddler can sit comfortably with his feet on the ground or supported on the foot bar of a high chair.*
- *Give him cutlery for toddlers that he can hold comfortably.*
- *Keep an open mind about how much your toddler needs to eat – he knows this better than you do.*

- *Eat together as a family – toddlers learn by copying you.*
- *Limit mealtimes to suit the attention span of your toddler – about 20 minutes is enough.*
- *Give him small portions and offer him more if he finishes the first portion.*
- *Eat in a calm, relaxed manner without distractions such as TV, games and toys so that he can concentrate on eating.*
- *Allow your toddler plenty of control over how much and what he eats by giving him finger foods to feed himself and allowing him to try spoon-feeding himself.*
- *Allow him to play with his food and make a mess.*
- *Give your toddler attention when he eats and praise him for eating well when he finishes.*

Ensure you smile with encouragement whenever you offer food. This is especially important if you are offering a food that is new to your toddler or a food you don't like yourself and you are concerned your child might not like. If you don't smile to conceal your concern, your child may sense your anxiety and consequently become reluctant to try the food.

Be positive. Make each meal a pleasant and sociable occasion that you, your toddler and the rest of the family enjoy. It is up to you to teach your children that eating is one of life's great pleasures and not something to be endured. If one meal turns into a disaster, don't feel guilty. Put it behind you and approach the next meal positively. Parents also learn by making mistakes. Nobody should expect to be a perfect parent.

HAVE A ROUTINE OF MEALS AND SNACKS

A regular pattern of meals and snacks has advantages because toddlers:

- *love ritual, routine and predictability – it helps them to feel safe and content*
- *do not eat well if they are tired or over-hungry.*

Give both a savoury and sweet course at meals. This gives two opportunities for nutrients to be consumed and increases the variety of foods he eats. Puddings are a valuable part of the meal and should not be used as a reward for eating the savoury course.

Toddlers are busy and active and can become tired very quickly. Organize a feeding routine around your toddler's daytime sleeps so that you don't feed him when he is tired or has gone too long without eating so that he is over-hungry. Snacks evenly spaced between meals will help to avoid the frustrations of being over-hungry. Here are two examples of feeding routines (depending on the number of daytime sleeps your toddler has).

Routine 1: for toddlers who have one daytime sleep

Early morning	Wakes – no milk feed
7.00am	Breakfast: cereal with milk; fruit; a drink. Or egg and toast; cup of diluted fruit juice
9.30am	Snack and drink
12.30pm	Light lunch: savoury course; fruit; cup of water
1.30pm	Sleeps for 1–2 hours
3.30pm	Snack and cup of milk
6.00pm	Tea: savoury course; milk-based pudding with fruit; cup of water
Evening	Bedtime routine: no milk feed

Routine 2: for toddlers who have two daytime sleeps

Early morning	Wakes – no milk feed
7.00am	Breakfast: cereal with milk; fruit; a drink. Or egg and toast; cup of diluted fruit juice
9.30am	Snack and drink

10.30am	Sleeps for 1–1.5 hours
12.00 midday	Lunch: savoury course; milk-based pudding with fruit; cup of water
2.30pm	Sleeps for 1–1.5 hours
4.00pm	Snack and cup of milk
6.30pm	Tea: savoury course; cake-style pudding with fruit; cup of water
Evening	Bedtime routine: no milk feed

Summary of dos and don'ts for feeding toddlers

Do...	Reason
Eat with your toddler as often as possible.	Toddlers learn by copying their parents and other children.
Develop a daily routine of three meals and two to three snacks around his sleeping pattern.	Toddlers don't eat well if they become over-hungry or very tired.
Check that your toddler isn't drinking too much milk – no large bottles of milk and no more than three 100–120 ml (3–4 oz) cups each day.	Too much milk will fill him up and leave him with little appetite for food.
Check that he is not drinking large quantities of fruit juice or other sweet drinks.	These will decrease his appetite for food.
Offer two courses at meals: one savoury course followed by a sweet course.	This gives two opportunities for him to take in the calories and nutrients needed and offers a wider variety of foods. It also makes the meal more interesting.

(Contd)

Do...	Reason
Always offer something you know your toddler will eat at each meal. In addition offer the foods you and others are eating.	Your toddler will be able to eat and enjoy some food while having the opportunity to become more familiar with other foods that you and others are eating.
Praise him when he eats well.	Toddlers respond positively to praise.
Make positive comments about the food.	Parents and carers are strong role models. If you make positive comments about foods, toddlers will be more willing to try them.
Offer finger foods as often as possible.	Toddlers enjoy having the control of feeding themselves with finger foods.
Eat in a calm, relaxed environment without distractions such as TV, games and toys.	Toddlers concentrate on one thing at a time. Distractions make it more difficult to concentrate on eating.
Finish the meal within about 20–30 minutes and accept that after this your toddler is not going to eat any more.	Carrying the meal on for too long is unlikely to result in him eating much more. It is better to wait for the next snack or meal and offer nutritious foods then.
Take away uneaten food without comment.	Accept that he has eaten enough.
Learn to recognize the signs that he has had enough to eat.	You will understand when he tells you that he has eaten enough.

Don't...	Reason
Insist that your toddler finishes everything on his plate or pressure him to eat more when he has indicated to you that he has had enough.	Toddlers should be allowed to eat to their appetite and parents and carers should respect this.
Take away a refused meal and offer a completely different one in its place.	He will soon take advantage if you do this. In the long run it is better to offer family meals and accept that he will prefer some foods to others. Always try to offer one food at each meal that you know he will eat.
Offer the sweet course as reward.	You will make the sweet course seem more desirable.
Offer large drinks of milk, squash or fruit juice within an hour of the meal.	Large drinks will reduce your toddler's appetite for the meal. Give water instead.
Offer snacks just before a meal.	The snacks will stop him feeling hungry enough for the food you are offering at the meal.
Give a snack very soon after a meal.	Many parents may do this if he hasn't eaten well at the meal just to ensure that their toddler has eaten something. However, it is best to have a set meal pattern and wait until the next snack or meal before offering food again.
Assume that because he has refused a food he will never eat it again.	Tastes change with time. Some toddlers need to be offered a new food more than ten times before they feel confident to try it.
Feel guilty if one meal turns into a disaster.	Put it behind you and approach the next meal positively. Parents also learn by making mistakes.

Dee has two daughters, Emma and Harriet. 'I treated them both exactly the same around food. Emma ate fairly well as a baby but became very fussy about food as a toddler. She would hardly eat anything and I used to worry that she wasn't eating the right things. When Harriet arrived just after Emma's second birthday I was too distracted with a new baby to worry too much about Emma's fussiness. Harriet is completely different to Emma in her attitude to food. Right from when I began weaning her, Harriet loved all food and would eat just about everything. She has always been like that, while Emma continues to be fussy and faddy with all food. Emma seems to eat less than Harriet but at four and six they are both really healthy. It's still frustrating to see Emma just pick at her food, though.'

TEST YOURSELF

1   *How much weight do toddlers gain each year?*

2   *Is this more, less or a lot less than babies in their first year?*

3   *How often do toddlers need to weighed and measured?*

4   *How do you know when your toddler is growing normally?*

5   *Is it normal or abnormal for toddlers to become fussy about the food they eat?*

6   *Is fussy eating evident in all toddlers?*

7   *Should the parent or the toddler decide how much the toddler should eat?*

8   *How does a toddler indicate to his parent/carer that he has had enough to eat?*

9   *What are the main reasons why a toddler may refuse to eat?*

10   *Why should you encourage your toddler to feed himself?*

2

Nutrients – what growing and developing toddlers need

In this chapter you will learn:
- *the nutrients that your toddler needs*
- *why he needs them*
- *which foods provide these nutrients*
- *the division of food into food groups, based on the nutrients they contain.*

What your toddler needs from food

Your toddler needs a combination of nutrients from his food, all of which perform different roles in his body. They combine together in a variety of ways to promote his growth and development and to boost his immune system so that he remains healthy and can fight off infections and illnesses.

Toddlers are growing at a fast pace compared with older children, and to support this growth they need more energy and nutrients per kilogram of their body weight than older children and adults. Toddlers need about 95 calories for every kilogram they weigh, whereas adults only need about one third of this – that is about 30–35 calories for every kilogram they weigh. At the same time, toddlers need larger amounts of most nutrients per kilogram of their body weight than adults. As toddlers' stomachs are quite small, they need very nutritious foods at all meals and snacks to ensure a good intake of nutrients.

A routine of two or three nutritious snacks in addition to three meals each day will help to give your toddler all the calories and nutrients he needs, in food portions that he can manage comfortably. It is important not to give toddlers only the low-fat, high-fibre foods which are recommended for a healthy, balanced diet for older children and adults. Too many high-fibre foods can make him feel full and could reduce the amount of food, and therefore energy and nutrients, he eats.

Nutrients: what are they and why does your toddler need them?

PROTEIN

Proteins are needed for building and maintaining all the cells in the body. Toddlers are creating vast numbers of new cells as they grow, and they need extra protein for this. Protein is made up of long chains of amino acids linked together. Some amino acids can be made by our body (non-essential amino acids), but others cannot and are called essential amino acids as we must get them from food. All the essential amino acids we need are found in protein in animal foods such as milk, eggs, meat and fish. Proteins in plant-based foods contain some of, but not all, the essential amino acids. The combination of a starchy food, such as bread, pasta, potatoes or rice, together with pulses or nuts will provide all the essential amino acids together. Examples of this are baked beans on toast, rice and peas, lentil soup and bread, or a hummus or peanut butter sandwich.

CARBOHYDRATE

Carbohydrates provide your toddler with energy and fibre. The energy comes from the starches and sugars. The body changes them into glucose which is used by the cells for energy. The brain can only use glucose for energy.

FIBRE

This is the term for the particular types of carbohydrates that are not digested in the small intestine for absorption into the blood. They stay in the small intestines and pass right through. They help the digestive system to work properly, preventing constipation and diarrhoea.

Prebiotics are the types of fibre that encourage the growth of good bacteria in the intestine. Prebiotic fibre is found in vegetables such as onions and leeks, garlic and bananas.

Probiotics are not fibre but are the bacteria in food that will colonize the intestine and provide health benefits. Beneficial bacteria in the intestine help the intestine to function optimally and may help to prevent diarrhoea in toddlers. Examples are bifidobacteria and lactobacicilli that are found in live yoghurt.

FAT

Most foods contain some fat but in certain foods there are only very small amounts. There are different types of fat, all of which provide the body with energy. Fat can be:

▶ *saturated*
▶ *monounsaturated*

- *polyunsaturated*
- *complex, such as cholesterol.*

The fat in foods is a mixture of all the types of fat, but certain foods have more of one type that the others. Complex fats such as cholesterol account for a very small proportion of the fat in foods.

Saturated fat
Most of the fat in meat, butter, cream, milk, cheese, coconut and palm oil is saturated fat. Processed commercial foods such as biscuits, cakes, pastries and ready meals also contain a lot of saturated fat as hydrogenated fat. This is because hydrogenating unsaturated fats to change them into saturated fat extends the shelf life of the foods because saturated fat is less likely to go 'off' than unsaturated fat.

Trans fats
The trans fats found naturally in milk and milk products are not harmful, whereas the trans fats found in processed food are now known to raise cholesterol in the same way as an excess of saturated fat.

Unsaturated fats: monounsaturated and polyunsaturated
Most vegetable oils, nuts and seeds contain more monounsaturated and polyunsaturated fat than saturated fat.

Essential fats: omega 3 and omega 6 fats
There are two key essential polyunsaturated fats that the body cannot make. These are omega 3 and omega 6 fats. A good balance of these two fats is vital for your growing toddler. Plant foods provide these essential fats in a shorter chain form and our body converts them to a long chain form to use in the cells in our body. Food from animal sources provides these essential fats directly in the long chain form.

Names and food sources of the essential omega 3 and omega 6 fats

		Omega 3 fats	Omega 6 fats
Short chain form (from plants)	**Names**	ALA (alpha-linolenic acid)	LA (linolenic acid)
	Main food sources	▶ walnuts, linseeds, and their oils ▶ rapeseed oil ▶ olive oil and soya oil have smaller amounts	▶ all nuts, seeds and vegetable oils
Long chain form (from animal foods)	**Names**	EPA (eicosapentaenoic acid) DHA (docosahexaenoic acid)	GLA (gamma linolenic acid) AA (arachidonic acid)
	Main food sources	▶ best source is oily fish* ▶ other sources are red meat and egg yolk, depending on how the animals and chickens are fed**	▶ fish, meat and egg yolk

*Oily fish include: salmon, mackerel, trout, fresh tuna, sardines, pilchards and eel.
**Animals that have grazed on grass, rather than been fed on cereals, have higher amounts of omega 3 in their meat. Chickens raised on a special feed high in omega 3 fats will produce eggs with yolks that are a good source of omega 3 fats.

The long chain form of omega 3 is particularly needed for the growing brain, the nervous system and for good vision. Babies can only make limited amounts of the long chain form and rely on getting plenty of long chain omega 3 in breast milk or infant formula, as well as some oily fish during weaning. Toddlers should be able to make adequate amounts of the long chain form, even if they eat a vegetarian diet without fish. However, some research shows that children who regularly eat oily fish a couple of times per week and have a good intake of omega 3 fat in the long chain form are less likely to get asthma.

Balancing omega 3 and omega 6 fats in toddlers' diets
Up until about 50 years ago, our diet had roughly equal quantities of these two essential fats, but nowadays we eat a much higher proportion of omega 6 fats and very little omega 3 fats. This change is thought to be one of the factors causing increased rates of allergy, asthma and hay fever in children.

Insight

There is a lot of talk about omega 3 fats at present and many supplements containing them have come onto the market. It is better to give your toddler oily fish each week rather than supplements.

VITAMINS

Vitamins are chemicals that we need for the proper functioning of our body, but we cannot make them ourselves. They are made by certain plants, animals or bacteria and so we must eat those plant and animal foods to obtain the vitamins. The bacteria in our intestines provide two of the vitamins – vitamin K and vitamin B_{12}.

Vitamins A, D, E and K are fat-soluble vitamins and are found within the oils and fats in some foods. When we eat plenty of these vitamins we can store reasonable amounts of them in our body. Vitamin C and the B vitamins are water soluble and any excess amounts of them that we eat are excreted in urine. The stores of these vitamins that we can build up are much smaller and having them regularly in our diet is more crucial.

Vitamin A comes in two forms: retinol in some animal foods (full-fat milk, butter, margarine, egg yolks and liver) and carotene in fruits and vegetables. Carotene is the orange colour in fruits and vegetables and it is also present in dark green vegetables such as spinach and broccoli.

Vitamin A is very important for growth and development as well as vision. As an antioxidant it is part of the immune system helping to prevent infections and illness. It is a crucial vitamin for toddlers and about one in two toddlers do not eat enough vitamin A, which is why the Department of Health recommend a daily supplement for all toddlers. In the developing world many toddlers have impaired vision due to a deficiency of vitamin A; fortunately this deficiency is not seen in the UK.

Excess vitamin A taken as retinol in too many vitamin supplements could be a problem for toddlers as excess amounts are stored in the body and this could cause liver and bone damage, hair loss and other abnormalities. Liver is very high in vitamin A now that animal feed is enriched with it. The Food Standards Agency recommends that toddlers and the rest of the family should only consume liver once per week.

B vitamins are thiamine, folate (or folic acid), niacin (nicotinamide), riboflavin, pyridoxine, biotin, pantothenic acid and vitamin B12.

They are all important for growth and development of a healthy nervous system, and are needed to convert food into energy. Vitamin B12 and folate are important for preventing types of anaemia. Good sources include meat, milk products, fish, eggs, cereals, seeds and vegetables. Dark green vegetables are high in folate.

Vitamin C is also known as ascorbic acid. It is essential for the immune system, for increasing the iron absorption from plant foods, protecting cells from damage and for maintaining blood vessels, cartilage, muscle and bone. Vitamin C is also involved in wound healing. A severe deficiency causes scurvy, where gums become swollen and bleed, teeth become loose, skin is dry and bruises easily, old wounds reopen and pain in joints and bones is experienced.

Vitamin D is sometimes called the sunshine vitamin as most vitamin D is made in our skins when we are outside in daylight in the summer months. We need to build a store of this vitamin during the summer months to last us through the winter as very few foods contain vitamin D – oily fish is the best source. Margarines, formula milks and one or two breakfast cereals are fortified with vitamin D. Meat and egg yolks contain tiny amounts.

Although it is important not to let your toddler's skin burn in the sunshine, it is important for them to spend time outside every day in summer in order to make plenty of vitamin D and build up a good store. Sunscreens prevent vitamin D being made in the skin so they should only be used to prevent sunburn when your toddler is outside for extended periods in the middle of the day. If he is unlikely to burn then allow him some time in the sunshine without applying sunscreen.

Vitamin D is crucial for the absorption of calcium from food and for depositing calcium and other minerals into bone to give it strength. It is also a key vitamin in the immune system. Many toddlers have low vitamin D levels and rickets, the disease which causes soft misshapen bones, is unfortunately on the increase in toddlers in the UK. Those most at risk are those with dark skins as they need longer in the sun to make enough vitamin D.

Because this vitamin is so crucial for young children, a daily supplement is recommended for all toddlers. It used to be taken in cod liver oil, but vitamin drops are now recommended (see Chapter 3, page 65).

Insight

Many parents are surprised that even toddlers who eat well need a vitamin D supplement. It is our mainly indoor lifestyles that have created this need. Because we now spend less time outside compared to previous generations we don't make enough vitamin D in our skins.

Vitamin E is an important antioxidant that protects cell structures in the body. It is found in many foods such as vegetable oils, butter and margarines, meat, fish and eggs. Toddlers usually have plenty of vitamin E in their food.

Vitamin K is needed to ensure normal blood clotting and is provided mostly by the bacteria in the intestine. Green leafy vegetables are the best food source of vitamin K.

MINERALS

Minerals are also needed for our bodies to function properly. They are found in varying quantities in plants and animal foods. By eating the right combination of foods, we will get the minerals in the appropriate amounts that we need.

Calcium is needed to build strong healthy bones and teeth. It is also needed for many key functions in the body, and the calcium in bone acts as a store so that there is always a ready supply enabling the muscles, including the heart, to contract and the nerves and cells to function as necessary. Milk, cheese and yoghurt are the best sources. Soya beans are a reasonable source of calcium but soya milk needs to be fortified with extra calcium to provide the same amounts as cows' milk. White bread has been fortified with calcium since the 1940s and tinned fish with edible bones – such as sardines – is another good source.

Copper is involved in energy and protein production. It is found in tiny amounts in all foods, and toddlers will get enough from their daily diet.

Fluoride strengthens tooth enamel and makes it resistant to attack by the bacteria that cause tooth decay. A smear of fluoride toothpaste (containing 1000 ppm of fluoride) on a toothbrush twice a day for teeth cleaning usually provides enough. In order to retain the fluoride in the toothpaste in their mouth, toddlers should not rinse their mouths out with water after brushing. There are areas of the UK where tap water contains significant amounts of fluoride – either because fluoride has been added or the water naturally contains high levels of fluoride. However, there are large areas of the UK where water does not contain adequate fluoride. In these areas dentists may recommend fluoride drops for toddlers. Ask your dentist for advice before beginning these drops, as giving a toddler too much fluoride can cause permanent brown spots on teeth.

Insight

Toddlers over three years of age can have more toothpaste – a pea-sized amount with 1350–1500 ppm of fluoride.

Iodine forms part of the hormone thyroxine, which has several key roles in the body: converting food into energy and enabling growth and physical and mental development. Iodine deficiency is common in some areas of Europe but is not often seen in toddlers in the UK. This may be because the amount of iodine in the soil in the UK is adequate. Good sources of iodine in foods in the UK are fish, milk, yoghurt and eggs.

Iron is part of the structure of haemoglobin, the chemical that carries oxygen to all the cells in the body via the blood. Oxygen is needed by cells to produce energy. Many toddlers do not eat enough iron, and anaemia due to iron deficiency is common among toddlers in the UK. It causes tiredness, delayed growth and development and more illness, as iron is also part of the immune system. Poor appetite is another consequence that creates a vicious circle as less iron will be eaten by a toddler with a poor appetite. See Chapter 9, page 173 for more information on iron deficiency anaemia.

Iron in food is found in two forms:

▶ *haem iron, which is readily absorbed – good sources are red meat such as beef, lamb, pork, dark poultry meat such as chicken legs and thighs, and oily fish*
▶ *non-haem iron, which is poorly absorbed unless vitamin C is present – good sources of non-haem iron are pulses, nuts, fortified breakfast cereals and some vegetables.*

Magnesium is also involved in the process of converting food into energy as well as building bone and protein production.

The best sources are wholegrain bread and breakfast cereals, milk and yoghurt. Other good sources are meat, eggs, pulses and some vegetables.

Phosphorus forms the main structure of bones along with calcium. It is found in milk, but unlike calcium it is also found in most other foods, so toddlers will usually have plenty in their food.

Potassium plays a key role in fluid balance, muscle contractions and proper nerve function. The best sources are milk, fruit, vegetables, cocoa and chocolate.

Selenium is an antioxidant and plays a role in the production of the thyroid hormone as well as energy production. The best sources for toddlers are bread, meat, fish, eggs and other foods made from flour. Brazil nuts and cashew nuts are particularly rich in selenium – but only give them to toddlers as chopped nuts, not whole nuts.

The amount of selenium in the soil determines how much is in the food grown on that soil. Selenium levels in UK soil are on the low side compared with the United States where levels are higher.

Sodium plays a key role in fluid balance and maintaining blood pressure. Toddlers will get enough sodium from bread, milk, meat and fish. Salt contains sodium and too much salt can raise blood pressure in adults, creating a higher risk of heart disease. Toddlers will have too much salt if they eat a lot of processed snack foods and ready meals which all have added salt. Older children who eat too much salt are likely to have blood pressure that is higher than normal for their age.

Zinc helps wounds heal and is part of the immune system. In toddlers it is important for growth as it is part of two hormones: the growth hormone and insulin. The best food sources are meat, fish, milk and eggs. Bread and breakfast cereals are also good sources.

Other phytonutrients include antioxidants that are the brightly coloured pigments in plant foods; that is in fruits, vegetables, spices, herbs, nuts, cocoa beans and foods made from cereals. Tea and coffee also contain them but these drinks are not recommended for toddlers. They are called a variety of names including flavanoids, flavanols, isoflavones. We have only become aware of their importance to our health over the last 30 or so years.

There are probably hundreds of these chemicals in food and to date little research has been done on them. Some of the commonly known names are:

▶ *lycopene in tomatoes*
▶ *quercetin in apples, onions, grapes and berries*
▶ *anthocyanins in berries.*

These antioxidants have not been shown to be of critical importance to your toddler's day-to-day health. However, it is important that during his toddler years and early childhood he learns to like the foods that contain them because they are known to prevent diseases that develop over time and will affect his health as an adult, such as cancer and heart disease.

HOW DO ANTIOXIDANTS BOOST THE IMMUNE SYSTEM?

Our bodies create free radicals during their normal functioning and in response to stress from the environment, such as excess pollution or cigarette smoke. Free radicals are harmful chemicals which damage cell structures that are required for a healthy functioning body. Antioxidants mop up the free radicals by deactivating them before they can damage the body.

How much of each nutrient does your toddler need?

Experts have agreed Reference Nutrient Intakes (RNIs) for different age groups of children in the UK. This is the average amount of a nutrient that children of that age group should have each day. The RNIs for children aged one to three years are shown in the table below.

Nutrients: the Reference Nutrient Intake (RNI), function and food sources

Nutrients needed, with RNI	Function in the body	Food sources
Protein RNI = 14.5 g	Provides structure for all the cells in the body. Enzymes and carrier molecules are made of protein. It can be broken down to provide energy if necessary.	The main sources are milk, yoghurt, cheese, meat, fish, eggs, nuts (chopped and ground or as butter). See page 46 for caution with whole nuts*. Other sources are pulses such as dhal, lentils, baked beans, hummus and other starchy beans (chickpeas, butter beans and red kidney beans). Breakfast cereals and foods containing flour such as bread, chapatti and pasta also provide some protein.
Carbohydrate No RNI, but should provide about 50% of daily energy (calories).	Starch and sugar provide energy (calories).	Potatoes, yam, breakfast cereals, couscous, rice and any foods containing flour (such as bread, chapatti, pasta, biscuits and cake).

Nutrients needed, with RNI	Function in the body	Food sources
There are three types of carbohydrate: ▶ simple sugars (such as lactose in milk), fructose in fruit and added sugar – sucrose and glucose ▶ starch ▶ fibre is made up of carbohydrate complexes that are not absorbed in the intestine.	Provides energy.	Milk contains the sugar lactose. Fruit contains the sugar fructose. Sweetened foods contain the sugars sucrose and glucose.
Fibre (also called non-starch polysaccharides) No RNI, but 5–7 g is an average intake for toddlers.	Fibre keeps the intestines functioning normally. Too little will cause constipation, but too much can cause diarrhoea and could slow growth.	Fruits, vegetables, cereals and foods made from flours. White flour and breads contain some fibre, while wholemeal or wholegrain contain more.
Fibre includes: ▶ non-digestible carbohydrates, mostly derived from plant material, that are fermented in the colon		Wholegrain cereals such as porridge, Ready Brek and Weetabix contain more fibre than highly processed cereals.

(Contd)

Nutrients needed, with RNI	Function in the body	Food sources
▶ prebiotics.	Prebiotics feed the bacteria in the colon that are important in the normal functioning of the intestines.	Prebiotics are found in onions, leeks, garlic and bananas.
Probiotics Bacteria in food that will colonize the intestine and provide health benefits.	Increasing the number of beneficial bacteria in the intestine can consequently reduce the effects of harmful bacteria that may cause infection.	Live yoghurt.
Fat No RNI, but should provide about 35–40% of daily energy (calories). It is made up of: ▶ fatty acids that are: – saturated – monoun- saturated or	Provides energy (calories) and carries some vitamins around the body. All cells have fats in their structure.	Oils and fats used in cooking foods. Butter, margarine and other spreads for bread. Nuts and cheese. Cakes, biscuits, ice cream and cream.

Nutrients needed, with RNI	Function in the body	Food sources
– polyun-saturated, including omega 3 and omega 6 ▶ complex fats, for example cholesterol and phospholipids.	We can make all the fats we need, except the omega 3 and omega 6 fats which we have to source from our food. They are needed for all cells in the body (brain, nerves and skin contain very high amounts of omega 3 and omega 6 fats).	Small amounts in whole milk and yoghurt, egg yolks and lean meat.

Toddlers need a good balance of omega 3 and omega 6 fats. There are usually plenty of omega 6 fats in the diet.

Oily fish are good sources of omega 3 long chain fats, DHA and EPA.

Rapeseed oil and walnut oil are good sources of omega 3 ALA. Most pure vegetable oil in the UK is made from rapeseed.

Olive and soya oils have a good balance of omega 3 and omega 6. |
| **Water** No RNI, but six to eight cups of about 100–120 ml (3–4 fl oz) should be offered daily. | For maintaining normal hydration, blood pressure and fluid balance.

Toddlers' bodies are about 70% water. | Most water comes from drinks: milk, fruit juices and diluted squashes are all about 90% water.

Soups, sauces, fruit and vegetables have high water contents. Drier foods contain less. |

(Contd)

Nutrients needed, with RNI	Function in the body	Food sources
Vitamins Vitamin A (retinol and carotene) RNI = 400 mcg	Ensures normal growth and development; strengthens the immune system; important for healthy intestines and skin and good vision.	Full-fat cows' milk. Egg yolks. Butter and other fat spreads (margarines). Orange, red and dark green fruit and vegetables such as carrots, red peppers, tomatoes, sweet potato, pumpkin, apricots, mangoes, cantaloupe melons, broccoli. Oily fish. Liver and liver pâté have very high levels of vitamin A, so only give them to your toddler once per week at the most.
B vitamins They are: thiamine RNI = 0.5 mg folic acid RNI = 70 mcg niacin RNI = 8 mg riboflavin RNI = 0.6 mg	Growth and development of healthy nervous system. Involved in the processes that convert food into energy.	Liver pâté and yeast extracts such as Marmite are the only foods that contain all the B vitamins. Most breakfast cereals are fortified with extra B vitamins.

Nutrients needed, with RNI	Function in the body	Food sources
pyridoxine RNI = 0.7 mg biotin (no RNI) pantothenic acid (no RNI) Vitamin B12 RNI = 0.5 mcg		Other good sources are meat, milk, yoghurt, cheese, fish, eggs, seeds, bread and vegetables.
Vitamin C (ascorbic acid) RNI = 30 mg	Helps absorb iron from non-meat sources. Is part of the immune system and protects cells from damage. Maintains blood vessels, cartilage, muscle and bone.	Most fruit and vegetables contain some vitamin C. The richest sources are blackcurrants, kiwi fruit, citrus fruits, tomatoes, peppers and strawberries. Potatoes, sweet potatoes and mangoes are also good sources. Certain fruit juices such as blackcurrant and orange have higher levels than other fruit juices.
Vitamin D RNI = 7 mcg	Needed to absorb calcium into the body. Also regulates calcium levels, ensures bone growth and is part of the immune system.	Most vitamin D is made in the skin when toddlers are outside during the summer months (April to September in the UK).

(Contd)

Nutrients needed, with RNI	Function in the body	Food sources
		The few food sources are oily fish and foods fortified with vitamin D which include margarine, some yoghurts and fromage frais, one or two breakfast cereals and formula milks.
Vitamin E No RNI	Antioxidant that protects cell structures throughout the body.	Contained in a wide variety of foods. Rich sources are vegetable oils and margarine, avocados, almonds, meat, fish and eggs.
Vitamin K No RNI	Aids blood clotting.	Mainly produced by bacteria in the large bowel. Food sources are green leafy vegetables and broccoli.
Minerals Calcium RNI = 350 mg	Needed for growing bones and teeth. Needed for muscle contractions and for the structure and functioning of all cells and the working of nerves.	Richest sources are milk, cheese, yoghurt and fortified soya milk. White bread is fortified with calcium. Ground almonds. Canned fish with edible bones, such as sardines.

Nutrients needed, with RNI	Function in the body	Food sources
Copper RNI = 0.4 mg	Making energy and protein.	In small amounts in most foods.
Fluoride Safe daily intake is 0.12 mg per kg body weight	Strengthens tooth enamel and makes it resistant to attack by the bacteria that cause tooth decay.	A smear of fluoride toothpaste on toothbrush when cleaning teeth twice a day provides enough for your toddler. In some areas of the UK, tap water is fluoridated or the water naturally contains adequate levels of fluoride. However, large areas of the UK have water that contains very little fluoride.
Iodine RNI = 70 mcg	Part of the hormone thyroxine, which helps convert food into energy and is needed for mental and physical development.	Fish, milk, yoghurt and eggs.
Iron RNI = 6.9 mg	Necessary for carrying oxygen around the body in the blood and needed for growing muscles, energy metabolism and the immune system.	Best sources are red meat (beef, lamb and pork) and dark poultry meat (chicken legs and thighs). White meat such as chicken breast has less.

(Contd)

Nutrients needed, with RNI	Function in the body	Food sources
		Other sources are: ▶ fortified breakfast cereals ▶ ground or chopped nuts (see page 46 for caution with peanuts and whole nuts*) ▶ dhal, lentils, hummus ▶ poppadums made with lentil flour ▶ bhajis and bombay mix made with chickpea flour. Smaller amounts are in fruit and vegetables.
Magnesium RNI = 85 mg	Helps in bone development, making protein and converting food into energy.	Best sources are wholegrain breakfast cereals, milk and yoghurt. Also in meat, egg, dhal, lentils, hummus, potatoes and some vegetables.
Phosphorus RNI = 270 mg	Building bone growth and using energy.	Richest source is milk and it is present in most other foods.
Potassium RNI = 800 mg	Important for fluid balance, muscle contraction and nerve conduction.	Milk, vegetables and potatoes.

Nutrients needed, with RNI	Function in the body	Food sources
		Bananas, dried apricots, prunes, dates and kiwi fruit are also good sources.
Selenium RNI = 15 mcg	Antioxidant and necessary for the production of the thyroid hormone thyroxin.	Bread, meat, fish, nuts, eggs and other foods made from flour.
Sodium RNI = 500 mg	Regulation of fluid balance and blood pressure.	Salt is the main source of sodium and salt is used in the production of bacon, ham, cheese and bread.

Salt is added to most ready meals, sauces, soups, snacks and other processed foods.

Sodium is also found naturally in small quantities in most fresh foods, particularly meat, fish, eggs, milk and yoghurt.

Foods with added salt such as crisps and processed foods should be kept to a minimum. |

(Contd)

Nutrients needed, with RNI	Function in the body	Food sources
Zinc RNI = 5 mg	Helps wounds heal and is involved in the function of many enzymes and hormones.	Best sources are meat, fish, shellfish and eggs. Other good sources are milk, wholegrain breakfast cereals such as porridge, Shredded Wheat, Weetabix, and bread. Some in potatoes, dhal, lentils, hummus and leafy vegetables.
Other phytonutrients Substances in plants, which provide long-term protection against cancer and heart disease. Also called flavanoids, flavanols, isoflavones. Examples are lycopene, lutein and quercetin.	They act as antioxidants protecting all cells from damage and are an important part of the immune system.	Fruits, vegetables, spices, herbs, nuts, and foods made from cereals. Particularly those that are brightly coloured. Cocoa and chocolate.

*Whole nuts should not be given to children under five years of age because of the risk of inhaling them or choking on them.

Make sure your toddler is getting all the nutrients he needs

You could slave over a computer to work out if your toddler is getting all the right nutrients in the right quantities – that would be on average the RNI for each nutrient every day. However, even then you wouldn't necessarily arrive at the correct figures as the data in the computer might not match exactly the food you had bought or prepared. Fortunately you do not need to do this because:

▶ *It is not necessary for your toddler to eat the required amount of each nutrient each day – most nutrients are stored in the body and these stores will last them some time. If he doesn't have milk one day his bones will not crack. Your toddler will eat more of some nutrients on certain days and less on other days. Over a period of two weeks or so he will be getting on average what he needs.*
▶ *Experts have grouped foods into food groups, and all the foods within each food group provide a similar range of certain nutrients. By combining foods from each of the food groups in certain quantities, each day you will be automatically providing all the nutrients he needs.*

There are four food groups that contain most of the nutrients and they are:

1 *bread, rice, potatoes, pasta and other starchy foods*
2 *fruit and vegetables*
3 *milk, cheese and yoghurt*
4 *meat, fish, eggs, nuts and pulses.*

There is a fifth food group that comprises foods that are high in either fat, sugar or both. These provide fewer nutrients and are high in energy (calories). They can be included in small quantities but should not replace foods in the food groups 1 to 4.

The nutrients that each food group provides are as follows:

Food group	Foods included	Main nutrients supplied
1 Bread, rice, potatoes, pasta and other starchy foods	Starchy foods: bread, chapatti, breakfast cereals, rice, couscous, pasta, millet, potatoes, yam, and foods made with flour such as pizza bases, buns, pancakes.	▶ carbohydrate ▶ B vitamins ▶ fibre ▶ some iron, zinc and calcium
2 Fruit and vegetables	Fresh, frozen, tinned and dried fruits and vegetables. Also pure fruit juices.	▶ vitamin C ▶ potassium ▶ phytochemicals ▶ fibre ▶ carotenes which are a form of Vitamin A
3 Milk, cheese and yoghurt	Cows' milk, goats' milk, growing-up formula milks, yoghurts, cheese, calcium enriched soya milks and desserts, tofu.	▶ calcium ▶ phosphorus ▶ protein ▶ iodine ▶ riboflavin
4 Meat, fish, eggs, nuts and pulses	Meat, fish, eggs, nuts and pulses (lentils, dhal, chickpeas, hummus, kidney beans and other similar starchy beans).	▶ iron ▶ protein ▶ zinc ▶ magnesium ▶ B vitamins ▶ vitamin A ▶ omega 3 and omega 6 fats

Food group	Foods included	Main nutrients supplied
		▶ omega 3 long chain fatty acids: EPA and DHA from oily fish

5 Foods high in fat and sugar: Foods high in fat	Cream, butter, margarines, cooking and salad oils, mayonnaise, crisps and other fried snacks.	▶ fat
		▶ some foods provide:
		  − vitamins D and E
		  − omega 3 and omega 6 fats

Foods high in sugar	Jam, honey, syrup, confectionery.	▶ sugar
Foods high in fat and sugar	Ice cream, biscuits, cakes, chocolate, toffee.	▶ sugar ▶ fat ▶ small amounts of some vitamins and minerals

Within each food group you need to offer as much variety as possible so that your toddler learns to eat all these foods. The more variety of foods eaten within each group, the better the balance of nutrients provided.

Chapter 3 teaches you how to combine the food groups and make up balanced meals and snacks each day.

TEST YOURSELF

1 *Which three nutrients do most toddlers not eat enough of?*

2 *Do toddlers normally eat enough protein?*

3 *Which food is the best source of omega 3 fats?*

4 *Which food is the best source of iron?*

5 *What are the best sources of fluoride?*

6 *Why do toddlers need a vitamin D supplement each day?*

7 *Why do toddlers need a vitamin A supplement very day?*

8 *How can you make sure your toddler gets all the nutrients he needs?*

9 *What are the four nutritious food groups?*

10 *Should your toddler avoid fat and sugar?*

3

Healthy eating for toddlers

In this chapter you will learn:
- *how to combine the five food groups to offer a healthy, balanced meal pattern*
- *the best drinks to offer*
- *foods that should not be given to toddlers*
- *the recommended vitamin supplements*
- *how to assess and make changes to your toddler's daily intake to ensure he gets a balanced diet.*

The challenge of getting your toddler to eat a healthy diet may seem overwhelming having learnt:

▶ *in Chapter 1 that he will go through a developmental stage of becoming very fussy about his food and he may use food refusal as an opportunity to exert his independence;*
▶ *in Chapter 2 the importance of giving him a huge range of nutrients to make sure he remains healthy and grows and develops as expected.*

If you observe these three cardinal rules you will find meals can become less stressful and more enjoyable.

Rule 1: It is up to you to offer your toddler a healthy, balanced diet of nutritious foods, but...

Rule 2: It is up to your toddler to decide what he will eat and how much he will eat and you must respect this.

Rule 3: Make each meal an enjoyable, social occasion.

Offering your toddler a balanced diet

In this chapter you will learn how easy it is to fulfil your responsibility to offer nutritious meals and snacks by combining the five food groups in the correct proportions. Toddlers do not always eat well, but if you make sure each meal and snack is nutritious when your toddler does eat well, he will be getting plenty of nutrients.

Toddlers are constantly learning; by offering your toddler nutritious foods he will learn for himself that the normal way to eat is eating nutritious foods. You will be teaching him valuable information that will help him maintain his health as he becomes older and more independent.

FOR HEALTHY EATING: THINK FOOD GROUPS NOT NUTRIENTS

Healthy eating involves combining food from five different food groups and serving them in the correct proportions. The combination also involves a mixture of some high-calorie foods and some low-calorie foods so that an excess of calories is not eaten.

The food combinations suitable for toddlers differ a little from those for older children and adults, as toddlers need a diet higher in nutrients and energy and a little lower in fibre.

The amount of each nutrient needed to keep toddlers healthy is an average amount. By offering your toddler the right combination of foods from the five food groups you will automatically offer him the average amount of nutrients he needs.

Don't worry if there are days when this combination doesn't happen. Toddlers store nutrients, so if they don't eat well for a few days they will come to no harm. As long as they are getting a good balance of the five food groups with some variety within each group, they are doing well.

What are the food groups?

The five food groups are:

1 *bread, rice, potatoes, pasta and other starchy foods*
2 *fruit and vegetables*
3 *milk, cheese and yoghurt*
4 *meat, fish, eggs, nuts and pulses*
5 *foods high in fat and sugar.*

FOOD GROUP 1: BREAD, RICE, POTATOES, PASTA AND OTHER STARCHY FOODS

This group includes bread, chapatti, pasta, rice, couscous, potatoes, sweet potatoes, yam, green banana, breakfast cereals and foods made from flour and other cereals such as rye, millet and sorghum. Offer a mixture of some white and some wholegrain varieties as giving a toddler only wholegrain foods could provide too much fibre for him.

Recommendation: include one of these foods at each meal and also offer them at some snack times.

You might offer:

Breakfast: breakfast cereals, porridge, bread, toast or chapatti

Lunch and evening meal: potatoes, rice, pasta, couscous, bread, chapatti, yam or green banana

Snacks: bread, toast, breadsticks, rice cakes or crackers, other foods based on flour such as pancakes, currant buns, tea bread, and scones

FOOD GROUP 2: FRUIT AND VEGETABLES

This group includes fresh, frozen, tinned and dried fruit and vegetables. It is the food group that parents often report that their toddlers find the most difficult to eat – particularly vegetables, as some have a very bitter taste. How much toddlers eat of this food group is less important than learning that they are a normal part of every meal.

Offer as much variety of this food group as you can, but be patient as toddlers will take time to learn to like new fruits and vegetables offered.

> Recommendation: serve fruit and vegetables at each meal and aim for around five small portions each day.

> ▶ *Serve fruit at breakfast and at least one vegetable and one fruit at both lunch and the evening meal.*
> ▶ *Set a good example by eating fruit and vegetables yourself and making positive comments about them.*
> ▶ *Cut raw fruit and vegetables into slices, cubes or sticks as your toddler will find these easier to eat than a large, whole fruit or vegetable.*
> ▶ *Thread pieces of fruit and vegetables onto cocktail sticks to make mini kebabs. Break the tips off the cocktail sticks to blunt the ends once you have threaded the fruit on.*
> ▶ *Remove any pips or stones; your toddler should be able to manage the skin on fruits such as apples, pears, peaches, grapes, and so on.*
> ▶ *Toddlers often prefer the flavour of vegetables that have been stir-fried, roasted or baked, rather than boiled or steamed.*
> ▶ *Include dried fruit at mealtimes. Dentists recommend that it should not be given as a snack, as it sticks to teeth and can cause tooth decay in the same way that sweets do.*
> ▶ *Offering foods from this group at each meal will teach your toddler that a meal should always include fruit and vegetables.*

FOOD GROUP 3: MILK, CHEESE AND YOGHURT

This group includes: milk drinks of about 100–120 ml (3–4 fl oz); milk on cereals; milk in foods such as milk puddings, white sauces; cheese and cheese sauces; yoghurt and fromage frais.

Butter and cream are not included in this food group, which is often called 'dairy'; they are in group 5 with high-fat foods, as they have no protein and very little calcium.

One serving is:

- ▶ *about 100–120 ml or 3–4 fl oz glass or cup of milk*
- ▶ *about 120 g pot of full-fat yoghurt or fromage frais*
- ▶ *a serving of cheese in a sandwich, or on top of a pizza slice*
- ▶ *a serving of custard or another milk pudding made with whole milk*
- ▶ *a serving of food in a white cheese sauce, such as macaroni cheese.*

To ensure your toddler has his three daily servings, you might offer foods from this group as:

Breakfast: milk on cereal and a small cup of milk

Mid-morning: cup of milk

Evening meal: yoghurt with fruit as a pudding

Another day your toddler's three servings might come from:

Breakfast: cup of milk in hot chocolate

Lunch: custard with pudding

Evening meal: cheese on pasta

This is the food group that some toddlers may have too much of. Toddlers do not need a pint of milk each day as is often recommended. Nor should they still be drinking bottles of milk. Toddlers who continue to drink too much milk will be obtaining too many calories from milk; this will fill them up and they may not then eat enough iron-containing foods from food group 4.

Milk from feeding bottles should have been discontinued before or around your toddler's first birthday so that all milk drinks are now from a cup or glass. Three cups of milk of about 120 ml (4 fl oz) will provide him with enough calcium and riboflavin which are the two key nutrients this group provides. If he is eating other milk products such as cheese and yoghurt then he can have these in place of each of the three cups of milk as they provide the same nutrients.

Full-fat milk and yoghurt should always be given to toddlers under two years as they provide more vitamin A. Those who are eating well can be changed to semi-skimmed milk after two years if this suits your family, but it is not necessary. Skimmed milk should not be given to toddlers as it very low in calories and the skimming process removes all the vitamin A from the milk.

FOOD GROUP 4: MEAT, FISH, EGGS, NUTS AND PULSES

This group provides protein and the richest sources of iron, zinc and other minerals in the diet. Pulses are peas, chickpeas, lentils and starchy beans like kidney beans (not green beans). Foods made from pulses such as hummus and dhal are also in this group.

Recommendation: serve foods from this group to non-vegetarians once or twice a day and to vegetarians two or three times a day.

▶ *Most toddlers prefer softer cuts of meat such as chicken, minced meat, sausages, pâté or slowly baked meat. Some find it difficult to eat the hard, chewy textures of less tender meat and will refuse it. Choose sausages and minced meat products – such as burgers – with a high lean meat content and low fat content to make sure adequate levels of nutrients are provided. Chapter 5 includes some recipes for slow-cooked and soft meat.*
▶ *Oily fish are a rich source of omega 3 fats and should be offered regularly – about twice each week. As they*

may contain traces of toxins, the Food Standards Agency recommends they are not given to boys more than four times each week and not more than twice each week for girls; the weekly recommendation is lower for girls as a precaution against the small risk of them accumulating toxins into their childbearing years.

▶ *The vegetarian options in this group include eggs, ground or chopped nuts, and pulses such as beans, chickpeas, hummus, lentils and dhal. A food or drink high in vitamin C should also be included in the meal to ensure that the non-haem iron in these foods is well absorbed. High vitamin C foods to include are tomatoes, peppers, citrus fruits, kiwi fruit, strawberries, pineapple and potatoes. Fruit juices high in vitamin C are blackcurrant or citrus juices; they can be served diluted with water and offered as a drink with the meal.*

Care with nuts:

▶ *Do not use whole nuts as they could be inhaled or may cause choking. Nut butters and ground or chopped nuts in recipes are fine.*

To ensure your toddler has his recommended daily servings, you might offer foods from this group as:

Breakfast: egg

Lunch: ham sandwich

Another day your toddler's servings might come from:

Lunch: shepherd's pie

Evening meal: fish fingers

A vegetarian toddler might have:

Breakfast: egg

Lunch: baked beans on toast

Evening meal: lentil soup

FOOD GROUP 5: FOOD AND DRINKS HIGH IN FAT AND/OR SUGAR

> Recommendation: offer these foods in small amounts in addition to, but not instead of, foods from the other four food groups.

Foods containing large amounts of fat and/or sugar do not need to be removed from your toddler's diet altogether. Having a sweet pudding with some fruit as a second course at lunch and in the evening makes the meals more delicious and enjoyable.

You do need to limit the quantity of foods high in fat and sugar that you offer your toddler as they are high in calories and contain fewer nutrients than foods in the other food groups. Sweet foods should be limited to a maximum of four times per day to decrease the likelihood of dental caries (see Chapter 9, page 187). Toddlers who snack on a lot of crisps, sweets and chocolate will not have any appetite to eat the more nutritious foods from food groups 1 to 4.

Foods high in fat

▶ *Oils, butter, margarine and cream provide toddlers with energy from fat and can also provide key nutrients such as omega 3 and omega 6 fats and the vitamins A, D and E, depending on the oils or fat used.*

▶ *Use rapeseed oil for cooking and walnut oil in dressings as they are high in omega 3 fat.*

▶ *Olive oil and soya oil have a good balance of omega 3 and omega 6 fats and can be used in dressings and cooking.*

▶ *Butter and margarines can also be used in cooking or spread on bread. Margarines are fortified with vitamins A and D by law, but choose one with a low level of trans fats as there is now concern about the large amounts of these in processed food.*

▶ *Crisps and other similar snacks are also included in this group. They are usually high in salt as well as fat and provide few other nutrients. They have no place in a toddler's diet on a regular basis. If you do give them to your toddler, give him just a few occasionally – for example, once a month – do not give him a whole packet. Crisps and similar snack foods will fill him up so that he does not eat more nutritious foods.*

Foods high in fat and sugar

▶ *Cake, biscuits and ice cream all contain nutrients in addition to fat and sugar. They also increase enjoyment of meals. You can combine them with fruit as a second course or pudding at mealtimes.*

Foods high in sugar

▶ *Your toddler will soon learn that sweets and other confectionery have a sweet taste which all toddlers naturally enjoy. However, they offer virtually no nutrients other than sugar so they should be given occasionally if at all. Indulgent grandparents and friends may bring them as presents, even if you do not buy them. Get into the habit of putting them away in a special box and give them occasionally with pudding or at the end of a meal. Never use them as rewards or bribes. If you deny your toddler all confectionery you may make them more desirable to him and he may behave badly on social occasions when he is offered them.*

▶ *Honey and jam provide some antioxidants in addition to sugar and small amounts can be used in meals to add flavour and a little sweetness.*

▶ *Sweetened drinks are also in this group. They are not recommended for toddlers but if you do offer them, ensure they are well diluted. Drinking sweetened drinks with food at a meal will lessen their tendency to cause dental decay and erosion of tooth enamel. Never give them to your toddler in a bottle between meals or just before bed; this increases the risk of dental caries considerably.*

Portion sizes – how much food should you offer?

There are no accepted and set portion sizes for toddlers as the amount toddlers eat is extremely variable. Some eat much more or much less than the average intake, and yet grow and develop normally. The amount each toddler eats may vary from meal to meal or snack to snack – often toddlers eat well at one or two meals each day and less well at the third meal. The amount eaten can also vary from day to day.

Do offer smaller portions than adults eat, as toddlers can find large servings overwhelming and this may put them off eating anything. Offer small amounts and offer more if your toddler finishes it all. Generally their portion sizes will increase as they grow.

GUIDE TO AVERAGE FOOD AMOUNTS TO OFFER YOUR TODDLER (THESE ARE NOT SPECIFIC SERVING SIZES – ALLOW HIM TO EAT AS MUCH AS HIS APPETITE DICTATES)

Food	Average food amounts to offer
Bread	½–1 slice
Breakfast cereal	3–6 heaped tablespoons or ½ –1½ Weetabix
Pasta, mashed potato	1–3 heaped tablespoons
Rice, couscous,	2–5 tablespoons
Fruit	¼–½ piece fruit such as an apple, orange, pear or banana ½ –1 satsuma/clementine/plum 3–10 small berries, grapes or cherries
Vegetables	1–3 tablespoons
Meat, fish, pulses	2–4 tablespoons
Egg	½ –1
Cheese	2–4 tablespoons grated cheese or 2–4 small cubes
Puddings/desserts	3–6 tablespoons ½–1 small carton yoghurt

	1 digestive biscuit or 1–2 biscuits
	1 small slice cake
Drinks	100–120 ml (3–4 fl oz)
Spreads	1 teaspoon butter, mayonnaise or oil
	1 teaspoon jam, honey or sugar
Occasional foods	3–4 crisps or sweets
	1 small fun-sized chocolate bar

Drinks

Busy, active toddlers can get very thirsty and need several drinks each day. Offer drinks with each meal and snack. This will be about six to eight drinks each day. Each drink will be about 100–120 ml (3–4 fl oz).

Toddlers can become dehydrated quite quickly in hot weather or if they have a temperature or a runny nose. A young toddler will not be able to tell you if he is thirsty, so always offer a drink of water if he is crying for no other apparent reason. He will push it away if he does not want it.

Too little fluid can be a cause of constipation (see Chapter 9, page 185). However, a large fluid intake – particularly in toddlers that are drinking 240 ml (8 fl oz) bottles of fluid – can also be a cause for concern. Large amounts of fluid can fill toddlers up so that they have little appetite for nutritious foods.

Milk and water are the safest drinks to offer between meals as they do not harm teeth. Diluted fruit juices can be given with meals but should not be offered between meals as they are acidic and contain fruit sugar.

Other sugary drinks, such as fruit juice drinks and squashes, have no place in a toddler's diet as they contribute only sugar with few other nutrients. They are also acidic. Sugar will decay teeth if offered frequently and the acid can cause your toddler's delicate tooth enamel to erode.

Some toddlers are given sweet milky tea. However, the tannin in tea reduces the amount of iron that your toddler can absorb from food. It is best not to give tea to toddlers but if you do so, do not offer it with a meal.

FINISHING WITH BOTTLES

If your toddler is still drinking from a bottle then change the drinks from bottles to drinks in cups one by one. Toddlers who continue drinking from bottles tend to use bottle drinking as a comfort. They can become very stubborn about insisting on their bottle as they get older.

Drinking from a bottle or a cup with a teat or valved spout is not recommended by dentists as it increases the time that the fluid is in contact with the teeth. For any drink other than water this is a problem as they all contain some sugar – milk contains lactose as sugar. Fruit juices contain the fruit sugar fructose and squashes contain the sugars glucose and sucrose.

When your toddler drinks from an unlidded cup or a cup with a free-flow spout he has to sip the fluid, lessening the time the sweet fluid is in contact with the teeth.

REMOVING ANY REMAINING BOTTLES OF MILK

Toddlers who carry on drinking a large bottle of milk first thing in the morning, at bedtime or during the night are those most at risk of iron deficiency anaemia. If your toddler is still drinking bottles of milk, it is important for the balance of his diet that you cut these out as soon as possible. As toddlers become older they can become very resistant to stopping habits that they associate with comfort.

Some mothers continue giving a bottle of milk when a toddler first wakes in the morning and are then surprised that the toddler eats very little breakfast. I always advise giving breakfast first thing in the morning and offering a small cup of milk after breakfast. It usually means an early breakfast for one parent but as the toddler becomes used to having breakfast first he will become amenable to waiting a little.

If he is still having a bedtime bottle of milk, you need to change the bedtime routine so that instead of giving milk you spend some extra time with him to comfort him before he goes into bed, for example:

▶ *give him a bath*
▶ *dress him in his pyjamas*
▶ *cuddle him, talk to him and then spend some time looking at a book with him*
▶ *put him into his bed while he is still awake and say good night. Allow him to settle on his own with a comforter such as his favourite toy or a special cloth or blanket he may have chosen.*

CHOOSING A MILK FOR YOUR TODDLER

The choice of milk drinks for your toddler over one year is:

▶ *cows' milk*
▶ *continue with breast milk or formula milk*
▶ *'growing-up' milk or toddler milk.*

From 12 months your toddler can begin drinking cows' milk in place of formula, or when you stop breastfeeding. Cows' milk is cheaper than formula milks and it is quite suitable for toddlers over one year who are eating well.

Cows' milk
Full-fat cows' milk should be used until at least two years of age. Semi-skimmed cows' milk can be drunk by those over two years,

but there is no necessity to change. Skimmed milk should not be offered to toddlers below five years.

Growing-up milks

These milks are promoted as being suitable from 12 months up to three years. They contain less protein than cows' milk but more vitamins and minerals, particularly iron and zinc. If a toddler is eating well then he will be getting these vitamins and minerals from his food so the extra expense is not necessarily justified. However, growing-up milks will provide useful extra nutrients for a toddler or young toddler who eats poorly. There are now five on the market and they are fairly similar, although one is based on goats' milk and one on soya protein:

▶ *Aptamil Growing Up Milk*
▶ *Cow & Gate Growing Up Milk*
▶ *Hipp Organic Growing Up Milk*
▶ *Nannycare Goat Growing Up Milk*
▶ *SMA Toddler Milk*
▶ *Alpro Soya Junior Milk.*

Drinks

▶ *Milk and water are the only safe drinks to offer between meals.*
▶ *Dilute pure fruit juices with water and only offer them with meals.*
▶ *Give all drinks in unlidded cups, or lidded cups with free-flowing spouts.*
▶ *Phase out bottles, teats and cups with valved spouts.*
▶ *Limit milk drinks to three cups of 100–120 ml (3–4 fl oz) each day.*
▶ *Do not offer bottles of milk during the day or night.*
▶ *Do not offer tea, sweetened fruit juice drinks, squashes or fizzy drinks.*

Foods that should not be offered to toddlers

Toddlers should be able to eat all family foods but there are a few that should be avoided:

▶ *Very spicy food, such as hot chilli.*
▶ *Undercooked eggs and shellfish; these can sometimes cause food poisoning and toddlers can become severely ill with food poisoning.*
▶ *Large fish that live for many years, such as swordfish, marlin and shark; they may contain high levels of mercury and are best avoided.*
▶ *Whole nuts because if a toddler inhales a nut he may have a severe reaction; toddlers may also choke on them. Ground or chopped walnuts, almonds and other tree nuts are acceptable and are a good source of protein and nutrients, especially for vegetarian toddlers.*
▶ *Tea, because the tannin reduces the amount of iron absorbed from foods. It is best not to give tea to toddlers but if you do so, do not offer it with a meal.*
▶ *Additives and sweeteners; it is best to offer your toddler foods without large amounts of additives or sweeteners. However, if your family foods include some, keep them to a minimum for your toddler. See Chapter 12, page 251 for more information, but do avoid the following:*
  Colours: *tartrazine E102*
  ponceau 4R E124
  sunset yellow E110
  carmoisine E122
  quinoline yellow E104
  allura red AC E129
  Preservative: *sodium benzoate E211*

Vitamin supplements

Toddlers all need a vitamin supplement containing vitamins A and D because having enough of these two key vitamins is crucial for good health and toddlers will not necessarily get enough of these two vitamins from their food.

This is particularly important for toddlers:

▶ *with dark skins – that is those of Asian, African, Afro-Caribbean and Middle-Eastern origin – because they do not make vitamin D in their skins as efficiently as white toddlers*
▶ *who live in northern areas of the UK where there is less sunlight to make vitamin D*
▶ *who were born prematurely*
▶ *who are on restricted diets such as vegetarian diets*
▶ *who are picky, fussy eaters.*

There are a variety of vitamin supplements containing vitamins A and D, but the more expensive preparations contain a number of other nutrients that your toddler does not need if he is eating foods from all the food groups. The NHS Healthy Start children's vitamin drops contain vitamins A, C and D and are the cheapest but are only sold in some NHS child health clinics. Ask your health visitor where to get them.

Toddlers who do not eat a healthy balanced diet may need a supplement with a wide range of nutrients (see Chapter 12, page 249).

Combining the food groups for healthy eating

The ideal daily meal plan for your toddler is that each day you offer:

▶ *three meals*
▶ *two to three snacks*
▶ *six to eight drinks*
▶ *vitamins A and D in a supplement.*

The meals and snacks should include:

▶ *two courses at each main meal*
▶ *bread, rice, potatoes, pasta and other starchy foods at each meal*
▶ *fruit and vegetables at each meal*
▶ *three servings of milk, cheese or yoghurt per day*
▶ *two to three servings of meat, fish, eggs, nuts or pulses per day*
▶ *some high-fat foods.*

Food group	How much?
Bread, rice, potatoes, pasta and other starchy foods	Include at each meal, and some snacks
Fruit and vegetables	Include at each meal, and some snacks
Milk, cheese and yoghurt	Three servings per day
Meat, fish, eggs, nuts and pulses	Two to three servings per day
Foods high in fat and foods high in sugar	Very small amounts with meals Limit sweet foods to four times per day
Drinks	Six to eight per day or one with each meal and snack
Vitamin drops	Vitamins A and D daily

DAILY MEAL PLAN COMBINING THE FIVE FOOD GROUPS

A variety of different eating plans, depending on your family routine, can provide a healthy eating regime with the desired combination of the food groups.

There are two examples below. They both have:

▶ *three meals*
▶ *two snacks*
▶ *six drinks*
▶ *vitamins A and D in a supplement*
▶ *two courses at each main meal*
▶ *bread, rice, potatoes, pasta and other starchy foods at each meal*

- *fruit and vegetables at each meal*
- *three servings of milk, cheese or yoghurt*
- *two to three servings of meat, fish, eggs, nuts or pulses*
- *some high-fat foods*
- *sweet foods – a maximum of four times per day.*

Example: Eating Plan 1
In this example, breakfast is a quick meal based on cereal with fruit and milk – a quickly prepared breakfast that would suit a family that has little time in the morning. The midday meal might be served at nursery and the evening meal is a cooked meal that the family might eat together. The three milk servings are taken at breakfast, mid-morning snack at nursery and for the evening meal pudding.

		Food groups to include	Sample menu
Breakfast		▶ Bread/rice/potatoes/ pasta/starchy food ▶ Milk/cheese/yoghurt ▶ Fruit ▶ Drink	breakfast cereal milk on cereal blueberries pure fruit juice diluted with water
Snack		▶ Fruit ▶ Milk/cheese/yoghurt	apple slices cup milk to drink
Midday meal	1st course	▶ Meat/fish/eggs/nuts/ pulses ▶ Bread/rice/potatoes/ pasta/starchy food ▶ Vegetables	mini meatballs pasta cauliflower florets
	2nd course	▶ High fat/high sugar group ▶ Fruit	apple crumble with ice cream
		▶ Drink	pure fruit juice diluted with water
Snack		▶ Bread/rice/potatoes/ pasta/starchy food ▶ Drink	crackers with marmite water

		Food groups to include	Sample menu
Evening meal	1st course	▶ Meat/fish/eggs/nuts/ pulses ▶ Bread/rice/potatoes/ pasta/starchy food ▶ Vegetables	fish and potato pie carrot and cucumber sticks
	2nd course	▶ Milk group ▶ Fruit group	plain yoghurt mixed with puréed mango
		▶ Drink	water

Example: Eating Plan 2

In this example there is a more substantial breakfast that might suit a family that is not rushed in the morning, or it might work at the weekend. The evening meal is a lighter meal with no food from the meat/fish/eggs/nuts/pulses group as there are already two servings from this group: one at breakfast and one at lunch.

		Food groups to include	Sample menu
Breakfast		▶ Bread/rice/potato/pasta/ other starchy food ▶ Meat/fish/eggs/nuts/pulses ▶ Fruit as drink	boiled egg with toast fingers diluted orange juice
Snack		▶ Milk/cheese/yoghurt ▶ High fat/high sugar group	glass milk one biscuit
Midday meal	1st course	▶ Meat/fish/eggs/nuts/ pulses ▶ Bread/rice/potatoes/ pasta/starchy food ▶ Vegetables	chicken curry and rice broccoli florets
	2nd course	▶ Milk/cheese/yoghurt ▶ Fruit	banana with custard
		▶ Drink	water

(Contd)

		Food groups to include	Sample menu
Snack		▶ Bread/rice/potatoes/pasta/ starchy food ▶ Drink	buttered scone water
Evening meal	1st course	▶ Bread/rice/potatoes/pasta/ starchy food ▶ Milk/cheese/yoghurt ▶ Vegetables	cheese and tomato sandwiches
	2nd course	▶ High fat/high sugar group ▶ Fruit	mini muffin and peach slices, few chocolate buttons
		▶ Drink	water

Is your toddler eating a healthy and balanced diet?

To check whether your toddler is currently eating a nutritious diet you can check the combinations of the food groups you are offering.

Make a list of all the food and drinks your toddler has in one day. Record this as each meal and snack. Using a form such as the one on the page opposite makes it easy: list the foods in the left hand column; now put a tick in the food groups columns for each food eaten from that food group.

If your toddler had eaten as per the sample Eating Plan 1, for breakfast you would put '1' in the 'Bread, rice, potato, pasta, other starchy food' column for the bowl of breakfast cereal. Then put '1' in the 'Milk, cheese and yoghurt' column for the cup of milk added to the breakfast cereal. If your toddler, like many others, leaves half of the milk in the bowl, then change this column entry to '½'. Now put '1' in the 'Fruit and vegetables' column for the blueberries eaten with the cereal.

Continue in the same way for all the food and drink. Then add up the 1s and ½s and put this amount in the 'Totals' row and you will be able to compare your toddler's diet with the daily recommendation.

Sample assessment using the foods in the sample Eating Plan 1 (page 68)

All food and drinks	*Food groups*					*Fluid*
	Bread, rice, potato, pasta, other starchy food	*Fruit and vege-tables*	*Milk, cheese, yoghurt*	*Meat, fish, eggs, nuts, pulses*	*Foods high in fat and/ or sugar*	*Drinks*
Breakfast						
breakfast cereal	1					
milk on cereal			½			
blueberries		1				
pure fruit juice diluted with water						1
Mid-morning snack						
apple slices		1				
cup milk to drink			1			1
Lunch						
mini meatballs				1		
pasta	1					
cauliflower florets		1				
apple crumble with ice cream		1			1	
pure fruit juice diluted with water						1
Mid-afternoon snack						
crackers with Marmite and cheese cubes	1		1			
water to drink						1

(Contd)

All food and drinks	Food groups					Fluid
	Bread, rice, potato, pasta, other starchy food	Fruit and vege-tables	Milk, cheese, yoghurt	Meat, fish, eggs, nuts, pulses	Foods high in fat and/ or sugar	Drinks
Evening meal fish and potato pie	1			1		
carrot and cucumber sticks		1				
plain yoghurt mixed with puréed mango		1	1			
water to drink						1
extra drinks of water						2
TOTALS	4	6	3½	2	1	7
RECOMMENDED DAILY INTAKE	3–5 (at each meal and some snacks)	5 (at each meal and some snacks)	3	2–3	some high-fat foods	6–8 cups

Of course these totals add up perfectly because the example is a meal plan recommendation!

Case study

Ellie is two years nine months and goes to nursery in the morning. She still has a sleep after lunch and her mother is concerned that she eats very poorly at lunchtime. She usually gives her bread and jam just to make sure she has had something. There are no problems with her growth and I asked her mother to write down everything Ellie had eaten the day before:

'Breakfast: cornflakes and milk, orange squash to drink. Milk to drink and fruit at break time at nursery. Lunch: jam sandwich and cake. A packet of Wotsits and a carton of a fruit juice drink in the afternoon with her older brother on the way home from school. Fish fingers with chips for tea and a bottle of milk on going to bed.'

Now, let's plot Ellie's daily diet:

All food and drinks	Food groups					Fluid
	Bread, rice, potato, pasta, other starchy food	Fruit and vege-tables	Milk, cheese, yoghurt	Meat, fish eggs, nuts, pulses	Foods high in fat and/or sugar	Drinks
Breakfast cornflakes with milk diluted fruit juice to drink	1 —		½			1
At nursery pieces fruit and milk to drink		1	1			1
Lunch jam sandwich and cake milk to drink	1		1		2	1

(Contd)

All food and drinks	Food groups					Fluid
	Bread, rice, potato, pasta, other starchy food	Fruit and vege-tables	Milk, cheese, yoghurt	Meat, fish eggs, nuts, pulses	Foods high in fat and/or sugar	Drinks
Afternoon one packet Wotsits carton of fruit juice drink					1 1	1
Evening meal fish fingers and chips chocolate biscuit milk to drink	1		1	1	1 1	1
Before bed full bottle of milk			2			2
TOTALS	3	1	5½	1	6	7
RECOMMENDED INTAKE	3–5 (at each meal and some snacks)	5 (at each meal and some snacks)	3	2–3	some high-fat foods	6–8 cups

Ellie is getting enough calories to keep growing for the time being. She is probably tired when she comes home from her busy morning at nursery which is why she is not eating well at lunchtime. After her afternoon sleep she is hungry and eats well, but is given the same snack as her brother, which is not nutritious enough to replace the nutrients she hasn't had at lunch.

The combination of the food groups is very poor and by comparing the totals with the recommendations, you can see she has too much milk and foods that are high in fat and sugar and not enough foods from the other food groups. Consequently Ellie's diet will be low in iron and other minerals. If she continues to eat like this, she would become deficient in iron and might get iron deficiency anaemia.

Insight

Ellie's diet is quite typical of toddlers I have seen with iron deficiency anaemia.

As the rest of the family do not eat fruit and vegetables, Ellie is not being offered them at home. The only fruit she is having is that offered as a snack at nursery.

There are several changes that Ellie's mother can make to improve Ellie's diet:

▶ *cut out the bottle of milk before bed as soon as possible*
▶ *change her lunch to a more nutritious sandwich, for example she could try a peanut butter and jam sandwich*
▶ *change her afternoon snack to a more nutritious snack, such as carrot sticks with breadsticks (which are crunchy like the Wotsits). She could also add some pieces of cold meat, such as ham or cooked chicken to make up for the small lunch that is being eaten*
▶ *the whole family need to begin eating more fruit and vegetables so that they are offered at each meal. As this change will take some time, Ellie could be given diluted pure fruit juice in place of a fruit juice drink that only contains about 5 per cent fruit juice (the rest will be sugar and colouring). The pure fruit juice will provide more nutrients from fruit than squash.*

If Ellie's mother makes these changes, then her one day's intake would be (see page 76):

All food and drinks	Food groups					Fluid
	Bread, rice, potato, pasta, other starchy food	Fruit and vege-tables	Milk, cheese, yoghurt	Meat, fish eggs, nuts, pulses	Foods high in fat and/ or sugar	Drinks
Breakfast cornflakes with milk diluted fruit juice to drink	1		½			1
At nursery pieces fruit and milk to drink		1	1			1
Lunch jam and peanut butter sandwich fruit pieces milk to drink	1	1	1	1	1	1
Afternoon carrot sticks and breadsticks few chunks of cold chicken diluted fruit juice	1	1		1		1
Evening meal fish fingers and chips with peas chocolate biscuit fruit pieces milk to drink	1	1 1	1	1	1 1	1
Before bed extra water to drink						1
TOTALS	4	5	3½	3	3	6

All food and drinks	Food groups					Fluid
	Bread, rice, potato, pasta, other starchy food	Fruit and vege-tables	Milk, cheese, yoghurt	Meat, fish eggs, nuts, pulses	Foods high in fat and/ or sugar	Drinks
RECOMMENDED INTAKE	3–5 (at each meal and some snacks)	5 (at each meal and some snacks)	3	2–3	some high-fat foods	6–8 cups

WHAT TO DO IF YOUR TODDLER IS NOT EATING A HEALTHY AND BALANCED DIET

If you find one sample day does not show a healthy and balanced diet, do not despair. A one-day record of your toddler's intake may not be indicative of his average intake. All toddlers will eat well some days and not so well on other days. His eating pattern during the week may be quite different from how he eats at the weekend. Your toddler's eating pattern could be quite different on the days that he goes to nursery or to a childminder, compared with the days when he stays at home. Birthday party days will also be quite different. It is best to assess your toddler's intake over a week rather than just concentrating on one day.

Assessing the average intake of each food group over a week
Write down the food and drinks your toddler consumes over a week and then assess each day using a form like the one used above. Add together the totals for each food group for each day and then divide this total by seven days to get an average for this food group for the week.

For example:

Day	Food groups					Fluid
	Bread, rice, potato, pasta, other starchy food	Fruit and vege-tables	Milk, cheese, yoghurt	Meat, fish eggs, nuts, pulses	Foods high in fat and/or sugar	Drinks
Sunday	5	5	3	2	2	6
Monday	6	4	4	1	3	8
Tuesday	4	6	2	2	2	5
Wednesday	5	3	1	2	4	6
Thursday	3	3	3	3	2	7
Friday	6	4	3	2	1	6
Saturday (went to a birthday party)	4	2	3	1	5	9
Totals for the week	33	27	19	13	19	47
Daily average for the week	4.7	3.8	2.7	1.9	2.7	6.7
RECOMMENDED DAILY INTAKE	3–5 (at each meal and some snacks)	5 (at each meal and some snacks)	3	2–3	some high-fat foods	6–8 cups

In this example the combination of the food groups over the week is good enough. The average for each food group is very close to the recommendation.

If the combination of the food groups over the week is not ideal, look at which food groups your toddler is not having enough of and think of ways to increase his intake by substituting this food group for another food group he may be having too much of. Chapter 5 gives ideas for nutritious meals and meal plans. Choosing more nutritious snacks is one way of improving his intake.

Nutritious snacks for your toddler

The table below lists some healthy snacks for your toddler and shows which food groups the snacks are from. You can see how snacks can make a valuable contribution to food combining for a healthy diet. Alternatively you can use these snacks to provide food groups not eaten at the previous meal, because your toddler did not eat well for whatever reason.

Healthy snacks and their food groups

Healthy snacks	Food groups				
	Bread, rice, potato, pasta, other starchy food	Fruit and vege-tables	Milk, cheese, yoghurt	Meat, fish eggs, nuts, pulses	Foods high in fat and/ or sugar
slices of fruit with a small cup of milk		1	1		
ham sandwich and a cup of water	1			1	
peanut butter and banana sandwich	1	1		1	
slices of apple spread with cream cheese		1	1		

(Contd)

Healthy snacks	Food groups				
	Bread, rice, potato, pasta, other starchy food	Fruit and vege-tables	Milk, cheese, yoghurt	Meat, fish eggs, nuts, pulses	Foods high in fat and/ or sugar
pancakes spread with fruit purée	I	I			
pancakes spread with chocolate spread	I				I
breadsticks or crackers with cubes of cheese	I		I		
pitta bread with hummus and a cup of water	I			I	
muffin with a small cup of milk	I		I		I
crumpet spread with honey and a cup of water	I				I
scone with jam and a cup of milk	I		I		I
yoghurt or fromage frais and fruit slices		I	I		
small piece fruit cake and a cup of milk	I	I	I		I
small slice of pizza and a cup of water	I	I	I		
small bowl of breakfast cereal and milk	I		I		
toast with peanut butter and a cup of water	I			I	

TEST YOURSELF

1 *How often should you offer foods from food group 1 (bread, rice, potatoes, pasta and other starchy foods)?*

2 *How often should you offer foods from food group 2 (fruits and vegetables)?*

3 *How often should you offer foods from food group 3 (milk, cheese and yoghurt)?*

4 *How much should you offer as a serving of milk?*

5 *When should bottles of milk be discontinued?*

6 *How often should you offer foods from food group 4 (meat, fish, eggs, nuts and pulses)?*

7 *How often should you offer foods from food group 5 (foods high in fat and/or sugar)?*

8 *How many drinks should you offer your toddler each day?*

9 *Which are the best drinks to offer your toddler?*

10 *Which foods should not be offered to toddlers?*

4

Ideas for nutritious meals and meal plans

In this chapter you will learn:
- *how to put nutritious meals together from what's in the cupboard and fridge*
- *how to plan meals using seasonal food*
- *ideas for nutritious picnics, packed lunches and party food.*

As long as you are combining foods from the four main food groups to make up meals and snacks you will be offering nutritious meals. Many meals can be taken straight from your cupboard or fridge and with the occasional use of a toaster you can have these meals ready in a few minutes – some will take less than a minute! Ideas for these meals and snacks are in section one. Section two lists ideas for meals for when you have time to cook and plan ahead by making things for the freezer. Recipes for some of these foods follow in the next chapter.

> **Insight**
>
> I do enjoy cooking when I have time but I have to admit my children ate a lot of meals from this first section below. Some parents think a warm meal is better for a child but in fact cold and quickly prepared meals can be just as nutritious.

1 Ready meals – meals you can toss together from your cupboard and fridge (as well as using a toaster)

BREAKFASTS

Packet breakfast cereals with fruit and milk or yoghurt
Choose breakfast cereals which are fortified with iron and extra
B vitamins – these replace the nutrients that are lost during the
processing. These cereals will all have some sugar in them but
choose those with lower amounts that are not sugar coated.
Adding fruit to the lower-sugar varieties provides flavour and
extra sweetness along with extra nutrients.

Add seasonal fruit or a tablespoon of dried fruit such as sultanas,
or ready-to-eat dried apricots if you have no fresh fruit. Banana
slices are always popular and available all year round.

Muesli with milk or yoghurt and a glass of diluted fruit juice
The oats in muesli are a reasonable source of iron. Choose
low-sugar muesli or you can make your own using the recipe on
page 99.

Diluted fruit juice as a drink or fresh fruit that is high in vitamin C
(strawberries, kiwi fruit, citrus fruits) will help the absorption of
iron from muesli or cereals.

Toast or breads
This can be offered with a variety of spreads: low-sugar jam, fruit
spread or honey. Only use a scrape of butter or margarine and
offer a glass of milk to include some protein. You could offer the
milk as a cup of hot chocolate on cold mornings.

For a more nutritious spread, offer cream cheese, smoked salmon or
peanut butter along with a glass of diluted fruit juice. Some families
may have cold cuts of meat or fish pâtés with toast for breakfast.

Crumpets, pancakes or toasted English muffins can all be offered with different spreads as an alternative to toast.

Hot cross buns or toasted tea bread are available all year round and make an alternative breakfast served buttered with a small glass of milk and some slices of fresh fruit.

> **Insight**
> This last breakfast was a favourite in our household.

FIRST COURSE FOR MAIN MEALS

'Just put it on the plate' meals
By just putting a food from each of food groups 1, 2 and 4 you will be offering a nutritious meal. For example: cold cuts of cooked meat with vegetable sticks and a starchy food such as bread, breadsticks, crispbread, crackers or plain popcorn.

Use cold leftover meat that you may have cooked the day before, for example roast chicken, lamb, beef or pork. Or buy some sliced turkey, ham or salami. Examples of simple combinations:

▶ *cold chicken with tomato wedges, green pepper sticks and a slice of buttered bread*
▶ *pieces of ham, celery and carrot sticks with some plain popcorn*
▶ *slices of cold roast meat cut into pieces with cucumber slices, cherry tomatoes and mini rice cakes or breadsticks.*

Sandwiches or toppings on toast, crackers, rice cakes or crispbread
Sandwiches are a nice soft finger food and can be made with any type of bread. Try mixing a slice of white bread with a slice of wholemeal. Use a thin scrape of butter, margarine or mayonnaise to stop the bread becoming soggy, although this will not be necessary if you have a dry filling.

Sandwich fillings are listed below. Cut the sandwiches diagonally into four triangles so that only one side has a crust. Your toddler will find it easier to eat the sandwich and if he wants to, let him leave the crusts.

You can also use any of the fillings listed below spread onto toast, crackers, rice cakes or crispbread to make a crunchy alternative to sandwiches. Serve the raw vegetables on the side.

Pitta bread with fillings
Cut pitta bread into pockets about the size of a small sandwich. They can be warmed in a toaster for about 10–15 seconds if desired. Any of the sandwich fillings can then be popped into the pocket. Serve them with some vegetable sticks on the side if you don't include diced vegetables in the filling.

Sandwich fillings and toppings for toast, crackers, rice cakes or crispbread

- *cold meats such as ham, lean salami or cold roast meat with lettuce or tomato*
- *liver pâté or liver sausage*
- *peanut butter with mashed banana or jam*
- *1 tbsp drained tinned tuna with 1 tsp mayonnaise and 1 tsp plain yoghurt*
- *1 tbsp tinned sardines with a squeeze of lemon juice*
- *1 tbsp of smoked fish such as smoked mackerel or smoked trout mixed with ½ tbsp of plain yoghurt and ½ tbsp of mayonnaise*
- *fish pâtés such as mackerel or salmon*
- *slices smoked salmon*
- *1 tbsp hummus mixed with ½ tbsp finely diced red pepper*
- *bean spreads such as black bean spread*
- *mashed avocado or guacamole or tofu and avocado spread (see recipe in Chapter 5, page 103)*
- *grated hard cheese with sliced tomatoes*

(Contd)

▶ *1 tbsp cream cheese with ½ tsp chopped herbs such as chives or parsley*

▶ *1 tbsp cream cheese and a scrape of Marmite*

Some toddlers may not like mixed fillings. They may prefer a plain filling like hummus with slices of pepper on the side, rather than diced pepper mixed in with the hummus.

If your toddler is wary of mixed foods being hidden in a sandwich then get him to help you make the sandwich so that he knows exactly what is in it.

Breadsticks and vegetable sticks with dips
You can buy breadsticks or they are very easy to make yourself. They can be served with a variety of dips:

▶ *hummus*
▶ *cucumber, mint and yoghurt dip*
▶ *avocado dip such as guacamole*
▶ *fish or meat pâté mixed with some extra plain yoghurt or mayonnaise to make them a suitable consistency for a dip.*

As previously suggested, you can mix diced vegetables into the dip or serve vegetable sticks on the side.

PUDDINGS OR SECOND COURSES FOR MAIN MEALS

Make this second course a combination of something sweet and some fruit – fresh, dried or tinned in juice not syrup:

▶ *sliced fresh fruit with yoghurt, fromage frais, ready-made custard or ice cream*
▶ *fruit slices with a biscuit, muffin or piece of cake*
▶ *carrot cake or a fruit cake that contains plenty of dried fruit.*

You can add a couple of small sweets or chocolate to this pudding if you have some. Confectionery as part of a meal will not harm your toddler's teeth.

Insight

'What's for pudding? Not fruit and yoghurt again!' was a common cry in my household. Adding a biscuit or small piece of chocolate made it much more exciting and just as nutritious.

SNACKS

Nutritious snacks should also be combinations of foods from one or two of the four main food groups, for example:

▶ *slices of fruit with a small cup of milk*
▶ *ham sandwich with cherry tomatoes and a cup of water*
▶ *peanut butter and banana sandwich*
▶ *slices of apple spread with cream cheese*
▶ *pancakes spread with fruit purée and a cup of milk*
▶ *pancakes spread with chocolate spread and a cup of water*
▶ *breadsticks or crackers with cubes of cheese and celery sticks, with a cup of water*
▶ *pitta bread with hummus and apple slices and a cup of water*
▶ *muffin with grapes and a small cup of milk*
▶ *crumpet spread with honey and a cup of milk*
▶ *scone with butter and jam, clementine segments and a cup of milk*
▶ *yoghurt or fromage frais and fruit slices*
▶ *small piece fruit cake and a cup of milk*
▶ *small slice of pizza and a cup of water*
▶ *small bowl of breakfast cereal with banana slices and milk*
▶ *toast with peanut butter, carrot sticks and a cup of water*
▶ *hot cross buns or tea bread with a cup of milk*

2 Meals for toddlers with parents who are happy to cook

With a few basic cooking skills, you can prepare a much wider variety of food for your family and toddler. Recipes for a variety of family foods that are popular with toddlers are included in Chapter 5.

COOKED BREAKFASTS

Porridge

Porridge is an easy hot cereal and can be prepared in a few minutes in a microwave. Alternatively you can make it in a saucepan following the instructions on the packet. Topped with fresh or dried fruit and yoghurt it makes a delicious start to the day. Make it with milk rather than water, or half milk/half water, to add more nutrients.

Eggs

A scrambled, poached or boiled egg with toast or bread makes an alternative to cereal with milk.

French toast is made by dipping bread into an egg whisked with a tablespoon of milk. The bread is then fried on both sides, in a little butter, until pale golden. You can serve it plain or with a topping such as jam or honey or just a shake of cinnamon mixed with a little sugar.

Pancakes are made with milk, flour and eggs and make a nutritious alternative to toast or bread to have with different spreads.

Muffins

Muffins can make an alternative breakfast and can be eaten on the run if you are really pushed for time. These can be made in batches and then frozen. You just need to remember to take them out of the freezer the night before or you can defrost them in a microwave in the morning if you forget.

COOKED LIGHT MEALS

Here are some suggestions for light, nutritious meals that you can cook yourself:

▶ *vegetable soups with toast or bread*
▶ *baked beans on toast – serve with some raw vegetable sticks*
▶ *pasta with vegetable sauce – include some pulses or dhal in the sauce or sprinkle with cheese*
▶ *grilled cheese on toast with salad or vegetable sticks*
▶ *pieces of quiche cut into small squares to be eaten as finger food*
▶ *pizza can also be cut into squares and eaten as finger food. Choose commercial pizzas carefully, as some are much higher in fat than others. Thin, crispy pizza bases are preferable to bases that are pan-fried and higher in fat. If you buy a marguerita pizza you can top it with diced vegetables that your toddler likes and add some extra grated cheese on top. Alternatively, quick pizzas can be made using pitta bread bases (see Chapter 5, page 116).*

COOKED MAIN MEALS

Ideally these should be family meals that you all eat together.

Toddlers prefer soft cuts of meat rather than meat that is chewy and hard. Use good-quality lean minced meat in meat loaf, meat balls or home-made burgers. Choose meat cuts than can be slow cooked to keep them soft. Stews and casseroles can usually be prepared quickly and left slow-cooking in the oven; use a timer so the meal is ready when you are. Always include vegetables – you can incorporate them into the sauce, if not as separate pieces.

COOKED PUDDINGS

These can make a delicious end to a meal. Fruit tarts or pies or crumbles are popular. They can be served with a little yoghurt or, for a treat, ice cream or cream. You can also offer cake, cookies or muffins along with some fresh fruit or a fruit coulis. By baking

your own cakes, cookies and muffins you will be eliminating the
additives present in commercial foods that are used to extend the
shelf life of the product.

Insight

A home-cooked pudding beats a purchased one every time
because it tastes so much better. It's definitely worth the
effort for the appreciation you get from your family.

SEASONAL MEAL PLANS

Family meals are the ideal for your toddler. Below are some
seasonal meal plans for family foods using produce that will be
cheap and locally produced in each season. However, you can
always substitute tinned and frozen foods and toddler favourites
for foods that your family may not eat or have in stock.

▶ *Vegetables popular with toddlers: tinned or frozen sweetcorn,*
  frozen peas, frozen spinach, frozen mixed vegetables.
▶ *Fresh fruits popular with toddlers and available year round:*
  bananas and kiwi fruit.

Meal plan for spring

		Day 1	*Day 2*	*Day 3*
Breakfast		porridge with dried fruit and milk	poached egg with toast fingers; kiwi fruit slices	toasted hot cross bun and slices of pear
	Drink	diluted fruit juice	diluted fruit juice	hot chocolate
Midday meal	1st course	chicken nuggets with new potatoes and purple sprouting broccoli	salmon fish fingers with pasta pieces, spinach and radish salad	roast lamb with potato wedges and broccoli florets

		Day 1	Day 2	Day 3
	2nd course	chocolate almond cake with orange segments	rhubarb crumble with custard	yoghurt and stoned cherries
	Drink	water	water	water
Evening meal	1st course	hummus and rocket sandwich	baked beans on toast with carrot sticks	cheese omelette with bread sticks and asparagus spears
	2nd course	fruit salad with yoghurt	mini muffin and apple slices	lemon tart with banana slices and ice cream
	Drink	water	milk	water

Meal plan for summer

		Day 1	Day 2	Day 3
Breakfast		toddler muesli with blueberries	pancake with strawberries	breakfast wheat biscuit with milk and peach slices
	Drink	diluted fruit juice	milk	diluted fruit juice
Midday meal	1st course	cold chicken pieces with rice salad and fresh peas	monkfish kebabs with new potatoes and cherry tomatoes	tuna pasta with green beans and carrot sticks

(Contd)

		Day 1	Day 2	Day 3
	2nd course	gooseberry fool	summer pudding	strawberries and ice cream
	Drink	water	milk	water
Evening meal	1st course	tomato omelette with toast fingers and sliced peppers	breadsticks with hummus dip and cucumber slices	ham sandwich with cucumber and courgette sticks
	2nd course	melon pieces with yoghurt	chocolate biscuit and nectarine slices	drop scones with raspberries
	Drink	water	water	milk

Meal plan for autumn

		Day 1	Day 2	Day 3
Breakfast		toddler muesli with milk and blackberries	boiled egg with toast fingers; grapes	breakfast wheat biscuit with milk and sliced pears
	Drink	diluted fruit juice	diluted fruit juice	diluted fruit juice
Midday meal	1st course	chicken nuggets with stir-fried vegetables	mackerel fish cakes with roast butternut squash and parsnips	mini meatballs with potato wedges and cauliflower florets

		Day 1	Day 2	Day 3
	2nd course	apple crumble with custard	cooked plums with fromage frais	apple and blackberry pie with custard
	Drink	water	water	water
Evening meal	1st course	mushroom omelette with toast fingers and cherry tomatoes	mini pizza topped with ham, tomato and diced peppers served with carrot and cucumber sticks	pasta and red pepper sauce with grated cheese
	2nd course	chocolate cake and grapes	mini muffin and plums	autumn fruit salad and shortbread
	Drink	water	water	water

Meal plan for winter

		Day 1	Day 2	Day 3
Breakfast		boiled egg with toast fingers; kiwi fruit slices	porridge with dried apricots and yoghurt	breakfast wheat biscuit with milk; apple slices
	Drink	diluted fruit juice	diluted fruit juice	diluted fruit juice

(Contd)

		Day 1	Day 2	Day 3
Midday meal	**1st course**	chicken and vegetable curry and rice	fish and potato pie with peas	slow-cooked beef stew with potato and swede mash, cauliflower florets and brussels sprouts
	2nd course	fromage frais and pear slices	apple crumble and custard	warm fruit salad with yoghurt
	Drink	water	water	water
Evening meal	**1st course**	pasta and red pepper sauce with grated cheese	toast fingers with chicken liver pâté and celery sticks	butternut squash and lentil soup with a bread roll
	2nd course	tangerine segments with chocolate biscuits	slice of date and walnut loaf	drop scones with clementine segments
	Drink	water	water	water

Meal plans for vegetarians – not eating meat or fish
This meal plan can be adapted for any season by adding the
seasonal fruit and vegetables from the previous seasonal plans.

		Day 1	Day 2	Day 3
Breakfast		porridge with dried fruit, ground almonds and milk	baked beans on toast; kiwi fruit slices	toddler muesli with extra chopped or ground nuts and milk

		Day 1	*Day 2*	*Day 3*
	Drink	diluted fruit juice	milk	diluted fruit juice
Midday meal	**1st course**	lentil burgers with roasted vegetables and pasta pieces	rice and dhal with stir-fried vegetables	mini falafel with potato wedges and vegetables
	2nd course	fromage frais and fruit slices	banana with custard	yoghurt and fruit slices
	Drink	diluted fruit juice	diluted fruit juice	diluted fruit juice
Evening meal	**1st course**	tortilla (Spanish omelette) with toast fingers	tofu and avocado spread on toast fingers with vegetable sticks	butternut squash and lentil soup with a bread roll
	2nd course	fruit salad with ice cream	slice of date and walnut loaf	chocolate almond mini cakes and fruit slices
	Drink	diluted fruit juice	diluted fruit juice	diluted fruit juice

PICNIC AND PACKED LUNCH IDEAS

Always pack a picnic or packed lunch in a cool bag. A good tip is to freeze the drinks in cartons to make the ice bricks to keep the lunch cool and the drinks will have melted by the time you are ready to eat.

Pack two courses and a drink as with other meals.

- *Savoury course ideas: sandwiches, slices of quiche, pizza slices, wraps, samosas, pieces of cold meat and breadsticks or crackers, mini falafels and pasta pieces. Always include some raw vegetable sticks. Cut them so that they are ready to eat and wrap them tightly in cling film.*
- *Sweet course ideas (some fruit with something sweet): a yoghurt or fromage frais are easy to pack as they will be sealed – don't forget to include a spoon; a piece of cake, muffin or biscuit can also be included; peel, segment or cut the fruit so that it is ready to eat – you can wrap slices tightly together in cling film to stop them going brown.*
- *Drink: pack a small bottle or carton of water, unsweetened fruit juice, milk or flavoured milk.*

BIRTHDAY PARTY FOOD AND OTHER CELEBRATORY MEALS

It is fun and important to teach your toddler about traditional celebratory meals by following traditions such as chocolate eggs at Easter and Indian sweets at Divali. These high-fat and sweet foods are often part of celebratory food, which is fine if eaten occasionally for annual events. However, birthday parties are now frequent events for toddlers if they have a large circle of friends from their nursery or playgroup. When arranging your toddler's birthday party, you could use food that is attractive but nutritious as well by including foods from food groups 1 to 4, as this planner shows.

Healthy party food

Hot food

- *pizza slices*
- *chicken nuggets*
- *chipolatas or mini sausages which are lean and have a high meat content*

▶ *avoid foods coated in pastry (such as sausage rolls) as
these are very high in fat.*

Cold food

▶ *sandwiches*
▶ *fairy bread – slices of buttered bread sprinkled with
coloured sugar strands*
▶ *crispy chocolate clusters (see recipe, Chapter 5, page 123)*
▶ *chocolate almond cupcakes (see recipe, Chapter 5,
page 123) – decorate with a little face*
▶ *jelly with fruit and ice cream*
▶ *traditional favourites, such as decorated gingerbread men*
▶ *birthday cake (cakes usually have the nutritious
ingredients flour, eggs and milk) – decorate it with a few
sweets; take care to minimize the amount of icing that is
used to decorate cakes and biscuits, as this is pure sugar*
▶ *do not give large amounts of sweets and confectionery –
however, you can use a few to decorate the more
nutritious foods, such as cupcakes with little faces*
▶ *avoid snack foods high in fat such as crisps.*

Drinks

▶ *diluted fruit juice – you can dilute it with fizzy water to
have a bubbly drink*
▶ *flavoured milk – a little extra sugar in the flavouring will
do no harm considering how nutritious the milk is.*

5

....

Recipes

In this chapter you will learn:
- *recipes for breakfasts*
- *recipes for vegetarian dishes using pulses*
- *recipes for meat and fish dishes*
- *recipes for puddings*
- *recipes for snacks.*

Breakfasts

PORRIDGE WITH FRESH FRUIT

(Makes 1–3 servings)

Porridge is a wonderfully warming breakfast on a cold day.
You can cook the porridge in a saucepan on a hob, but using a
microwave makes it much quicker and easier. You can make it
plain and add fresh fruit to it, or make it with dried fruit mixed in.

5 tbsp porridge oats
90 ml/3 fl oz milk
90 ml/3 fl oz water

Put the oats in a deep cereal bowl and pour in the milk and water.
The bowl should be about half full. Microwave on full power,

uncovered for 2½ minutes. Top with fresh fruit and serve with extra milk or yoghurt.

PORRIDGE WITH DRIED FRUIT

(Makes 1–2 servings)

5 tbsp porridge oats
4 dried apricots (diced) or 1 tbsp sultanas
90 ml/3 fl oz milk
90 ml/3 fl oz water

Put the oats and dried fruit in a deep cereal bowl and pour in the milk and water. Microwave on full power, uncovered for 2½ minutes. Serve with extra milk and 2 tbsp plain yoghurt.

TODDLER'S MUESLI

(Makes 2 servings)

By making your own muesli you can choose the ingredients you wish and keep the sugar content down, as commercial brands often have large amounts of sugar. It will also save you some money.

2 tbsp rolled oats
2 tbsp wheatgerm
2 tbsp ground almonds
2 tbsp dried fruit – sultanas, raisins or chopped apricots
1 tbsp desiccated coconut
1 tsp brown sugar

Mix all the ingredients together. Serve with milk or yoghurt and some extra fresh fruit, if desired.

Egg dishes for breakfast or light meals

MUSHROOM OMELETTE

(Makes 1–2 servings)

1 egg
½ tbsp water
small pinch pepper
1 tsp butter or oil
2 button mushrooms, thinly sliced

Using a fork, beat the egg and water with the pepper in a small
bowl. Melt the butter in a small non-stick frying pan and add the
mushroom slices and sauté until softened. Remove from the pan.
Add a little more butter to the pan and allow it to melt and cover
the base, then turn up the heat. Once sizzling, pour in the egg
mixture and add the mushrooms to one half of the egg mixture.
Cook over a medium to high heat until the egg is cooked through.
Fold the half without mushrooms over the half with mushrooms.
Cut into finger-sized pieces for your toddler to feed himself. Serve
with toast fingers.

TORTILLA (SPANISH OMELETTE)

(Makes 2–4 servings)

This is a complete savoury course containing egg, potato and
vegetables together.

2 tsp rapeseed oil
1 spring onion, finely chopped
1 medium potato (about 100 g), peeled, diced and steamed
2 tbsp diced fresh vegetables that have been cooked, or use
*   frozen mixed vegetables*

2 *eggs, beaten*
2 *tbsp grated cheese*

Heat the oil in a small non-stick frying pan. Add the spring onion, potatoes and vegetables and fry over a gentle heat, stirring occasionally, until the potatoes are slightly brown and the vegetables are hot (about 6–8 minutes). Sprinkle in the grated cheese and then pour in the beaten eggs. Carry on cooking without stirring until the underside is cooked. Place the pan under a preheated grill until the top is golden brown and the eggs are cooked all the way through. Lift the tortilla onto a chopping board and slice into fingers or triangles.

Vegetarian dishes using pulses

BUTTERNUT SQUASH AND LENTIL SOUP

(Makes 3–4 servings)

1 tbsp rapeseed oil
1 medium onion
1 clove garlic, peeled and chopped finely or crushed
½ butternut squash, peeled, deseeded and cut into cubes
6 tbsp red lentils
½ litre/17 fl oz water or stock
½ tsp ground ginger
½ tsp ground coriander
½ tsp ground cumin
pepper to taste

Heat the oil in a large saucepan and sauté the onion and garlic for about 5 minutes. Then add the rest of the ingredients and bring to the boil and simmer for about 20 minutes until the butternut squash and lentils are soft. Blend in a liquidizer until smooth, adding a little more water if it is too thick.

Serving suggestion: add 1 tbsp of plain yoghurt to each bowl and sprinkle on some chopped fresh herbs such as coriander, chives or parsley.

RED LENTIL DHAL

(Makes 2–4 servings)

3 tbsp split red lentils
250 ml/8 fl oz water
2 small spring onions very finely chopped
1 garlic clove, peeled and finely chopped
½ tbsp of melted ghee or rapeseed oil
½ tsp ground turmeric
½ tsp ground cumin

Thoroughly wash, drain and place the lentils in a small saucepan with the water and bring to the boil. Simmer uncovered for 10 minutes, stirring frequently and removing any scum that forms.

Cover and cook for a further 10–20 minutes or so, stirring occasionally until the lentils are soft and form a moist 'porridge'. In a separate pan, gently heat the ghee or rapeseed oil, add the onion and fry until nicely browned. Add the garlic and fry for a further 2–3 minutes. Next, add the ground spices and fry for a further 2 minutes. Finally add the contents of the pan to the lentils and stir to fully combine for 2 minutes. If the dhal is too thick, add further water; if too thin, simmer gently until reduced.

COOKING GREEN PUY LENTILS

Wash the lentils and rinse well. Place in a pan and cover with cold water and bring to the boil. Boil rapidly for 10 minutes, then reduce the heat and simmer for 30–40 minutes or until tender. Drain. These lentils can be added to pasta sauces in place of meat, such as in a bolognaise sauce.

HUMMUS

(Makes 6–10 servings)

Making your own hummus is quick and easy.

400 g/14 oz can chickpeas, drained and rinsed
3 tbsp olive oil
juice of ½ lemon
1 tsp cumin
1 clove garlic, crushed

Put all the ingredients into a bowl and purée with a hand-held blender. Stir the hummus into any combination of vegetables or use as a sandwich filling or dip.

TOFU AND AVOCADO SPREAD

(Makes 4–6 servings)

½ ripe avocado, stone and skin removed
55 g/2 oz tofu, broken into pieces
juice of ½ lemon
1 small clove garlic
½ tbsp fresh parsley
1 tsp olive oil

Put all the ingredients in a bowl and purée with a hand-held blender until the mixture is smooth. Spoon into a serving bowl and garnish with a slice of lemon. Store in the refrigerator tightly covered with cling film.

PASTA WITH LENTIL BOLOGNAISE SAUCE

(Makes 2–3 servings)

3 tbsp puy lentils, rinsed
½ tbsp olive oil

2 spring onions, finely sliced
½ small courgette, diced
2 small button mushrooms, washed and diced
2 tbsp chopped tomatoes
1 tsp tomato purée
½ tsp dried mixed herbs
pinch of black pepper
55 g/2 oz pasta spirals

Put the lentils into a saucepan and add water to cover them. Bring to the boil and simmer until the lentils are tender (about 25 minutes). Meanwhile, heat the oil in a pan and add the onion, garlic, courgette and mushrooms. Stir-fry for 5–10 minutes, until tender. Add the chopped tomatoes, tomato purée, herbs and pepper. Cover and cook gently for about 5 minutes. Drain the cooked lentils and stir into the vegetable sauce. Cook pasta according to the instructions on the packet. Drain well. Mix the pasta into the lentil sauce. Serve sprinkled with grated cheese.

BUTTERNUT SQUASH AND CHICKPEA RISOTTO

(Makes 5–8 servings)

1 litre (1¾ pints) water
1 clove garlic, peeled
1 tsp ground cumin
1 tbsp tomato purée
3 bay leaves
1 small butternut squash, peeled, deseeded and cut into
    small cubes
1½ tbsp butter
1 small onion, peeled and chopped
220 g/8 oz risotto rice
400 g/14 oz can chickpeas, drained
1 tbsp chopped parsley
30 g/1 oz grated parmesan cheese

In a pan place the water, garlic, cumin, tomato purée, bay leaves and butternut squash cubes. Simmer for 10–15 minutes until the squash is just tender. Using a slotted spoon, transfer the squash to a plate and set aside. Remove the garlic cloves and bay leaves and discard. Melt the butter in a heavy-based pan and add the onion and sauté for a few minutes until soft. Add the rice, stir well and continue to cook gently over a low heat for a minute or two. Gradually add the stock a ladle at a time. Stir constantly, gradually adding more liquid as the rice absorbs it. When the rice is just tender, add the squash and the chickpeas. Keep adding stock and stirring until the rice is creamy and all the stock is absorbed. When cooked, stir in the cheese and sprinkle with chopped parsley. Serve with a green vegetable.

MINI FALAFEL

(Makes 4–6 servings)

400 g/14 oz can chickpeas, rinsed and drained
1 small onion finely chopped
1 clove garlic, peeled and finely chopped
1 tbsp fresh coriander leaves, washed and chopped
1 tsp ground coriander
1 tsp ground cumin
½ tsp ground turmeric
2–4 tbsp flour
1–2 tbsp rapeseed oil

Place the chickpeas in a food processor with the onion, garlic, cumin and both types of coriander. Process until the mixture resembles a smooth purée. Let the mixture rest for at least half an hour. Take walnut-sized portions and shape each into a small flat round shape 1 cm/½ inch thick. Roll them lightly in the flour and chill for another 30 minutes. Heat the oil in a frying pan and cook the falafel over a gentle, medium heat for about 10 minutes, turning frequently.

SPICY CANNELLINI BEANS WITH MUSHROOMS

(Makes 4–6 servings)

2 tbsp olive oil
2 medium onions, sliced
1 tsp ground cumin
1 tsp ground coriander
1 tsp ground turmeric
½ tsp ground cinnamon
220 g/8 oz mushrooms, chopped
1 red pepper, deseeded and sliced
400 g/14 oz tin cannellini beans, drained
400 g/14 oz chopped tomatoes
1 tsp tomato purée
pinch of black pepper
2 tbsp fresh coriander leaves, chopped

Heat the oil in a large non-stick frying pan and cook the onions
until transparent and soft. Add all the spices and stir for a minute
then add the mushrooms and pepper. Cook for another minute
or so then add the beans, tomatoes, tomato purée and pepper.
Cover and simmer for 15 minutes. Sprinkle with coriander or
parsley before serving. Serve with pasta or rice and a green
vegetable.

TOFU STIR-FRY

(Makes 2–4 servings)

1 tbsp yellow bean sauce
1 tbsp smooth peanut butter
juice of 1 lemon
1 tbsp olive oil
1 tsp grated fresh ginger
pinch of mild chilli powder
1 clove garlic, peeled and crushed
115 g/4 oz firm tofu, drained and sliced

1 courgette, diced
1 red pepper, deseeded and diced
85 g/3 oz fresh bean sprouts

In a bowl, mix together the yellow bean sauce, peanut butter and lemon juice. Heat the oil in a non-stick frying pan and stir-fry the ginger, chilli and garlic for a minute. Add the tofu slices and fry for a minute turning once. Add the courgette, red pepper and bean sprouts and continue stir-frying for 2–3 minutes. Add the sauce mixture and stir-fry for 1–2 minutes until well combined. Serve with noodles or rice.

Meat recipes

TOAST FINGERS WITH CHICKEN LIVER PÂTÉ

(Makes 2–3 servings)

55 g/2 oz chicken livers
15 g/½ oz butter
2 spring onions, chopped
1 tsp chopped thyme
½ celery stick chopped
½ tbsp apple juice
2 slices thick white bread

Melt the butter in a non-stick frying pan and sauté the spring onions for a few minutes. Trim and chop the chicken livers and add in with the thyme, celery and apple juice. Cook for a further 10–12 minutes, stirring often. The livers should be cooked right through and the vegetables soft.

Remove from the heat and mash together with a fork or use a blender for a smoother texture. Toast the bread and spread with the pâté. Cut into fingers and serve with cherry tomatoes or slices of cucumber.

HOME-MADE CHICKEN NUGGETS

It's so easy to make these chicken nuggets that look similar to commercially produced nuggets, but are superior in quality and nutrients. They are also lower in salt. You can make your own breadcrumbs or use fine dried breadcrumbs available in the supermarkets.

(Makes 2–4 servings)

1 chicken breast
1 egg, beaten
3 tbsp plain, dried breadcrumbs
½ tsp dried mixed herbs

Preheat the oven to 200°C/400°F/Gas Mark 6. Lightly grease a non-stick oven tray by brushing it with olive oil. Cut the chicken breast into small strips. Put the beaten egg in one small bowl. Mix the breadcrumbs and herbs in a separate small bowl. Dip the chicken breast strips into the egg and then into the breadcrumbs. Place each nugget on the baking tray. Cook in the oven for 10–15 minutes until golden and cooked through, turning once to brown both sides. Serve with oven-roasted vegetable sticks.

MINI BURGERS OR MEATBALLS

(Makes 12 mini burgers)

1 small onion, peeled and cut into quarters
1 medium carrot, finely grated
2 tbsp breadcrumbs
1½ tbsp tomato purée
1 tsp dried mixed herbs
½ tsp ground coriander or cumin or ground mace
pinch of freshly ground black pepper
1 egg, whisked
220 g/8 oz very lean minced beef

Preheat the oven to 180°C/350°F/Gas Mark 4. Put the onion pieces in a food processor and process until finely minced. Add the carrot, breadcrumbs, tomato purée, mixed herbs and egg. Process for about 10 seconds. Add the minced beef and process for a further few seconds until the meat is well mixed through. Form little burgers and place them on a baking tray. Put into the oven for 25–30 minutes. Check they are cooked right through. Serve them on a toasted bread roll with a slice of tomato and some lettuce as a nutritious burger. Alternatively, serve the burgers as meatballs with the tomato and red pepper sauce (see recipe below) and either potato wedges or pasta shapes for a finger food meal.

MEATLOAF

(Makes 3–6 servings)

This is a popular way to serve soft meat. Serve it hot with the tomato and red pepper sauce below or you can serve it cold, cut into small cubes as a finger food, the next day.

Use the same ingredients and follow the instructions as for the mini burgers recipe, above. Rather than making burgers, form the mixture into a loaf shape on a baking tray. Bake uncovered in the oven at 180°C/350°F/Gas Mark 4 for 45 minutes.

TOMATO AND RED PEPPER SAUCE

(Makes 3–6 servings)

This accompanies the meatball and meatloaf recipes (above) but can also be used for pasta or chicken.

1 tbsp olive oil
½ onion, finely sliced
1 red or green pepper, deseeded and diced
1 clove garlic, crushed or thinly sliced

1 can/400 g chopped tomatoes
1 tsp oregano or basil
pinch of freshly ground black pepper

Heat the oil in a frying pan and add the onion. Fry gently for a few minutes then add the diced pepper and garlic. Continue frying over a gentle heat for another 5 minutes. Add the tomatoes and herbs and simmer until the onions and pepper are soft. Purée the sauce and keep warm to serve with meatloaf or meatballs.

Fish recipes

TOAST FINGERS WITH OILY FISH

(Makes 2–4 servings)

25 g/1 oz smoked mackerel or sardines/pilchards tinned in oil and
*   well drained*
½ tbsp natural bio yoghurt
½ tsp lemon juice
½ tsp tomato purée
2 slices thick white or brown bread

Mash the fish with the yoghurt, lemon juice and tomato purée.

Toast the bread and spread with the fish mixture. If you wish to serve it warm, place under a preheated grill for 1–2 minutes. Cut into fingers and serve with vegetable sticks.

HOME-MADE FISH FINGERS

These are quick and easy to make and contain more fish than commercial frozen fish fingers.

(Makes 2–4 servings)

110 g/4 oz fillet white fish (e.g. cod or haddock)
1 egg, beaten
4 tbsp dried breadcrumbs
1 tbsp rapeseed oil

Cut the fish into four pieces, taking off any skin and checking carefully for any remaining bones. Put the egg in one bowl and the breadcrumbs in another shallow bowl. Heat the oil in a frying pan. Dip the fish pieces first in the egg, and then coat all sides with breadcrumbs and drop into the hot oil. Fry for 4–5 minutes, turning once, or until the fish is cooked right through and the breadcrumbs are golden brown. Serve with mashed potato and steamed vegetable sticks.

SALMON FISH FINGERS

(Makes 4 servings)

110 g/4 oz salmon fillet, skin removed
4 tbsp dried breadcrumbs
1 egg, beaten in a shallow dish
1 clove garlic, crushed
2 tsp butter

Preheat the oven to 200°C/400°F/Gas Mark 6. Cut the salmon into fingers, checking that there are no bones. Beat the egg in a small bowl and put the breadcrumbs in another shallow bowl. Dip the salmon pieces in the egg and then coat in breadcrumbs. Place on a lightly greased baking tray. Mix together the crushed garlic and butter. Dot each piece of salmon with a little of the butter mixture. Bake in the oven for 5–6 minutes and then turn the salmon fingers and cook for a further 4–5 minutes until golden brown and cooked through. Do not overcook.

FISH CAKES

These work well with smoked, oily fish but you can use white fish for a milder taste.

(Makes 8 servings)

220 g/8 oz potato, peeled and cut into pieces
140 g/5 oz fillets of smoked mackerel, trout or eel, all bones
    carefully removed
1 egg, beaten
juice of 1 lemon
2 tbsp fresh chives or parsley, finely chopped
pinch of freshly ground black pepper

Steam or boil the potatoes until tender. Place the smoked fish in a
bowl and flake with a fork.

Tip in the cooked potatoes and chives and mash all together until
well mixed. Add in the juice of half the lemon and just enough
whisked egg to make a mixture that binds well but isn't too runny.
Mix well. Form fish cakes with a heaped tablespoon of mixture
and place on a grill lined with a sheet of aluminium foil. (Your
fingers will get quite sticky!) Place under a hot grill, turning once,
until golden brown (about 7 minutes either side). Drizzle with
lemon juice before serving.

FISH AND POTATO PIE

You can make this dish with all white fish, but by using some oily
fish you will be providing your toddler with more omega 3 fats.

(Makes 8–10 servings)

222 g/8 oz potatoes, peeled and cubed
222 g/8 oz sweet potatoes, peeled and cubed
450 g/1 lb mixed fish fillets such as mackerel, salmon, white fish
    and prawns
450 ml/16 fl oz milk
1 bay leaf
2 tbsp plain flour

½ tsp dried herbs
1 tsp wholegrain mustard
pinch of freshly ground black pepper
3 tbsp breadcrumbs
2 tsp chopped fresh parsley

Preheat the oven to 200°C/400°F/Gas Mark 6. Steam or boil the potatoes for about 20 minutes, until soft. While they are cooking, put the fish in a pan with the milk and a bay leaf and simmer gently until the fish is cooked and flakes easily. Lift the fish out and place in an ovenproof dish and flake. Make the sauce by melting the butter in a saucepan and adding the flour. Cook gently while stirring for 1–2 minutes – do not allow the flour to brown. Discard the bay leaf and gradually stir in the milk which the fish was cooked in. Stir over a low heat until the sauce thickens. Stir the herbs, mustard and pepper into the sauce and pour over the flaked fish. Mash the potatoes together with some extra butter and milk and spread them over the top of the fish in sauce. Sprinkle the breadcrumbs and parsley on top and bake in the oven for 25 minutes until golden brown.

MONKFISH KEBABS

Monkfish is an ideal fish for kebabs as it doesn't fall to pieces when cooked.

(Makes 4 servings)

114 g/4 oz monkfish tail, cut into cubes
1 medium tomato, cut into 8 wedges
1 red pepper, cut into cubes
8 button mushrooms
1 tbsp olive oil
juice of 1 lemon
pinch of freshly ground black pepper

Preheat the grill. Thread the cubes of monkfish onto cocktail sticks putting the wedges of tomato, the squares of red pepper and the button mushrooms between the cubes of fish. Mix the olive oil, lemon juice and pepper together in a small bowl to make a dressing. Place the kebabs on a grill pan lined with foil and brush with the olive oil dressing. Grill for about 6 minutes, then turn, brush the other side with dressing and grill for a further 5 minutes until the fish is cooked right through.

TUNA PASTA

(Makes 2–4 servings)

90 g/3 oz penne or other pasta shapes
½ small onion, peeled and finely chopped
1 garlic clove, peeled and crushed
2 tsp tomato purée
1 large ripe tomato, chopped or ½ tin chopped tomatoes
110 g tinned tuna in oil, drained (keep the oil)

Cook the penne or pasta in boiling water according to instructions on the packet. Meanwhile, put the oil drained from the tinned tuna in a small pan over a gentle heat. Fry the onion and garlic in the oil for about 10 minutes, until soft. Add the tomato purée and tomatoes. Simmer for 2–3 minutes. Flake the tuna and add it to the tomato sauce. Continue simmering for another 2 minutes. Drain the pasta when cooked and add to the tomato sauce. Serve with some vegetable sticks.

Vegetable recipes

Stir-frying or roasting vegetables gives them a more attractive flavour than simply steaming or boiling.

STIR-FRIED VEGETABLE STICKS

(Makes 2–4 servings)

1 tbsp olive oil
3 small broccoli florets
3 small cauliflower florets
4 baby sweetcorn, halved or left whole if they are small
4 mangetout, topped and tailed
4 button mushrooms
½ red pepper, cored, deseeded and sliced lengthways

Heat the oil in a non-stick frying pan. Add the cauliflower
florets first and cook for a couple of minutes. Then add the baby
sweetcorn, mangetout, mushrooms and pepper slices. Stir the
vegetables from time to time to stop them burning. Continue
cooking for another 5–8 minutes until the vegetables are slightly
softened, but still al dente. Serve with any of the savoury dishes.

ROASTED WINTER VEGETABLES

(Makes 4–6 servings)

2 tbsp rapeseed oil
1 tsp chopped fresh thyme
2 parsnips, peeled and sliced thickly lengthways
2 carrots, peeled and sliced lengthways
1 beetroot, peeled and diced
2 large red-skinned potatoes, scrubbed and diced – no need to peel
2 leeks, washed and sliced into about 2 cm/1 inch pieces
1 slice of pumpkin, peeled and cubed

Preheat the oven to 200°C/400°F/Gas Mark 6. Put the oil and
thyme in a large bowl. Add the prepared vegetables and toss in
the oil until well coated. Spread the vegetables out on a large oven
tray. Put in the oven and cook for about 35 minutes, until soft.

Mini pizzas

It takes just minutes to put these pizzas together.

HAM AND PEPPER PITTA PIZZA

(Makes 1–2 servings)

1 mini pitta bread
½ tbsp tomato purée
pinch of dried oregano
1 slice of ham, diced
3 thin slices courgette, cubed
½ red pepper, diced
1 tbsp grated parmesan cheese
1 tbsp cheddar cheese

Preheat the grill. Spread the tomato purée over one side of the pitta bread. Sprinkle over the oregano and then scatter the ham, courgette and pepper pieces evenly over the top. Lastly sprinkle on the two cheeses. Grill for 5 minutes or until the cheeses have melted and are just beginning to brown. Cool and cut into slices or triangles for serving.

MUSHROOM AND PEPPER PITTA PIZZA

(Makes 1 serving)

1 round mini pitta bread
½ tbsp tomato purée
1 small button mushroom, sliced
½ green pepper, diced
2 tbsp grated mozzarella cheese

Spread the sauce on one side of the pitta bread. Sprinkle on the mushroom and pepper followed by the cheese and the oregano. Cook under a hot grill for 2–3 minutes until the cheese is bubbling.

Desserts or puddings

FRUIT SALAD FOR SUMMER DAYS

These summer fruits are at their best in July and August.

(Makes 1 serving for your toddler and one for you)

1 ripe peach
1 ripe apricot
1 wedge of melon
4 strawberries
6 blueberries

Wash the peach, apricot and berries. Cut the peach and apricot in half and remove the stones. Most toddlers will be happy eating these two fruits with the skin left on but some may prefer them peeled. Cut the fruit into bite-sized pieces. Deseed the melon wedge, remove the rind and cut the remainder into bite-sized pieces. Remove the stalks from the berries and mix the fruits together.

Serve on its own or with a small scoop of ice cream.

FRUIT SALAD FOR AUTUMN DAYS

All these fruits are in season and at their best in October and November. This makes a refreshing dessert to follow a warm meal. Some toddlers will prefer it on its own but it can be served with fromage frais or yoghurt.

(Makes 1 serving for your toddler and one for you)

1 satsuma
1 ripe pear
4 blackberries or loganberries
4 small seedless grapes

Peel the satsuma and divide into segments. If there are pips, cut the segments in half and remove the pips. Wash the rest of the fruit well. Core the pear and cut into bite-sized cubes. Mix all the fruits together in a bowl.

WARM FRUIT SALAD

(Makes 4–6 portions)

55 g/2 oz dried peaches or pears
55 g/2 oz dried apple rings
40 g/1½ oz dried apricots
40 g/1½ oz sultanas
100 ml orange juice
100 ml water
1 clove
1 cinnamon stick

Place all the ingredients in a pan and bring to the boil. Cover and simmer for about 10 minutes, or until all the fruits are tender. Remove the clove and cinnamon and allow to cool. Chill until required. Serve with yoghurt, custard or ice cream.

TROPICAL FINGER FRUIT SALAD

(Makes 1 serving for your toddler and one for you)

½ small ripe mango
1 wedge melon
1 ripe kiwi fruit
1 slice of fresh pineapple
few slices of banana

Peel the mango and kiwi fruit. Cut the fruit into bite-sized pieces. Cut away the rind and hard core from the pineapple slice. Cut the remainder into bite-sized pieces. Mix all the fruit together.

RHUBARB CRUMBLE

(Makes 4–6 servings)

55 g/2 oz plain flour
45 g/1½ oz butter, cut into small cubes
30 g/1 oz rolled oats
3 tbsp ground almonds
45 g/1½ oz soft dark brown sugar
450 g/1 lb rhubarb
2 tbsp sugar

Preheat the oven to 180°C/350°F/Gas Mark 4. To make the crumble topping: put the flour, oats and butter into a food processor and process until the mixture resembles coarse crumbs; stir in the ground almonds and brown sugar. Prepare the rhubarb by cutting into chunks and cooking in a little water with the sugar until it begins to soften. Put the rhubarb in a small ovenproof dish.

Sprinkle the crumble on top and bake in the oven for 30–40 minutes until the top is lightly browned. Serve with ice cream or custard.

Milk puddings

Traditional milk puddings will be popular with your toddler if you introduced them while he was a baby. Count them as one of his three servings of milk each day.

RICE PUDDING

(Makes 4–6 servings)

2 tsp butter
3 tbsp pudding rice

1 tbsp soft brown sugar
4 tbsp sultanas
550 ml/1 pint milk
½ tsp ground nutmeg

Preheat the oven to 150°C/300°F/Gas Mark 2. Grease an oven-proof dish with a little butter. Put the rice, sugar and sultanas into the dish and stir in the milk. Float the rest of the butter on top and sprinkle with nutmeg. Cook for about 2–3 hours stirring once or twice after an hour. It will be ready when the rice is tender and the top is golden.

If your toddler prefers, you can make it without the sultanas. Serve it with some fresh fruit slices as finger food or with a fruit coulis sauce mixed through.

SAGO OR TAPIOCA PUDDINGS

These can be made in the same way as the rice pudding but only need 1–1½ hours to cook. Replace the rice with the same quantity of either sago or tapioca.

Sweet snacks

These can be offered with fruit as a pudding or as a between-meal snack.

DATE AND WALNUT LOAF

The fruit and nuts make this sweet, moist cake a nutritious snack. Walnuts are high in omega 3 fats. This loaf will keep well, in fact it becomes more moist when stored for a day or two.

110 g/4 oz soft butter or margarine
175 g/6 oz soft brown sugar
2 eggs

110 g/4 oz *wholemeal flour*
110 g/4 oz *plain white flour*
1½ tsp *baking powder*
110 g/4 oz *walnuts, finely chopped*
110 g/4 oz *pitted dates, chopped*
3–4 tbsp *water*

Preheat the oven to 180°C/350°F/Gas Mark 4. Grease a loaf tin.
Put the butter, sugar, eggs, flour and baking powder in a food
processor and process for a few seconds until mixed. Add the
walnuts, dates and water. Mix for another few seconds but do not
over-process. Turn the mixture into the loaf tin, spreading it out
evenly. Bake for 1 hour until the loaf feels springy. To test if it is
ready, insert a fine skewer and then remove; the skewer should
come out clean. Allow to cool in the tin for a few minutes before
turning out. Serve warm or cold. To store, wrap in foil.

DROP SCONES

(Makes about 24 little scones)

2 *eggs*
1 tbsp *sugar*
120 ml/4 fl oz *milk*
110 g/4 oz *self-raising flour*
1 tsp *baking powder*
1 tbsp *butter, melted*
butter for frying

Put the egg and the sugar in a bowl and beat with a hand-beater
until they are thick. Add the milk, flour, baking powder and melted
butter and beat until smooth. Leave the mixture to stand for at
least 10 minutes. Melt a little butter in a large, flat non-stick pan.
Drop heaped tablespoons of batter into the pan to make small
rounds, well-spaced apart. Allow them to cook until bubbles
appear on the surface and burst. Turn them over and cook for a
further 1–2 minutes until they are golden brown on both sides.
Make several batches until all the mixture is used. Serve them with
fruit fingers or topped with a thick fruit purée.

MINI SULTANA MUFFINS

(Makes 20 mini muffins)

85 g/3 oz wholemeal flour
130 g/5 oz plain white flour
100 g/3½ oz sultanas
3 tsp baking powder
50 g/2 oz soft dark brown sugar
45 g/1½ oz butter, melted
1 egg, beaten
250 ml/8 fl oz milk

Preheat the oven to 200°C/400°F/Gas Mark 6. Mix together all the dry ingredients in a bowl. Beat the egg and add the butter and milk. Pour the wet ingredients onto the dry ingredients and mix lightly until combined. Spoon the mixture into mini cupcake cases and bake for 8–10 minutes, until firm to the touch and lightly browned. Serve immediately with some slices of banana and a glass of milk.

MINI APPLE MUFFINS

(Makes 12 small muffins)

85 g/3 oz plain white flour
1 tsp baking powder
30 g/1 oz rolled oats
55 g/2 oz light muscovado sugar
2 small dessert apples, peeled, cored and diced
1 tbsp sultanas or raisins
25 g/1 oz butter, melted
1 egg

Preheat the oven to 200°C/400°F/Gas Mark 6. Line a 12-hole muffin tray with cupcake paper cases. Mix the flour, baking powder, oats and sugar in a bowl. Stir in the chopped apples and sultanas. In another bowl, beat together the butter, yoghurt and egg. Add this to the dry ingredients and stir quickly and briefly, until just incorporated. Do not over-mix. Divide the mixture between the paper cases and bake for about 12 minutes until just firm to the touch. Cool on a wire rack.

CHOCOLATE ALMOND CUPCAKES

These are milk-, wheat- and gluten-free and delicious for everyone.

(Makes 12 mini cakes)

100 g/3½ oz good-quality dark chocolate
60 g/2 oz butter
55 g/2 oz sugar
2 drops vanilla essence
55 g/2 oz ground almonds
2 eggs, separated

Preheat the oven to 180°C/350°F/Gas Mark 4. Line a 12-hole mini muffin tin with cupcake paper cases. Put the chocolate, butter and sugar in a glass bowl and melt in the microwave on a low power setting. Leave to cool a little then stir in the almonds and vanilla. Separate the eggs and stir the egg yolks into the chocolate mixture. In a clean bowl, whisk the egg whites until stiff and fold them into the chocolate mixture using a metal spoon. Spoon the mixture into the 12 cupcake paper cases. Bake for 15–20 minutes. Allow them to cool slightly before removing from the tin.

CRISPY CHOCOLATE CLUSTERS

(Makes 12 servings)

These are a fun and nutritious snack, suitable for a party.

225 g/8 oz good-quality dark or milk chocolate
110 g/4 oz Rice Krispies, cornflakes or other breakfast cereal

Melt the chocolate in the microwave or in a bowl over a saucepan of simmering water. Allow to cool slightly and then mix in the breakfast cereal. Spoon into 12 paper cupcake cases. Leave to cool and set hard (place in the fridge if it is a hot day). Store in an airtight container.

Savoury snacks

These two recipes make more nutritious alternatives to commercial snacks.

CHEESE STRAWS WITH PAPRIKA

(Makes 15 straws)

110 g/4 oz plain flour
1 tsp ground paprika
55 g/2 oz butter, diced
85 g/3 oz cheddar cheese
1 egg, beaten

Preheat the oven to 200°C/400°F/Gas Mark 6. Mix the flour, paprika and butter together in a food processor until the mixture resembles breadcrumbs. Stir in the cheese and egg until a soft dough forms. Roll out the dough, on a floured board, to about 1 cm/½ inch thick and cut into fingers, or shape into thin rolls. Put on a greased baking sheet and bake for 10 minutes. Cool on a wire rack.

TORTILLA CRISPS

(Makes 4 servings)

1 large flour tortilla

Preheat the oven to 180°C/350°F/Gas Mark 4. Cut the tortilla into small wedges. Place the pieces on a baking sheet, making sure they are in a single layer. Bake in the oven for approximately 10 minutes until golden and crisp, but watch them as it is easy to over-cook them. Serve on their own as a snack, or with a dip.

6

Coping with fussy eating and food refusal

In this chapter you will learn:

- *how food battles between parents and toddlers can develop very easily*
- *how parents can unwittingly exacerbate fussy eating*
- *why the common strategies that parents resort to are not always helpful*
- *the behaviour changes needed to help resolve your toddler's fussy, faddy eating.*

As discussed in Chapter 1, fussy eating is a normal stage of development which all toddlers will pass through. It will be more evident in some toddlers than others, and the parents of toddlers who continue to eat well throughout this stage may remain blissfully unaware that this developmental stage even exists. However, for parents of those toddlers that are very cautious about trying new foods it can become an exasperating time. Try to remember it is not your toddler's fault that he is very cautious and wary of new foods. He is not necessarily behaving this way to annoy you. In families of two or more children, where the parents have treated all their children in the same way, one toddler may be noticeably fussy and faddy about eating while the other children were not.

Insight

I have met many families that have one very fussy faddy eater. One was the middle child of five children who had been

(Contd)

treated and fed exactly the same as the other four children. It was easy for his parents to accept that it was not their fault that he was fussy about food.

If you are a parent or carer of a toddler who has become noticeably fussy and faddy about eating, your reaction and how you manage the situation can have a large influence on how quickly and easily your toddler passes through this phase.

How food battles can develop

The responsibility of feeding a toddler well weighs heavily on the shoulders of some parents. They often overestimate the amount of food he needs to keep healthy, and worry that he may become ill or not grow properly if he doesn't eat as much as they expect him to. They may think they have a better idea than their toddler of how much he should eat.

Parents who find coping with fussy eating very challenging can exacerbate the problem by giving their toddler more attention when he doesn't eat, than when he does.

Insight
When parents are very worried about their child not eating they automatically give their child a lot of attention at mealtimes, trying to coerce the child to eat more. Children love their parents' attention whether their parents are cross, anxious or happy.

OVERESTIMATING HOW MUCH FOOD YOUR TODDLER NEEDS

You may overestimate how much food your toddler needs because you really have no idea how much he should eat. Alternatively, you may have noticed he is eating less than another toddler of a similar age or a toddler who is younger than he is.

Even if your toddler is very fussy about food, he knows better than you how much food he needs because he can regulate his appetite to meet his growth needs. This means that your toddler's hunger will vary depending on the amount of food that he needs to eat. Toddlers' appetites can change from day to day depending on many factors. If a toddler is growing normally then he is eating as much as he needs.

Once parents have decided they would like their toddler to eat more than he wants, they may do a number of things:

▶ *Plead with him to eat more. You may hear yourself saying, 'Come on, be a good boy and eat up these vegetables' or, 'Have a spoonful for Mummy and then one more for Granny'.*
▶ *Extend mealtimes in the hope that he will eat more.*
▶ *Keep him at the table after everyone else has left, insisting that he finishes his food.*
▶ *Bribe him to eat more with a promise of a reward. You may promise a pudding or sweets if he eats his savoury course.*
▶ *Give snack food after a poorly eaten meal, just to make sure he has eaten something.*
▶ *Insist on feeding him rather than encouraging him to feed himself.*
▶ *Play games to trick him into opening his mouth to put some more food in.*
▶ *You may even begin to force-feed by restraining your toddler in some way and forcing food into his mouth.*
▶ *You may continue to try to feed him after the meal is finished, while he is playing. You may follow him around the house or garden, waiting for an opportunity to put a spoonful of food in his mouth while he is playing.*

WHY THESE STRATEGIES DO NOT WORK

None of these strategies will make your toddler willingly eat more. In fact they usually exacerbate the situation by making your toddler feel confused and anxious. Either of these feelings can result in your toddler eating less and less, making you more anxious or more determined to increase the quantity he eats.

Extending mealtimes and pleading with him to eat more
When you extend mealtimes your toddler will become bored because his attention span is quite short. Most toddlers eat whatever food they are going to eat in the first 20 minutes of the meal. No matter how much longer you keep him sitting in front of his food, he is unlikely to eat any more willingly. You will just be making him feel miserable and bored and he will begin to associate this negative experience with meals and food.

Insisting he eats a particular food
There are many valid reasons why your toddler may be refusing to eat a particular food:

▶ *It may be because the food is new to him and he needs to see it several more times before he is confident enough to try tasting it.*
▶ *It may not be exactly the same as what he is used to, for example: it may be a broken biscuit rather than a whole one; it may have a small blemish on it (such as a mark on the skin of an apple). Because the food looks different he will be wary of eating it.*
▶ *It may be because he does not like the taste of that food.*
▶ *It may be because that food resembles something he considers disgusting.*
▶ *It may have been touched by another food he does not like.*
▶ *It may be on the same plate as a food he does not like.*

Your toddler may not be able to explain to you why he does not want to eat this particular food, but for him he has a very valid reason for refusing to eat it. If you do not keep insisting he eats the food, in time he may move on and be very happy to try this food and learn to like it, or his tastes may change or his associations with the food will change. If you insist he eats a food when he does not want to, you may set up a negative association with that food in his mind and he may continue to avoid that particular food throughout the rest of his life.

Using bribes

If you use bribes to coerce your toddler to eat more of a particular food, you are essentially telling him that eating this food is so unpleasant that he needs a reward to eat it. If you offer food B as a reward for eating up food A, in essence you are telling him that food B is a desirable food and food A is an undesirable food. For example, if you say, 'Eat up your meat and vegetables and you can have your pudding', you are telling him that meat and vegetables are unpleasant but the sweet pudding is very desirable. This is in fact the reverse of the long-term nutritional message that your toddler can learn even at this age – that meat and vegetables are very nutritious and can be delicious and enjoyable.

Feeding him rather than allowing him to feed himself

Your toddler may want to be more involved in the meal than you are allowing him to be. Anxious parents often want to control the meal and prefer to do the spoon-feeding themselves. However, your toddler needs to be allowed to feed himself and to make a mess. He needs to learn about food, and playing with it helps him become more familiar with that food and more likely to learn to like it. He also needs to become more adept at feeding himself. Soon he will be off to nursery and school and needs to be able to feed himself when you are not there.

Insight

Parents who like to be in control and those who don't like mess are the most likely to prefer to feed their toddler rather than allow their toddler to feed himself.

Giving him more attention when he does not eat

Toddlers love your attention. The strategies listed in the previous paragraphs give your toddler plenty of your attention when he is not eating. If you are giving him more attention when he does not eat than when he does, he may begin to refuse to eat to get your attention. To him the attention of a cross parent is better than no attention.

Always give your toddler attention and praise for desirable behaviour and ignore undesirable behaviour. Praise him when he does eat and do not give him attention when he is not eating.

Giving snack foods when he does not eat

If you are anxious that your toddler has not eaten at a mealtime you may give him a snack soon after the meal – just to make sure he has had something to eat. If he prefers the food you give him as a snack after the meal, he may begin refusing his meals in order to receive the snack food afterwards. If you carry on giving him this snack food he will become less and less likely to eat well at mealtimes.

> ### Insight
> Many parents give their toddler snacks because they are worried that he will become ill or stop growing if he does not eat enough.

Playing games or trailing around behind him to pop food into his mouth

You will be confusing him. Your toddler does not know if he should be playing or eating. He needs to learn that mealtimes are for eating and not playing with toys and that play time is for playing and not eating or grazing on food.

Preparing an alternative meal when he refuses food that you first offer him

Your toddler will soon take advantage if you do this and will wait for you to prepare his preferred foods. However, you will not be giving him the opportunity to become familiar with other foods and to learn to like foods he is currently refusing. In the long run, it is better to offer family meals and accept that he will prefer some foods to others. Always try to offer one food at each meal that you know he will eat.

Force-feeding

Some parents resort to force-feeding when they become very anxious that their toddler is not having enough to eat, or not eating particular foods they think he needs for nutritional reasons. However, force-feeding will make your toddler anxious and frightened around food and mealtimes. You may even make him vomit. As he associates very negative experiences with food and meals, he will lose his appetite as soon as mealtimes approach and you will have reduced the quantity of food he will willingly eat.

EXACERBATING THE FOOD BATTLE

Once meals have become stressful for a toddler, he will become anxious as mealtimes approach and lose his appetite, thus reducing further the quantity he will eat. This can make a parent even more anxious and more determined to make their toddler eat.

Escaping the food battle cycle

Once a food battle is established no one will enjoy the meal. It is best for you to change the behaviour that is exacerbating the food battle.

There are several very valid reasons why you may become over anxious about the quantity of food and type of food your toddler eats, for example:

▶ *If your toddler was born prematurely and his survival was in doubt, you may become very anxious about everything, including how much food he eats.*

- *If your toddler had a hospital admission soon after birth because there were feeding problems or he became dehydrated, you may continue to feel anxious about not being able to feed your toddler properly.*
- *A healthcare professional may have implied that your toddler has not gained enough weight.*
- *Your toddler may be smaller than other toddlers of the same age or younger.*
- *You may think your toddler eats much less than others the same age or younger.*

It may be difficult to stop feeling anxious, but if you understand why you feel anxious you may be able to manage these feelings and put them into perspective.

ARE YOU DEPRESSED?

A parent who is unhappy or even depressed for whatever reason may not interact with their toddler as much as their toddler would like and needs. If your toddler finds the only way to elicit a response from you is to refuse to eat, he will do this.

If you are unhappy and suspect you may be depressed then speak to your GP as soon as possible. Your GP will be able to help you find a solution to overcome the depression so that you are able to look after your toddler and to interact with him as he needs.

ARE YOU WORRYING UNNECESSARILY?

When there are particular foods your toddler refuses, you may begin to worry that he is not getting enough nutrients to keep him healthy, growing and developing. The amount of each nutrient needed to keep him healthy is an average amount. Most nutrients are stored in the body and these stores will last him some time so he does not need to eat well at every meal, every day. If he does not have milk one day, his bones will not crack up.

Often a toddler will eat well at one or two meals each day but their parents tend to focus on and worry about the one meal when he does not eat well. Over a period of a week or so, by eating more on some days and less on others, your toddler may be getting, on average, what he needs. To assess this, write down everything he eats and drinks over a week and then fill in a food group chart (see Chapter 3, page 71) for each day. You will be able to see how often he is eating foods from each food group and you can compare this with the recommendations for healthy eating.

If you add the totals for each food group over the seven days you can work out an average intake for the week as explained in Chapter 3.

Now you can assess:

▶ *Are you combining the food groups and offering your toddler foods from all five food groups each day? If he is refusing one particular food you may find that there are other foods from the same food group that he will eat at other meals and snacks, so that overall he will be getting the key nutrients from that food group by eating foods that he is happy to accept.*
▶ *Is there some variety within each food group over the week? Make a list of all the foods your toddler eats from each food group over the seven days and count all the different foods he eats in each food group. You may find there is more variety than you expected.*

Case study

Kate came to see me about her son Ashley who was almost three years old. She was concerned he was not eating enough. He ate virtually nothing at lunch before he went to nursery and she would often give him a small cake or a biscuit to make sure he had eaten something. In the evening he would eat a few mouthfuls. He usually ate much better on the weekends. I asked if he liked his nursery and she said no, she was going to change him to another one soon. We agreed that maybe he was tense about going to nursery which is why he didn't eat well at lunch. He may have been too tired to eat well in the evening after nursery. When I asked

(Contd)

her what he ate for breakfast she reeled off the following list: two Weetabix with milk, an egg and two slices of toast with jam, all washed down with about ½ pint of milk. Effectively he was eating most of what he needed for the day at breakfast because he was hungry and happy to eat then!

Changing your behaviour to overcome food battles

If you recognize that meals have become an unpleasant time for you and your toddler then it is time to change your behaviour so that eventually your toddler will change in the way you wish.

Remember the three cardinal rules from Chapter 3:

Rule 1: It is up to you to offer your toddler a healthy balanced diet of nutritious foods, but...

Rule 2: It is up to your toddler to decide what he will eat and how much he will eat and you must respect this.

Rule 3: Make each meal an enjoyable, social occasion.

KEEP AN OPEN MIND ABOUT THE QUANTITY YOUR TODDLER NEEDS

Respect his decision when he indicates to you that he has had enough and honour it. In the long term, it is important that children learn to know when they are full and no longer hungry. Some obese children have no idea when they feel satiated and consequently eat larger quantities of food than they need.

Toddlers will survive for a very long time, even though they are eating very little. When they are ill they will eat very little while they are feeling miserable. They may lose a little weight but when they begin eating well again they will regain this weight quite quickly.

PLANNING CHANGES

It may be useful to make a list of what you would like to change and then think about what would be the most easy to change. You can make those changes first, before you move onto the more difficult changes.

When you have decided what you are going to change, chat about it with other members in your family so that everyone can make the change and no one will undermine this change by doing the opposite or giving in to your toddler's tantrums when he notices things have changed.

HOW WILL YOUR TODDLER REACT TO A CHANGE IN YOUR BEHAVIOUR?

When you begin to change the way you manage mealtimes your toddler will probably notice the change and be surprised. His behaviour may seem to get worse before it gets better as he notices that things are different and he tests out the new rules and limits. He may throw a tantrum. This is a good sign so do not give up but carry on persevering with the change.

Making changes

Positive changes you might make	Reason for changing
Begin eating more meals with your toddler.	Toddlers learn by copying their parents and other children.
Make positive comments about the foods you are offering and show him you are enjoying those foods.	Parents and carers are strong role models. If you make positive comments about foods your toddler will be more willing to try them.

(Contd)

Positive changes you might make	Reason for changing
Develop a daily routine of three meals and two to three snacks around his sleeping pattern.	Toddlers don't eat well if they become over-hungry or very tired.
Cut out large bottles of milk and offer a maximum of three small cups of 100–120 ml/ 3–4 fl oz each day.	Too much milk will fill him up and leave him little appetite for food.
Cut back on sweet drinks if he is drinking large quantities of fruit juice or other sweet drinks.	These will decrease his appetite for food.
Offer two courses at meals: one savoury course followed by a nutritious pudding or sweet course.	This gives two opportunities for him to take in the calories and nutrients needed and offers a wider variety of foods. It also makes the meal more interesting for him.
Praise him when he eats well.	Toddlers respond positively to praise.
Offer finger foods as often as possible.	Toddlers enjoy having the control of feeding themselves with finger foods.
Eat in a calm, relaxed environment without distractions such as TV, games and toys.	Toddlers concentrate on one thing at a time. Distractions make it more difficult for him to concentrate on eating.
Finish the meal within about 20–30 minutes and accept that after this time he is probably not going to eat any more.	Carrying the meal on for too long is unlikely to result in him eating much more. It is better to wait for the next planned snack or meal and offer nutritious foods then.

Accept that your toddler has eaten enough when he signals to you that he doesn't want any more and take away any uneaten food without comment.

He is indicating he has had enough when he:

▶ *says no*
▶ *keeps his mouth shut when food is offered*
▶ *turns his head away from food being offered*
▶ *pushes away a spoon, bowl or plate containing food*
▶ *holds food in his mouth and refuses to swallow it*
▶ *spits food out repeatedly*
▶ *cries, screams, shouts, gags or retches when you try to feed him. When he has eaten enough he is unlikely to eat much more, no matter what you do.*

Negative behaviours you might stop	Reason
Insisting he finishes everything on his plate.	Toddlers should be allowed to eat to their appetite and parents and carers should respect this.
Pressuring him to eat more when he has indicated to you he has had enough.	
Taking away a refused meal and offering a completely different one in its place.	He will soon take advantage if you do this. In the long run, it is better to offer family meals and accept that he will prefer some foods to others. Always try to offer one food at each meal that you know he will eat.
Offering the sweet course or pudding as a reward for eating the savoury course.	You will make the sweet course seem more desirable.
Offering large drinks of milk, squash or fruit juice within an hour of the meal.	Large drinks will reduce your toddler's appetite for the meal. Give water instead.

(Contd)

Negative behaviours you might stop	Reason
Offering snacks just before a meal.	The snacks will stop him feeling hungry for the food offered at the meal.
Giving a snack very soon after a meal if he hasn't eaten well at the meal.	Many parents may do this just to ensure their toddler has eaten something. However, it is best to have a set meal pattern and wait until the next snack or meal before offering food again.
Assuming that because he has refused a food, he will never eat it again.	Some toddlers need to be offered a new food more than ten times before they feel confident to try it. Tastes also change over time.
Feeling apprehensive about mealtimes and feeling guilty if one meal turns into a disaster.	Parents also learn by making mistakes, and making changes can be hard. Forget about any disasters and approach each meal positively.

PLANNING SOME OF THE MORE DIFFICULT CHANGES

Introduce a routine of meals and snacks throughout the day and respect your toddler's decision when he says he has had enough

Make sure each meal is balanced and nutritious so that when your toddler does eat well he is getting plenty of nutrients. Plan a feeding regime for your toddler around his daytime sleeps so that he never goes longer than 2½–3 hours awake without being offered some food. For examples, see the sample routines in Chapter 1.

Remember:

▶ *Let your toddler eat as much as he wishes.*
▶ *When he indicates he has had enough, ask him once or twice if he would like some more.*
▶ *If he indicates he has had enough, take the food away and say something positive like, 'Good boy, you have eaten some potato.' Say this even if he has eaten very little.*
▶ *Don't coerce him to eat more.*
▶ *Don't look anxious.*
▶ *Don't make any negative comments.*
▶ *Offer him a second course and repeat as above.*

This may seem a difficult routine to follow if he has eaten very little, but you can be confident that you will be offering him food again in another 2½–3 hours. He can eat more then if he is hungry.

Cut back on milk or fruit juice and other sweet drinks
If your toddler is not eating enough food because he is drinking too much, you will need to reduce the quantity of drinks he is having. Ideally you need to be offering about 6–8 small drinks per day – a drink with each meal and snack and another one or two if he becomes thirsty while playing. An average drink for a toddler is about 100–120 ml/3–4 fl oz in a cup or beaker.

Drinks in feeding bottles should have been phased out by the time he was about 12 months old. If he is still having drinks in bottles you need to change these to drinks in cups. Just change one drink at one time per day and when that is accepted, change another drink at another time.

TOO MUCH MILK
If your toddler is having too much milk from cups you can reduce the amount you offer in each cup. Alternatively, you could change one cup of milk at one time each day to a cup of water.

If he insists on having his milk drinks in a bottle, then reducing the amount of milk can be more difficult as he probably associates the bottle of milk with comfort. Take him out at times when he usually has a bottle of milk and give him some food and some milk in a cup, not a bottle. Give him less milk than he usually has. Repeat this as often as possible so that he becomes used to having food in place of milk and accepts milk in a cup rather than a bottle. When he is familiar with this regime, he will accept it at home as well.

If you are still giving an evening bottle of milk at bedtime this may be difficult for your toddler to relinquish. You may be able to change to a cup, but just gradually reduce the amount of milk you are offering and then cut it out altogether.

Giving milk drinks during the night should be phased out because this will reduce your toddler's appetite for food during the day. If he habitually wakes for a bottle during the night, the volume of milk should be gradually reduced until he has started to eat more during the day. You can do this by reducing the volume of milk or gradually diluting the milk with some water so that he is having fewer calories this way and it slowly becomes less satisfying.

TOO MANY SWEET DRINKS

Too much fluid from sweet drinks such as fruit juices, squashes and fizzy drinks will suppress your toddler's appetite for food. Some parents think it is cruel to give toddlers water rather than sweet drinks; however, water is much safer for teeth than sweet drinks.

Gradual changes to make if your toddler demands sweet drinks:

- ▶ *Only use unsweetened pure fruit juice, not squash and fruit juice drinks. This is because fruit juice contains fructose while the others contain sucrose. Fructose is sweeter than sucrose so you need less fruit juice to give a sweeter taste.*
- ▶ *Gradually dilute the drinks with more and more water.*
- ▶ *Give only water with meals.*
- ▶ *Give only water within an hour of a meal or snack.*
- ▶ *Change all drinks between meals to water.*

IF YOU CONTINUE TO BE WORRIED

If you have tried changing your behaviour and have persisted for some time but you do not think there is any improvement in what your toddler is eating, ask your health visitor to weigh and measure him and plot these measurements on the growth charts in his Personal Child Health Record book. If his height and weight are normal for his age, reassure yourself that he is eating enough even though you have been expecting him to eat more than he does.

If you and your health visitor continue to have concerns, ask your GP to check that there are no underlying medical problems that are preventing your toddler from eating well.

Case studies

Carolyn: 'My son used to drive me to distraction with his fussy eating when he was about two years old. I knew it was supposed to be normal but I couldn't help panicking that a) he was not getting the right nutrition and b) he was picking up bad eating habits.

He would eat any number of bread-type products, biscuits and cakes (of course), yoghurt, cheese sticks and fruit. But I had a real battle with the "main courses". Sometimes he would eat pasta, but then he would refuse to eat it, despite quite happily gobbling it down two days before. For tea I would cook a first course but sometimes he would refuse to touch it. If he didn't eat any of the first course, I tended to relent and give him a yoghurt or cheese and fruit anyway as I felt he should be eating something. My husband and I were bad at eating with him – breakfast happened sometimes but he was often napping when I had my lunch. His tea was before my husband came home. We did try to eat with him on the weekends, though.

After my health visitor suggested I eat with him more often I did change and made an effort to eat some of what he was eating each time he ate. Things got better slowly and since he has been at nursery, his eating is much better.'

(Contd)

Esra: 'At 18 months my son decided he would eat nothing but fromage frais. And I mean NOTHING. This went on for five weeks. I was hysterical. Then he would eat only beige food for a further two years, for example pasta, biscuits, Ready Brek. And I tried every strategy, trick, persuasive tactic, threat, begging, everything. He was still a nightmare eater until he was seven years old. Today, aged nine, he has the appetite of six horses and will eat and try absolutely anything and everything.'

TEST YOURSELF

1 Why do toddlers refuse to eat certain foods?

2 How do parents usually react when their toddlers are fussy about food?

3 What are the main concerns of parents when their toddlers do not eat as much as they expect them to?

4 What are the three cardinal rules to observe when feeding toddlers?

5 If a toddler does not eat much at a meal, should parents give a snack or drink of milk just to make sure the toddler has had something to eat?

6 When parents make changes to how they manage mealtimes how are toddlers likely to react?

7 If changes do not seem to improve their toddler's behaviour at first should parents give up or persist with the changes?

8 Why should parents cut back on large sweet drinks and drinks of milk if their toddler does not eat well?

9 Which behaviours should parents reward with their attention?

10 How should parent react when toddlers indicate they do not want to eat any more of the food before them?

7

Coping with extreme food faddiness and food refusal

In this chapter you will learn:
- *reasons for extreme food faddiness and food refusal*
- *why it is not the parents' fault*
- *how to cope with extreme food refusal and find support*
- *how autistic spectrum disorders and Asperger's Syndrome can affect food intake*
- *how to make calorie intake the priority so that growth is not affected*
- *about the supplements that can be used to make up for foods that toddlers refuse to eat.*

Most faddy eating and food refusal resolves with time, as toddlers slowly become more familiar with a wider range of foods. How to cope with this is discussed in Chapter 6. This chapter is for parents of those very few toddlers who are extremely fussy about their food and do not eat enough, so that it can begin to affect their growth. There are two main reasons why this can happen:

▶ *Your toddler has not had a lot of experience in eating different textured foods as a baby or as a very young toddler. Medical reasons may have caused this or it may be that you were reluctant or unable to move your toddler onto a wider variety of textures when he was the best age to learn to eat them.*

▶ *Your toddler's character is such that he is very reluctant to accept change and move onto a wider variety of foods.*

Whatever the reason for extreme food refusal, it is very demanding to cope with. It can be very easy to make mistakes and begin to plead, coerce or try to force-feed a toddler. Once parents start to turn mealtimes into stressful situations, food refusal may get worse.

If you have tried and persisted with the strategies in Chapter 6 but feel that you are not making any progress, your toddler may fall into one of the two categories listed above which are discussed in more detail below. If you think your toddler's growth is being affected, ask your health visitor to check this – there may be a specialized feeding team in your area that you can be referred to. These teams can assess which factors are causing the feeding problem and can equip you with strategies to cope and make sure your toddler is eating enough.

Health professionals in a specialized feeding team usually include:

▶ *a paediatrician with experience of gastro-intestinal problems*
▶ *a child psychologist who can equip you with strategies to cope*
▶ *a speech and language therapist who can organize tests to assess whether your toddler can eat and swallow normally or if he has an oral-motor developmental problem. He/she can also guide you in offering suitable foods that will help your toddler learn to eat a wider range of foods*
▶ *a dietician who can help you ensure your toddler is eating enough in calories for his growth and can help you choose a vitamin and mineral supplement to make sure he is getting enough vitamins and minerals despite eating a narrow range of foods.*

Now let's take a look at the two main types of rare feeding problems in more detail.

Toddlers who did not learn to eat different tastes and textured foods at the appropriate time

This may have happened because your toddler:

- ▶ *was tube fed when he was a baby because he had a serious illness. Babies who had to be tube fed may not have the opportunity to get used to milk and weaning foods in their mouth. They may not have learnt to eat different textures and tastes when they were 6–12 months old and were happy and willing to accept them readily.*
- ▶ *has an oral-motor dysfunction or developmental delay which meant he was not able to learn to cope with different textures of food. He may cough and gag on more difficult food textures. Some babies and toddlers do not develop as quickly as others and may take much longer to learn to co-ordinate their tongue and mouth for feeding. Your health visitor or a GP should be able to diagnose this or they may refer you to a community paediatrician for assessment. A speech and language therapist should be able to give you advice and support to help you and your toddler make progress at the rate which he can cope with.*
- ▶ *had a poor appetite for whatever reason and was reluctant to eat. You may have just offered him food that you knew he would eat in order to be sure he was eating something. You may not have offered foods of other tastes and textures so that he would get the experience of eating these and learn to cope with them while he was the best age to learn to like these foods.*

There are many reasons why babies may have had a poor appetite. It is common in babies who:

- ▶ *have had very severe gastro-oesophageal reflux and therefore associate eating with discomfort and pain. This reflux would have made eating an unpleasant experience for your baby and he would have been reluctant to eat well.*

> *If the pain was very severe he may continue to consider eating an unpleasant experience.*

▶ *were born prematurely and had a lot of unpleasant experiences around their mouth in their early life, such as nasogastric tubes and unpleasant-tasting medicine syringed into their mouth.*

Toddlers who have not learnt to cope with a wide range of food and textures while they are babies reach the neophobic developmental stage (when they are wary of new foods) when they are familiar with just a few tastes and textures. They will often eat only soft or purée textures and mostly sweet tastes. The foods these toddlers prefer eating tend to be:

▶ *yoghurts and commercial baby food because they are soft*
▶ *'bite and dissolve' foods such as chocolate and some soft crisps (like Quavers and Skips), as these are foods that easily break down in the saliva.*

If these toddlers do eat a food like yoghurt, they will usually eat any flavour and any brand. This distinguishes them from the toddlers described in the following section who are reluctant to accept any change.

Processing textures within the mouth, chewing and moving food from side to side with the tongue are all difficult for these toddlers. They may also gag on foods, but will only gag and vomit when they are given a texture that is more difficult to cope with than a purée or a 'bite and dissolve' food. Your toddler needs to learn to eat different textures and flavours, but because of his age he will take much longer to learn to cope with different textures than a baby would. You will need to introduce changes very slowly – but with patience you will eventually get there.

The following table gives examples of foods and their textures, in order of increasing difficulty to eat. Use this table to find the texture which your toddler can happily manage now. Make up most of his meals with foods from this category so that he is able to eat well at three meals each day.

Once he is eating three meals well, you need to introduce foods from the next texture stage and give your toddler plenty of practice at trying these foods until he is able to eat them comfortably. This may take a few days or a few weeks. When you are happy that he is managing this texture, incorporate these foods into all his meals and you can now begin offering foods from the next texture stage.

Be careful not to offer your toddler foods with mixed textures as it will be more difficult for him to cope with two different textures at the same time. Examples of mixed textures are: yoghurt with pieces of fruit in it or soup with pieces or chunks of vegetables in it.

Food textures in order of increasing difficulty

Food texture	Description	Examples
1 Smooth purée	Quite runny or smooth with no lumps.	▶ puréed stewed fruit ▶ puréed stewed vegetables ▶ Weetabix soaked in milk or fruit juice ▶ fromage frais ▶ smooth yoghurt
2 Soft mash	Fairly smooth with small soft lumps. Foods are mashed with a fork rather than liquidized.	▶ banana mashed with a fork ▶ mashed potato ▶ mashed well-cooked vegetables ▶ well-mashed baked beans ▶ scrambled egg ▶ steamed fish ▶ dhal made with well-cooked lentils

Food texture	Description	Examples
3 'Bite and dissolve' finger foods	These dissolve in the mouth and do not need any chewing but do need enough control to hold food in the mouth until it dissolves.	▶ rice cakes ▶ pink wafer biscuits ▶ ice cream wafers ▶ most sponge fingers ▶ Wotsits ▶ Skips ▶ Quavers ▶ Monster Munch
4 'Bite and melt' finger foods	These melt in the mouth, similar to bite and dissolve but coat the mouth more.	▶ Maltesers cut in quarters ▶ chocolate buttons
5 Bite and soft chew	These need some preparation or munching in the mouth before being swallowed.	▶ very ripe peeled fruit (pear, melon, avocado, peeled grapes cut in half) ▶ soft pieces of cooked potato, sweet potato, carrot, beetroot, soft chips, cooked florets of cauliflower/ broccoli ▶ mini pasta shapes ▶ soft biscuits (malted milk, Rich Tea, digestive biscuits) ▶ sandwiches made with soft white bread (crusts cut off) and smooth fillings – for example, cheese spread, butter and Marmite, hummus, smooth peanut butter

(Contd)

Food texture	Description	Examples
		▶ soft cake, for example Madeira cake ▶ pancakes ▶ cheese triangles ▶ cubes of soft cheese ▶ small pieces of well-cooked fish ▶ corned beef ▶ fishcakes with the coating taken off
6 Bite and splinter	Need a little more chewing before being swallowed.	▶ breadsticks ▶ cream crackers ▶ crisps ▶ poppadums ▶ Ryvita ▶ Hula Hoops
7 Bite and lump	These need good chewing skills and are usually the last foods to be mastered by most children.	▶ raw apple ▶ chicken nuggets ▶ whole grapes ▶ crusty bread ▶ pizza ▶ sausages

Where you can, offer the foods that you eat as a family as this will help your toddler become familiar with the taste of those foods. You may need to offer a new taste more than ten times before your toddler gets used to it, so don't give up, and keep offering it each time you are eating it yourself.

Even if your toddler cannot cope with certain textures now, he will learn to do so eventually. Ask your health visitor if there is a local speech and language therapist who can give you extra help and support to move through these textures. If the problem persists, ask your GP, who may then refer you to the community paediatrician who will be able to check if there is a problem with the muscles or nerves that is exacerbating this problem.

Toddlers who are very reluctant to accept change

A very small number of toddlers are extremely wary of new foods and will only eat a small range. They do not move on and accept a wider range of foods as they get older but get stuck in this phase and continue to eat a very limited range of foods. It may be because they feel safe eating only the foods they are used to. They will often only eat certain brands of food or specific flavours of a food, such as one particular brand of strawberry yoghurt. The food has to look right or they will refuse it; for example, these toddlers may refuse a broken biscuit or toast that is 'too brown'.

Boys are more likely to have this problem, although it is seen in girls. One survey showed the ratio of boys with the problem compared to girls as 10:1. Toddlers and children with Asperger's Syndrome or autism can also behave in this way with food.

These toddlers quite often get fussier about food at around 18 months old, although they may have had problems with lumpy foods when first introduced to them. If your toddler falls into this category, you may have noticed that he gagged or vomited on lumps when you first offered them.

Another characteristic of these toddlers is that they are also likely to be more anxious and very sensitive to touch, taste, sound and smell. You may notice that your toddler:

▶ *refuses to wear certain clothes, and wants to stick to specific colours or textures*
▶ *does not like walking barefoot on textured surfaces such as grass or sand*

▶ *may worry about getting his hands dirty and his face sticky;*
if he does he may find it very difficult to handle food and feed
himself.

Insight

The family of one toddler told me that he used his elbows
to break a tumble in the garden so that his hands would not
touch the soil.

Such toddlers tend to be more emotionally responsive in general,
and less likely to be able to accept change. They also tend to be
very strong-willed and may not do something just because someone
else is doing it, or someone else wants them to do it. They will not
copy other children and family members, and so will not copy
others' eating behaviour. This does not mean that these toddlers
are naughtier – or more attention seeking – than those who easily
accept food, just that they have a different way of interacting with
the world around them.

A toddler who behaves in this way can be the third or fourth
child in a family who has been treated very similarly to his siblings.
Hence he is behaving this way because of his character and not
because of the way his parents have treated him. If it is your first
child who behaves this way then you may think it is your fault;
however, it is likely to be just down to your toddler's character
because of his genes.

No matter how much you encourage him to try new foods he may
stick very rigidly to a small number of foods which he is happy
with. This may continue for some years before he will gradually
accept change. If you try to force him to eat a food he dislikes he
will often gag and vomit. As he gets older he may begin to react
to the smells of foods that he dislikes, and have difficulties being
around others who are eating food that he does not like. He may
gag or vomit if he is given a disliked food or even if he just sees or
smells a disliked food.

WHAT CAN YOU DO?

▶ *Messy play: offer your toddler a session of messy play every day. Start with textures that he is happy to touch. This may be very dry textures such as rice and lentils. Then you can gradually move onto more messy wet substances. Make it as much fun as possible for him so that he enjoys it and gains confidence.*

Insight

Some parents do not like messy hands themselves and would find this difficult. If you are reluctant to do this with your toddler, find a playgroup or friends who will do this with him.

▶ *Make a list of all the foods your toddler is happy to eat.*
▶ *Offer meals including the foods your toddler is happy to eat. Your first priority for your toddler is to make sure he eats enough calories to ensure he grows and gains weight normally. You will need to give him the high-calorie foods that he likes such as ice cream, cakes, biscuits and chocolate. Do not withhold these foods in the hope that he will eat healthier foods that he does not like, such as fruit and vegetables. Do not worry that he will not eat foods from all the food groups as a dietician will be able to assess your toddler's current diet and advise on a supplement to make sure he is getting all the nutrients he needs.*
▶ *Offer small frequent meals as he may become very anxious at mealtimes and may eat very slowly. Small frequent meals may make it easier for him to eat enough food to get enough calories.*
▶ *Don't put foods he dislikes on the same plate as foods he likes. Some toddlers will simply refuse the whole plate of food if there are any foods on it that they dislike.*
▶ *Don't hide a disliked food inside another liked food. Your toddler will notice the smell or taste of the food he dislikes and will then refuse to eat the food he normally likes.*
▶ *Don't withhold foods your toddler accepts until he has eaten foods he doesn't like or is frightened of, for example: 'You can't have your pudding until you've eaten your vegetables.'*

▶ *Don't leave long gaps between meals to make him hungry. This will not work and may cause him to lose weight.*

▶ *Don't force your toddler to eat foods he dislikes. This will make him more anxious at mealtimes and he may vomit on the food you are forcing him to eat.*

A child psychologist will be able to help you to cope with your toddler's behaviour and gradually to introduce new foods into his meals. However, this can be a very long and slow process.

Case study

'As the mother of two teenage boys, 15 and 19, I find they are like chalk and cheese. I have spent the last 18 years of my life battling with guilt arising from my eldest son's diet. Since he was a year old he has refused to eat a varied diet. This has caused me more problems than him! Socially he does find it a little awkward but seems to persist in his idiosyncratic diet. I believe that, although it is restricted in variety, it is balanced! It includes: wholemeal bread and other breads, smooth peanut butter, butter, Vegemite, potatoes (fried or roast only), feta and halloumi cheese, smooth yoghurts, chocolate, fruit juice, lots of water, apples, grapes, raisins, dried apricots, biscuits and cakes. This list is in order of quantity of consumption. He will eat a plain pizza when out with friends, but that is pretty much his only concession. Friends and family were concerned when he was tiny that he would not grow properly. He has proved them wrong: being over six foot tall and very strong and fit. He is not at all fat, but quite broad. Certainly the texture of foods seems to play a part in his choices and he has no moral issue with meat eaters.

He has just gained excellent grades in his A-levels and secured a place at Bristol University to study electronic engineering next year after a 12-month work placement. So, I should not have stressed him or myself about this eating thing – just to please others really. Because he was thriving, the situation was never really brought to the attention of health visitors and so on. At the time I certainly felt I would not be able to cope with their intervention and the additional stress that would cause.

We always eat together as a family: three of us eat one meal and it has now become a way of life to prepare something additional that our eldest son will enjoy.'

Dianne

CAN CHANGING DIET HELP TODDLERS WITH AUTISM?

Toddlers with autism are often very particular about the foods they will eat and often restrict themselves to quite a narrow range of foods. There are several hypotheses that changing certain aspects of a toddler's diet may improve his autistic behaviour. However, there is a lack of consistent and good-quality evidence that changing an autistic toddler's diet will be beneficial. The diets that have been promoted for autistic toddlers are:

▶ *a diet free of gluten and casein – this entails cutting out wheat, rye, barley, oats and all milk products, limiting the variety of foods that can be eaten*
▶ *a diet free of all food additives*
▶ *a diet free of phenolic compounds and salicylates*
▶ *adding extra nutrients such as B vitamins, magnesium and zinc supplements to the diet*
▶ *adding fish oils and omega 3 supplements to the diet.*

Insight

Although some parents have reported improved behaviour with one of these regimes they do not help all autistic toddlers.

If you have an autistic toddler and you wish to try one of these diets, ask to see a dietician so that you can be sure that whatever you are trying will not harm your toddler. You will need to consider whether cutting something out of your toddler's diet – particularly if he eats only a very narrow range of foods – might mean he then eats so little that he will stop growing.

It can be very difficult to remain objective about whether your toddler's behaviour improves with a change in his diet. You will need to record symptoms of his behaviour carefully and to ask others such as nursery staff or grandparents to assess his behaviour objectively also. These diets can make life even more difficult for parents and if there is no obvious improvement after a few weeks, it is probably not worth persevering. What is important is making sure an autistic toddler gets all the nutrients he needs; a vitamin and mineral supplement may be necessary if he eats only a very restricted range of foods.

TEST YOURSELF

1 What are the two main characteristics of toddlers who are extremely fussy about the foods they will eat?

2 How can a specialized feeding team help with this extreme fussy, faddy eating?

3 Why does not learning to eat different foods and food textures between 6 and 12 months make toddlers more fussy around food.

4 What type of foods do these toddlers prefer?

5 What type of support do toddlers who are fussy about textures need?

6 Are boys or girls more likely to become fussy about food because they are reluctant to accept change?

7 What things may toddlers who are very sensitive to touch, taste and smell not like doing?

8 What can parents whose toddler is sensitive to touch do to encourage him to widen the range of foods he eats?

9 Why do very strong-willed and stubborn toddlers sometimes eat a limited range of foods?

10 Why are some toddlers with autism and Asperger's Syndrome very fussy about food?

8

Healthy eating for vegetarian toddlers

In this chapter you will learn:
- *about the different types of vegetarian diets*
- *the nutrients that are at risk in a vegetarian toddler's diet*
- *how to combine vegetarian foods for healthy eating.*

If you feed your toddler a vegetarian diet you will need a little more
care and planning to make sure your toddler is getting all the nutrients
he needs – particularly iron and zinc. If you are from a traditional
vegetarian culture then your traditional diet may be adequate.
However, if you have emigrated from one country to another, you
may not always be able to get all the traditional foods that made
up the eating pattern in your original homeland. If you have chosen to
become vegetarian yourself as an adolescent or adult, the food choices
you make for yourself may not necessarily provide your growing
and developing toddler with all the key nutrients he needs.

Types of vegetarian diet

There are several types of vegetarianism:

- ▶ *semi-vegetarian – only red meat is not eaten*
- ▶ *piscatarian – no meats and poultry are eaten but fish, milk and
  eggs are included*

- *lacto-ovo vegetarian – meat, poultry and fish are not eaten but milk and eggs are included*
- *lacto-vegetarian – meat, poultry, fish and eggs are not eaten but milk is included*
- *vegan – all animal products are excluded; that is meat, poultry, fish, eggs and milk and milk products. Soy milk and soy milk products are usually used in place of cows' milk.*

In each of these vegetarian diets there is a chance of not offering your toddler enough of certain nutrients unless you plan the combination of foods well. The nutrients that may be low in vegetarian diets are:

Type of vegetarianism	Nutrients which may be low
semi-vegetarian	iron
piscatarian	iron
lacto-ovo vegetarian	iron, zinc and omega 3 fats
lacto-vegetarian	iron, omega 3 fats and vitamin D
vegan	protein, iron, zinc, calcium, vitamins A, D, K, B2, B12

Ensuring adequate nutrients in your vegetarian toddler's diet

CHOOSING A MILK FOR DRINKS

For young toddlers it is better to continue with formula milk beyond one year of age rather than changing to cows' milk. Use either a follow-on formula or a growing-up milk, as these milks are enriched with extra iron, zinc and vitamin D along with other nutrients.

PROTEIN

Good-quality protein containing all the essential amino acids is provided by meat, fish, eggs, milk and milk products. Pulses, lentils and nuts which vegetarians need to eat in place of meat, fish and eggs contain protein which does not contain adequate amounts of all the essential amino acids. One essential amino acid in particular is too low. That amino acid is found in the protein of food group 1 – bread, rice, potatoes, pasta and other starchy foods. Hence when pulses, lentils and nuts are combined with a starchy food at a meal or snack, a similar quality of protein to that in meat, fish, eggs and milk is provided.

Combinations of food from groups 1 and 4 that provide first-class protein

▶ *muesli containing ground or chopped nuts and oats*
▶ *baked beans on toast*
▶ *lentil soup with bread or toast*
▶ *bean casserole with rice or potatoes*
▶ *lasagne made with textured vegetable protein (TVP)*
▶ *hummus and pitta bread*
▶ *peanut butter sandwich*
▶ *black bean spread with toast*
▶ *rice and peas*
▶ *tofu stir-fry with noodles*
▶ *minestrone soup (which usually contains both beans and pasta)*

IRON

Oily fish and dark poultry meat are good sources of iron in the haem form, which is the form more readily absorbable. Pulses and nuts and starchy foods contain some iron but it is the non-haem form which is less readily absorbed. When foods with non-haem iron are eaten with a fruit or vegetable high in vitamin C the iron will be better absorbed from these foods.

Foods containing nuts can contribute reasonable amounts of iron. Most toddlers should be able to manage foods containing chopped or ground nuts but they should not be given whole nuts as there is a risk of choking. If a toddler inhales a whole nut this can cause distress and may cause inflammation in the lungs requiring a hospital admission.

Choosing an iron-fortified breakfast cereal will provide a good source of iron. This can be offered at breakfast or given with some milk as a nutritious snack. Many processed breakfast cereals are fortified with iron, but check the packet to make sure. Porridge oats naturally provide some iron and are also a good choice for breakfast.

Dried fruit is also a good source of iron and can be added to breakfast cereals or used in milk puddings, cakes and biscuits or given as part of the pudding. It is best not offered as a snack as it is very sweet and can cling to teeth keeping the tooth surface in contact with sugar over a long period.

ZINC

Giving your toddler formula milk, such as a growing-up milk will provide extra zinc as formulas are all fortified with zinc. Wholegrain cereals are a good source of zinc and can be mixed with white cereals to add extra zinc.

OMEGA 3 FATS

The levels of these in the diet can be boosted by only using oils rich in omega 3 fats: rapeseed oil, walnut oil and to a lesser extent olive and soya oils.

VITAMINS A AND D

Vegetarian toddlers should all be given vitamin drops containing vitamins A and D. As discussed in Chapter 2, many toddlers do not get enough vitamin A from their food and certain toddlers are likely to have low vitamin D stores. The Department of Health recommends vitamin drops containing vitamins A and D for all toddlers but particularly those who are likely to have low vitamin D levels – that is those:

- *with dark pigmented skins*
- *who spend little time outside – for example, those who do not play outside every day during the summer months*
- *whose skin is well covered when they are outside*
- *living in northern areas of the UK.*

VEGAN TODDLERS

Vegan toddlers need a more comprehensive vitamin and mineral supplement to provide all the nutrients they need. As toddlers will all have different likes and dislikes each vegan toddler's diet should be assessed by a registered dietician so that a suitable vitamin and mineral supplement can be recommended to provide any nutrients which your toddler may not be getting enough of. Ask your GP or health visitor for a referral to a registered dietician.

Food combining for vegetarian diets

The combination of food groups for healthy eating is exactly the same as that discussed in Chapter 3; that is combining foods from the five food groups. The only difference is that when meat and fish are not offered, foods from group 4 should be offered three times a day and should always be in combination with a food high in vitamin C. You can offer this combination at each mealtime, but snacks are just as suitable if your toddler eats well at certain snack times.

The food groups and recommendations for vegetarians are similar to those for non-vegetarian toddlers as described in Chapter 3, but more care is needed with food group 4. Take care to:

- *include one item from food group 4 at each meal or three times per day;*
- *always offer it in combination with a starchy food and a food rich in vitamin C.*

A vegetarian diet can be quite a bulky diet with more fibre than a non-vegetarian diet, and adding in some extra fat will help to make sure there is enough energy. Using fats with a high omega 3 will boost levels of these important fats, particularly in diets where fish is excluded.

Recommended foods for a vegetarian diet

Food group	Foods to include	Recommendation
1 Bread, rice, potatoes and other starchy food	bread, chapatti, oat porridge or muesli, breakfast cereals with added iron, rice, couscous, pasta, millet, potatoes, yam, and foods made with flour such as pizza bases, buns, pancakes	Include one of these foods at each meal and also offer them at some snack times.
2 Fruit and vegetables	fresh, frozen, tinned and dried fruits and vegetables; also pure fruit juices; those foods high in vitamin C are: blackcurrants, kiwi fruit, citrus fruits, tomatoes, peppers and strawberries; potato, sweet potatoes and mangoes; citrus or blackcurrant fruit juices; dried fruit is high in iron	Serve them at each meal and aim for around five small portions each day. Serve fruit at breakfast and at least one vegetable and one fruit at the midday and evening meals. Always include a fruit or vegetable high in vitamin C at each meal to aid iron absorption.

(Contd)

Food group	Foods to include	Recommendation
3 Milk, cheese and yoghurt	breast milk, follow-on milks, growing-up milks, yoghurts, cheese, soy-based formula milks, calcium-enriched soya milk and yoghurts, tofu	Serve three times a day.
4 Meat, fish, eggs, nuts and pulses	poultry, fish, eggs, pulses and foods made from them such as dhal and hummus; use nuts which are ground or chopped	Serve at each meal and always in combination with a food from food group 1.
5 Food and drinks high in fat and/or sugar		Offer these foods in small amounts in addition to, but not instead of, foods from the other four food groups.
Foods high in fat	cream, butter, margarines and mayonnaise; oils high in omega 3 fats are rapeseed oil and walnut oil; oils with a good balance of omega 3 and 6 fats are olive oil and soya oil; crisps and other fried snacks	Use in cooking and to boost energy content of foods for toddlers who are not overweight.
Foods high in sugar	jam, honey, syrup, confectionery	Use in small amounts.
Foods high in fat and sugar	ice cream, biscuits, cakes, chocolate, puddings	Use in small amounts.

Alternatives to meat and fish

SEMI-VEGETARIAN: ONLY RED MEAT IS NOT EATEN

Offer poultry, oily fish, fish, eggs and pulses two to three times per day. When you serve poultry, give your toddler dark poultry meat such as legs and thighs as this has a higher iron content than light meat, such as that on the breast of a chicken or turkey. When you use eggs, pulses or nuts combine them with a high vitamin C food.

Sample menu plan

	Day 1	*Day 2*	*Day 3*
Breakfast	breakfast cereal with added iron; banana slices; glass of diluted orange juice	porridge with dried fruit; glass of diluted orange juice	muesli with added ground almonds and strawberries; small glass of diluted orange juice
Midday meal	chicken curry with rice and broccoli; yoghurt and strawberries	salmon and potato fish-cakes with cauliflower and carrot; rice pudding with mango slices	pasta with minced turkey in bolognaise sauce with green beans; egg custard and fresh peaches
Evening meal	tuna, sweetcorn and mayonnaise sandwich; pancake with raspberries and ice cream	cheese omelette with toast fingers, pepper slices and courgette sticks; pear slices and a muffin	pitta bread with hummus, carrot and cucumber sticks; slices of kiwi fruit with a biscuit

PISCATARIAN: MEAT AND POULTRY ARE NOT EATEN

Use fish frequently and use oily fish up to about four times per week for boys. The Food Standards Agency recommends that girls should be limited to oily fish twice per week. This is because oily fish can contain traces of some toxins which may build up to levels which girls can retain into their child-bearing years.

Offer one of the following at each of the three meals:

- ▶ *fish*
- ▶ *oily fish*
- ▶ *egg, nuts or pulses combined with a high vitamin C food.*

Sample menu plan

	Day 1	Day 2	Day 3
Breakfast	boiled egg and toast fingers; banana slices; glass of diluted orange juice	baked beans on toast; glass of diluted orange juice	muesli with added ground almonds and strawberries; glass of diluted orange juice
Midday meal	chickpea curry and rice with courgette and cauliflower; yoghurt and strawberries	salmon and potato fishcakes with broccoli and carrot; rice pudding and mango slices	pasta with lentils in bolognaise sauce with green beans; egg custard and fresh peaches
Evening meal	tuna, sweetcorn and mayonnaise sandwich; pancake with raspberries and ice cream	cheese omelette with toast fingers, pepper slices and courgette sticks; pear slices and a muffin	pitta bread with hummus, carrot and cucumber sticks; slices of kiwi fruit with a biscuit

LACTO-OVO VEGETARIAN: MEAT, POULTRY AND FISH ARE NOT EATEN

At each meal offer:

▶ *egg, nuts or pulses combined with a high vitamin C food*
▶ *a cereal food.*

To increase the omega 3 fats in the diet:

▶ *use rapeseed oil for cooking*
▶ *use walnut oil or olive oil for dressings*
▶ *use ground or chopped walnuts sprinkled onto breakfast cereal or fruit or mixed into puddings.*

Sample menu plan

	Day 1	Day 2	Day 3
Breakfast	boiled egg with toast fingers; banana slices; glass of diluted orange juice	baked beans on toast; glass of diluted orange juice	toddler's muesli with added ground almonds and strawberries; glass of diluted fruit juice
Midday meal	chickpea curry and rice with courgette and cauliflower; yoghurt and strawberries	dhal and rice with broccoli and carrot; rice pudding and mango slices	pasta with lentils in bolognaise sauce with green beans; egg custard and fresh peaches
Evening meal	tofu stir-fry with noodles, cherry tomatoes and spinach; pancake with raspberries and ice cream	cheese omelette with toast fingers, pepper slices and courgette sticks; pear slices and a muffin	pitta bread with hummus, carrot and cucumber sticks; slices of kiwi fruit with a biscuit

LACTO-VEGETARIAN: MEAT, POULTRY, FISH AND EGGS ARE NOT EATEN

At each meal offer:

▶ *nuts or pulses combined with a high vitamin C food*
▶ *a cereal food.*

To increase the omega 3 fats in the diet:

▶ *use rapeseed oil for cooking*
▶ *use walnut oil or olive oil for dressings*
▶ *use ground walnuts sprinkled on breakfast cereal or fruit or mixed into puddings.*

Sample menu plan

	Day 1	*Day 2*	*Day 3*
Breakfast	baked beans on toast; banana slices; glass of diluted orange juice	porridge with ground almonds and dried fruit; glass of diluted orange juice	muesli with added ground almonds and strawberries; glass of diluted orange juice
Midday meal	chickpea curry and rice with courgette and cauliflower; yoghurt and strawberries	dhal and rice with broccoli and carrot; rice pudding and mango slices	pasta with lentils in bolognaise sauce with green beans; egg custard and fresh peaches
Evening meal	tofu stir-fry with noodles, cherry tomatoes and spinach; raspberries and ice cream	peanut butter sandwich with pepper slices and courgette sticks; pear slices and a chocolate biscuit	pitta bread with hummus, carrot and cucumber sticks; slices of kiwi fruit with a biscuit

VEGAN: ALL ANIMAL PRODUCTS ARE EXCLUDED – THAT IS MEAT, POULTRY, FISH, EGGS AND MILK PRODUCTS

A vegan diet is very restrictive for a toddler and not usually recommended because of a toddler's high requirement of nutrients supplied in milk. If you do wish to embark on a vegan diet, breastfeed your toddler or use a soya-based formula milk until he is at least two years old. Ask to see a registered dietician to get some individualized advice on how suitable your family foods are for your toddler. A dietician will also be able to recommend a suitable vitamin and mineral supplement.

At each meal you need to combine foods to make sure your toddler is having good-quality protein and some high-iron foods at each meal, along with a food rich in vitamin C. At each meal offer a combination of:

▶ *a cereal-based food*
▶ *nuts or pulses*
▶ *a food high in vitamin C.*

Breastfeeding your vegan toddler
If you are still breastfeeding your vegan toddler, your breast milk may not contain adequate vitamin B12 for your toddler. Your own bones will act as a supply of calcium for your milk, but unless your diet contains sufficient calcium to replace these losses, you might be putting yourself at risk of osteoporosis in later life. While you are breastfeeding, take a vitamin supplement that contains both vitamin D and vitamin B12 and a calcium supplement.

Choosing a soya milk
There are two infant formulas suitable for vegan toddlers in the UK that are based on soya milk: Cow & Gate Infasoy and SMA Wysoy.

When you change from formula to an ordinary soya milk, choose one that is enriched with calcium. Although soya beans are a good source of calcium, there is not as much calcium in ordinary soya milk as cows' milk. A calcium-enriched soya or oat milk will have similar levels of calcium to those found in cows' milk. Other milks, such as those based on rice or nuts, are not suitable for toddlers as they do not contain the range of nutrients that toddlers need from their milk. Rice milk is also unsuitable as it may contain small amounts of arsenic.

MORE RESTRICTED DIETS

Diets with more restrictions than a vegan diet are unsuitable for toddlers and older children. Toddlers on macrobiotic and fruitarian diets have become severely malnourished with deficiencies of various nutrients. When parents have refused to change to a more nutritious diet on the advice of healthcare professionals, toddlers and children have been taken into care to prevent ill health and death as a consequence of malnutrition.

TEST YOURSELF

1 What does a piscatarian not eat?

2 What is not eaten on a lacto-ovo vegetarian diet?

3 What is not eaten on a lacto-vegetarian diet?

4 What do vegans avoid?

5 Are vegan diets suitable for toddlers?

6 When should toddlers on a vegetarian diet change from formula milk to cows' milk?

7 Which nutrient is likely to be low in all vegetarian diets?

8 Why should nuts and pulses always be combined with a starchy food?

9 Why should eggs, nuts and pulses always be combined with a food high in vitamin C?

10 What is the best oil to use for toddlers who do not eat fish?

9

Common nutritional problems in toddlers

In this chapter you will learn:

- *about common nutritional problems in toddlers: iron deficiency anaemia, obesity and being overweight, constipation, dental caries, inadequate weight gain, rickets and vitamin D deficiency*
- *how these nutritional problems arise and how to prevent them*
- *the effect of food on behaviour.*

The toddler years are a good time for encouraging healthy eating habits. As toddlers learn by copying, you need to set them a good example yourself and adopt the healthy eating behaviour that you wish your toddler to learn. If he is your first child then this might be a good time to reappraise your own eating pattern and make sure it is a healthy one, based on an ideal combination of the five food groups. If you are eating the food you would like him to eat and making positive comments about these foods then he will, in time, begin to eat these foods and learn to like them.

Toddlers need very nutritious food to support their growth and development but feeding is challenging at the same time because of the developmental stage of fussy and faddy eating. If toddlers eat poorly or are not offered sufficiently nutritious food the common nutritional consequences that may occur are:

- ▶ *iron deficiency anaemia*
- ▶ *obesity and overweight*

- *constipation*
- *dental caries*
- *inadequate weight gain*
- *vitamin D deficiency and rickets.*

Iron deficiency anaemia

Not eating enough foods rich in iron is the most common nutritional problem for toddlers in the UK. A lot of iron is needed at this age for their growth, but about one in four toddlers do not eat enough iron in their food. About half of those not eating enough iron go on to develop iron deficiency anaemia. There are some other rare causes of iron deficiency anaemia, but most toddlers become anaemic because there is not enough iron in the food they eat.

Iron is an essential part of the pigment in red blood cells called haemoglobin, which carries oxygen around the body. Without enough iron, growth and development will be delayed. The immune system will not be working optimally and so an anaemic toddler may pick up a lot of infections which may make him miserable and less likely to eat well. A vicious cycle of poor eating and consequently a lower iron intake can occur, making the deficiency worse and unlikely to be resolved without some help.

WHICH FOOD GROUPS PROVIDE IRON?

- *Food group 4 (meat, fish, eggs, nuts and pulses) provides the most iron in the diet. The recommended serving of two to three times per day will ensure that your toddler has sufficient iron in his diet.*
- *Both food groups 1 and 2, starchy foods and fruit and vegetables, also provide some iron.*
- *Food groups 3 and 5 do not provide iron.*

Which foods contain iron?

The best food sources of iron in food group 4 are red meat such as beef, lamb and pork. Dark poultry meat such as chicken legs and thighs and oily fish are also good sources. These animal foods provide iron in a readily absorbable form; that is as haem iron. Liver is a very rich source of haem iron but should only be offered once a week as all liver now contains very high levels of vitamin A.

Other foods containing iron provide it in the form known as non-haem iron, which is less readily absorbed than in the form haem iron. However, the amount of non-haem iron absorbed can be increased if foods high in vitamin C are eaten at the same meal. Foods rich in non-haem iron are pulses, nuts, fortified breakfast cereals and some vegetables. Follow-on formulas and growing-up milks also contain this form of iron.

Good sources of iron

Haem iron from:	Non-haem iron from:
beef and lamb	breakfast cereals fortified with iron
pork	bread (especially wholemeal)
dark poultry meat (for example, chicken legs and thighs)	pulses (for example, starchy beans and lentils, dhal, chickpeas and peas)
liver (this should be limited to just once per week because of the high levels of vitamin A)	green vegetables
	nuts
oily fish (for example, sardines, mackerel, salmon and tuna)	dried fruit

TODDLERS MOST LIKELY TO BECOME IRON DEFICIENT

Toddlers who do not eat sufficient high-iron foods because they are filling themselves up on foods with very little iron are those most likely to become deficient in iron. The foods that contain virtually no iron, which toddlers often eat to excess, are:

- *cows' milk*
- *packet snack foods such as crisps*
- *sweets and confectionery*
- *sweetened drinks.*

Some toddlers continue to drink excess amounts of milk. This is particularly so for those who continue to drink bottles of milk as a comfort food. Many continue to be given bottles of milk at bedtime or when they wake during the night.

Toddlers who are eating large quantities of packet snack foods, sweets and sweetened drinks will be filling themselves up on these very low-iron foods and consequently decreasing their appetite for iron-rich foods.

Toddlers who are most likely to develop iron deficiency anaemia are those who:

- *eat very few iron-rich foods*
- *still drink too much milk and consequently eat less foods containing iron*
- *were changed onto cows' milk as a main drink before 12 months of age – without the iron from breast milk or infant formula at this age, their iron stores would have been depleted*
- *are very fussy about foods, particularly those containing good amounts of iron*
- *drink tea with their meals – the tannin in tea prevents iron in food being absorbed*
- *were born prematurely – these toddlers did not have the opportunity to lay down good stores of iron prior to their birth*
- *vegetarian toddlers who do not eat iron-rich foods in combination with foods rich in vitamin C at all their meals*
- *are given a lot of high-fibre cereals or bran – the phytates in bran prevents some of the iron in food being absorbed.*

DIAGNOSING IRON DEFICIENCY ANAEMIA

Toddlers with anaemia may become pale and tired and have less resistance to infection, although sometimes there are no apparent symptoms. They may lose their appetite and eat less, thereby reducing their iron intake further. Undetected iron deficiency anaemia can cause slow growth and developmental delay. A blood test is needed to determine if a toddler is iron deficient, but this can now be done with just a finger prick to extract a couple of drops of blood. If iron deficiency is confirmed, your doctor can prescribe an iron supplement to treat the deficiency which will resolve over the next few weeks. Whether the effects of slow growth and delayed development while he was anaemic affect the toddler as he gets older is still debatable. Some studies have shown that children who had iron deficiency anaemia as toddlers have lower IQs later in childhood than children who were not iron-deficient as toddlers. Other studies show there is no difference.

PREVENTING IRON DEFICIENCY ANAEMIA

The most important steps you can take to prevent your toddler from developing anaemia are:

▶ *Make sure your toddler is regularly offered foods rich in iron so that he learns to like them.*
▶ *Do not offer bottles of milk.*
▶ *Reduce the amount of milk, cheese and yoghurt you offer your toddler to just three servings a day so that he is less reliant on milk and will eat more iron-rich foods. However, do not offer less than three servings per day, otherwise he will run short of calcium (see Chapter 2).*
▶ *Limit high-fat snack foods such as crisps and confectionery to very small amounts.*
▶ *Offer nutritious snacks containing foods from food groups 1, 2 and 4.*

Obesity

Even though obesity is rising and is constantly in the news, parents still worry more about their toddlers not eating enough than they do about them gaining too much weight. However, one toddler in ten is now considered to be obese.

CHECKING WHETHER YOUR TODDLER IS OVERWEIGHT OR OBESE

Young toddlers are normally quite chubby when they first begin to walk. As they become more mobile, their muscles will develop and they will lose some of their fat. They should slim down during their toddler years but it is difficult to know just by looking at them whether they are overweight or obese.

Insight

As we have all become used to toddlers and children being chubbier, even doctors and other healthcare professionals find it hard to judge whether a child is overweight or obese just by looking at them.

To check if your toddler is overweight or obese, you will need to have his height and weight measured accurately. Your health visitor at the local health clinic will be able to do this for you. You can then calculate his Body Mass Index (BMI). The BMI is equal to his weight in kilograms divided by his height in metres squared.

If your toddler weighs 15.1 kg and is 98 cm (0.98 m) tall, then his BMI is:

his weight ÷ (his height in metres)²
= *15.1 ÷ (0.98)²*
= *15.7*

The normal BMI range for a toddler depends on his age, and there are centile charts for BMI as there are centile charts for height and weight mentioned in Chapter 1. A BMI centile chart for boys is shown in the Appendix on page 290. Ask your health visitor or GP to mark his BMI on a BMI centile chart to check whether he is overweight or obese for his age. A toddler with a BMI over the 98th centile line is considered obese and a toddler with a BMI between the 91st and 98th centiles is considered overweight. Toddlers with a BMI between the 2nd and 91st centiles are considered to have a BMI within the normal range.

Alternatively, you can measure your toddler, calculate the BMI and compare it with the chart below. However, be aware that your measurements taken at home may not be accurate and if you have concerns, ask for them to be checked with carefully calibrated equipment at your health clinic.

Boys' BMI ranges for normal weight, overweight and obese

Age	BMI		
	Normal range	Overweight	Obese
2 years	14.3–18.5	18.5–19.7	Above 19.7
3 years	14.0–18.0	18.0–19.0	Above 19.0
4–5 years	13.7–17.6	17.6–18.7	Above 18.7

Girls' BMI ranges for normal weight, overweight and obese

Age	BMI		
	Normal range	Overweight	Obese
2 years	14.0–18.3	18.3–19.5	Above 19.5
3 years	13.7–17.8	17.8–19.0	Above 19.0
4–5 years	13.0–17.7	17.7–19.0	Above 19.0

CAUSES OF BECOMING OVERWEIGHT AND OBESITY IN TODDLERS

Medical causes of obesity are extremely rare and include:

- *endocrine disorders such as hypothyroidism, Cushings syndrome, growth hormone deficiency and leptin deficiency*
- *genetically inherited disorders such as Prader-Willi syndrome.*

The vast majority of toddlers are overweight or obese because they eat and drink too many calories for the amount of energy they expend in growing, developing and being active. This is usually due to the lifestyle pattern that the family follows and obese toddlers often have at least one parent who is overweight or obese.

The excess calories eaten are converted into fat which is stored around the body – often around the waist. This fat is metabolically active and is bad for your toddler's health, causing resistance to the hormone insulin.

WHAT TO DO IF YOUR TODDLER IS OVERWEIGHT OR OBESE

If your toddler is overweight or obese:

▶ *you do not have to put him on a strict diet*
▶ *he does not need to lose weight*
▶ *you do need to re-examine your family lifestyle and make some changes to the balance between what your toddler eats and drinks and the energy he expends through physical activity; the balance should be fewer calories in and more calories expended on physical activity. If you can achieve this, your toddler's weight gain will slow down and as he gets taller he will grow out of his obesity.*

The whole family must make changes together. Your toddler copies what you do so you must change your lifestyle and encourage your toddler to follow your example. The changes you need to make may be:

▶ *the food and drinks you buy and consume*
▶ *the amount of physical activity your family does*
▶ *the amount of time you spend in sedentary activities, such as watching TV*
▶ *bedtimes and the amount of sleep your toddler has.*

Small sustainable changes are the best to focus on, rather than radically altering everything overnight and finding you cannot maintain the changes. Experts suggest you think of three small changes and begin with them. When these are successfully incorporated into your lifestyle, consider another three to focus on.

As toddlers learn by copying you, you will need to make the changes yourself first. Don't expect your toddler to do things that you are not prepared to do yourself. As he follows your lead, praise him so that he will be keen to repeat that behaviour again. Praise yourself as well when you make changes and keep them up.

Discuss the changes you are making with those who come to your house – for example, your friends, extended family, babysitters, au pairs and nannies. Ask them to follow your example while in your house so that they do not undermine the changes you and your toddler are making.

The lifestyle changes you need to choose are the same as those that are discussed below in preventing obesity.

PREVENTING OBESITY IN YOUR TODDLER

Assess your family lifestyle
Your lifestyle is the lifestyle your toddler will grow up to think is a normal one. If you want him to learn a healthy lifestyle then that is what your family lifestyle must be. Are you eating a healthy, balanced diet and doing some physical activity each day – for example, walking, dancing or playing active games or a sport? If not, then now is the time to reassess this and make some changes.

Set up a routine of healthy meals and snacks
Eat healthy, well-balanced meals together as a family as often as possible. The more often your toddler sees you eating a combination of nutritious foods (as discussed in Chapter 3), the more he will be learning that these are part of a normal meal pattern. These meals will be a combination of both higher-calories foods such as meat, fish, cheese and sauces and the lower-calorie foods such as starchy foods, fruit and vegetables.

It may seem a fine balance between giving your toddler enough food to provide all his nutrients and energy for growth but at the same time not giving so much that he becomes overweight. However, toddlers often need to eat a smaller quantity of food than their parents suppose. When offered the healthy, balanced diet discussed in Chapter 3, most toddlers can regulate their calorie intake to suit their needs. It is important to allow your toddler to finish eating when he signals to you that he has had enough. Do not coerce him to eat more and never insist he finishes everything on his plate. He will be telling you he has had enough to eat when he:

• says no

• keeps his mouth shut when food is offered

• turns his head away from the food being offered

• pushes away the spoon, bowl or plate containing food

• holds food in his mouth and refuses to swallow it

• spits out food

• cries, shouts or screams

• tries to climb down from the table or out of his highchair

• gags or retches.

Limit sweet and high-fat foods to small amounts

Toddlers naturally like sweet, high-calorie foods and would just eat mainly these foods if they were given the chance. There is no need to cut out sweet food or foods containing sugar altogether, but you do need to limit them to small amounts. If your toddler asks for more sweet food during the day, say 'No' quite clearly and compromise by saying he can have a little of what he is asking for at the end of his next meal.

Toddlers like to have boundaries and limits because it makes them feel safe and secure. However, they will constantly test you to make sure the boundary is still there. So set the limits for sweet foods and stick to them. Even though your toddler may cry when you say no, he needs to learn that the pain of not having what he wants will go away. Comfort him and distract him or say he can have something at the next mealtime. Do not give in to a tantrum and change the limits you have set. This will confuse him about what the limits are.

Limit high-fat, low-nutrient foods

High-fat, low-nutrient foods such as crisps and other packet snacks provide plenty of calories but very few nutrients. Limit them to very occasionally, such as once a month, and offer other crunchy foods in their place – for example, carrot or cucumber sticks. If your toddler eats high-fat snacks regularly they will fill him up so that he refuses to eat more nutritious foods. He may end up with a deficit of nutrients such as iron, as discussed earlier in this chapter. Other nutrients which might be low are zinc and vitamin A.

Make sure your toddler gets enough sleep

Toddlers need about 12 hours of sleep in each 24 hours; this 12 hours includes any daytime sleeps your toddler may still be having. Studies have shown that toddlers who get less than 10 hours of sleep in each 24 hours are more likely to become obese. It is not known exactly how too little sleep makes toddlers more likely to become overweight and obese, but it may be that less sleep affects their growth in some way.

If your toddler has to be woken in the morning then this is an indication that he needs to go to bed earlier the night before so that he can sleep for a longer period until he is ready to wake himself.

Encourage active play and walking
Allow your toddler plenty of opportunity for active play each day. If you do not have a garden where he can run outside whenever he wishes, take him to a playground each day for about an hour. Let him walk when he wants to, even though this will slow you down; do not insist he always sits in his stroller or car seat when you are out and about.

Spend as much time as you have playing with him – throwing and catching balls and playing chasing and running games. Do praise him when he is active so that he becomes proud of his achievements and progress and enjoys being active. The more active he is, the more he will develop his physical co-ordination. This will make games and sport more pleasurable for him as he gets older.

Limit the time he is sedentary or not active
Studies show that toddlers who watch more than one hour of television or DVDs each day are more likely to become obese. Limit the time he is just sitting watching a screen to less than one hour so that he is more active for the majority of his day.

Eating out
Try and choose a balanced meal for your toddler when eating out – a meal that includes vegetables and fruit. Unfortunately the children's menu in many restaurants may only include foods high in fat and sugar. There is no need to deny your toddler this food altogether, especially if he can see others eating and enjoying it. However, limit the number of times you take your toddler to eat in such restaurants and keep portion sizes small. Do not go to restaurants where you can eat all you want for a set amount of money – the temptation is for the whole family to overeat.

Party food

Many toddlers are invited to birthday parties frequently, and eating large amounts of high-calorie but low-nutrient party food several times per month can unbalance the diet. On the days your toddler is going to a party, make sure you offer him a well-balanced meal as his other main meal for that day. Do not offer any fried food – just plain meat or fish and some vegetables and just a piece of fruit for dessert.

Observing a few simple rules will make sure you do not create a lifestyle pattern that will cause your toddler to become overweight or obese.

▶ *Offer your toddler a combination of the nutritious foods from food groups 1 to 4 (see Chapter 3).*
▶ *Allow your toddler to eat to his appetite and never insist he finishes everything on his plate.*
▶ *Do not coerce him to eat more when he has shown you he has had enough.*
▶ *Always combine some low-calorie foods with high-calorie foods at each meal. Fruit and vegetables are low-calorie foods, so include these in every meal.*
▶ *Only allow very small amounts of sweet or high-fat foods.*
▶ *Allow your toddler plenty of opportunity for active play each day. Let him walk when he wants to, even though this will slow you down – do not insist he always sits in his stroller or car seat when you are out and about.*
▶ *Make sure he has enough sleep each night and during the day – about 12 hours in every 24 hours is the average for toddlers.*
▶ *Change the lifestyle of your family if necessary, so that your toddler is growing up learning that eating nutritious foods and having plenty of physical activity is the normal way to live.*

WHAT ARE THE CONSEQUENCES OF REMAINING OBESE?

Toddlers who remain obese into their childhood and carry extra weight are likely to have more frequent respiratory infections. The extra weight will exacerbate their asthma and, sadly, overweight and obese children are more likely to be bullied.

> **Insight**
>
> Studies have also shown that obese children have lower self-esteem and lower academic performance along with a higher risk of depression – consequences that no parents would wish for their child.

Constipation

About one in 30 toddlers becomes constipated and passes infrequent stools which are hard and dry. These toddlers may strain excessively to pass the stool and they may cry with the pain of passing it. To avoid the pain of passing such a stool, some may withhold the stool.

Normally toddlers pass a stool anywhere from once every two days to two times each day. Anything within this range is considered normal, but constipated toddlers will pass them less frequently than this.

WHAT CAUSES CONSTIPATION?

Some toddlers develop constipation and there is no apparent reason for it. In some cases it may be because the toddler has a phobia about passing stools at the time of potty training or beginning to use the toilet and may withhold stools. Your toddler may have a medical reason for his constipation. In rare cases, an anal fissure may be causing constipation. This is a tear of the anal passage which can be treated. However, some cases of constipation are due to a poor diet and/or not enough fluid.

The dietary causes of constipation are:

▶ *not eating a healthy diet*
▶ *drinking too little fluid*
▶ *eating too little fibre – foods containing fibre are the foods in groups 1 and 2 in Chapter 3; that is fruit, vegetables and foods made from cereals such as pasta, rice, couscous, bread and other foods made with flour*
▶ *some food allergies and intolerances cause constipation (see Chapter 10).*

If you think your toddler is constipated, check:

▶ **the number of drinks he is having each day.** *Toddlers should be having about 6–8 drinks per day. This will be a drink with each meal and one in-between the meals.*
▶ **that fruit and vegetables are included at every meal.** *Make sure you are giving your toddler fruit at breakfast and at least one vegetable and one fruit at the other two meals.*
▶ **that potatoes or cereal-based food are part of each meal.** *Cereal-based foods are pasta, rice, couscous, bread and any foods made with flour. You could change to offering more wholegrain cereals such as Weetabix, Shredded Wheat or Cheerios for breakfast. You could also include some more wholemeal bread and crackers. Do not offer bran or cereals enriched with bran, as bran can decrease the absorption of some of the valuable nutrients in food that your toddler needs.*

If the constipation is a problem you should talk to your GP who can prescribe a simple laxative or stool softener to ease the passage of hard stools. You can then make changes to your toddler's food and fluid intake. If these changes do not resolve the problem you can consider whether an allergy or intolerance to food may be causing the problem (see Chapter 10).

If constipation in your toddler is not resolved quickly, he may begin to withhold his stool to avoid the pain of passing them. This can then set up chronic constipation and your toddler will become less aware of when his rectum is full and when he needs to pass a stool. Chronic constipation can be more difficult to resolve. Soiling where liquid faeces pass around the side of a hard stool and leak into a toddler's pants is an indication of chronic constipation. A psychologist may be able to help with changing behaviour that is causing constipation.

> **Insight**
> When toddlers are constipated their appetite is reduced, so encouraging them to eat or drink more is a losing battle. The first step should always be to begin laxatives and once the constipation is resolved, changes to the diet can begin.

Dental caries

Many toddlers develop dental caries and dental erosion in their first set of teeth. Both of these can cause pain and discomfort to your toddler. Although these first teeth will eventually be replaced, taking care of them is extremely important; they are necessary for the development of the jaw so that the permanent teeth can grow and develop normally in the gums. The foods most likely to cause decay are sugary foods and drinks. Acidic drinks cause erosion of the tooth enamel.

WHAT CAUSES DENTAL CARIES?

Sugar from foods is broken down by the bacteria in the plaque which accumulates on teeth. An acid is released by the plaque bacteria and this attacks the tooth. The risk of developing dental caries depends on how many times per day the teeth are exposed to acid attacks due to plaque bacteria breaking down sugar. If you limit the number of times your toddler has sugary or sticky food to four or less times per day, you will reduce the likelihood of him developing caries. If you only give sugary foods at the three meals and at one snack, that will be four times per day.

Toddlers who are given sweetened drinks in a bottle drink them more slowly over a longer time than toddlers who drink from a cup or glass quickly by sipping. The teeth of the slow drinkers are in contact with the sugar for a longer time.

Saliva in the mouth helps to minimize the acid attack. But night-time is a particularly vulnerable time for teeth, as the flow of saliva is minimal during periods of sleep. Giving sweet food and drinks just before a sleep is therefore very damaging for teeth. Giving a bottle of a sweetened drink to a toddler as he goes down to sleep is the surest way possible to inflict dental caries on him.

WHAT CAUSES DENTAL EROSION?

The tooth enamel of toddlers is very delicate and dissolves when teeth are bathed in acidic drinks. Sweet drinks such as pure fruit juices, squashes and fizzy drinks are all acidic drinks. The balance of sugar and acid in a drink improves the flavour, which is why acids such as citric acid are added to most sweet drinks. Water and milk are not acidic and are the only safe drinks to offer between meals.

Drinking acidic drinks slowly over a longer time is more damaging. This happens if toddlers are given acidic drinks in bottles or cups with a teat or valved spout, where the drink is taken by slow sucking.

PREVENTING DENTAL DECAY AND DENTAL EROSION

Healthy eating
Calcium, vitamin D and fluoride are all important in building strong teeth to withstand attacks by acid. Three servings of milk,

cheese or yoghurt each day will provide enough calcium. Vitamin D is present in the vitamin drops that are recommended for all toddlers and it will also be made in the skin when toddlers are playing outside in the summer months.

Brush teeth with fluoride toothpaste twice a day

Fluoride is adequate in the tap water in some areas of the UK, but not all. Brushing the teeth twice a day with fluoride toothpaste on a dry toothbrush will provide enough fluoride as well as removing the plaque that accumulates on teeth. You will have to do this for your toddler, but encourage him to try himself. You can finish off to make sure it has been done well.

Insight

For toddlers under three years of age use a smear of fluoride toothpaste on the toothbrush. Then once he is over three, increase to a pea-sized amount of toothpaste.

Limit sugary foods to four times per day (three meals and one snack)

For breakfast you may give your toddler a little jam or honey as a spread on toast, or you may offer a breakfast cereal that has had sugar added during the process of making it. For the two main meals give him a small sweet pudding after the savoury course and perhaps a sweet or chocolate to finish off. For a fourth serving of sugary food, you could offer a biscuit or small cake at one of his snacks.

Offer all drinks in non-lidded cups or glasses or cups with free-flow spouts

Toddlers drinking from non-lidded cups and glasses or cups with free-flow spouts will sip the drink and drink it more quickly than if the drink was being sucked through a valved spout on a lidded cup or a teat on a bottle.

Offer only 'safe' drinks

It is best to offer water from an early age so that your toddler is happy to drink water. Avoid squashes and fizzy drinks altogether. Fruit juices are useful for providing vitamin C to help iron absorption, especially with vegetarian meals. If you dilute fruit juice with water you will reduce the acidity, making it less damaging to teeth. As long as fruit juices are well diluted and only offered in cups at mealtimes they will be less harmful. Water and milk are the only 'safe' drinks to offer between mealtimes.

To prevent dental caries in your toddler:

▶ *Help him clean his teeth twice per day with a smear (if he is under three years) or a pea-sized amount (if he is three years and over) of fluoride toothpaste.*
▶ *Limit sugary foods to four or less times per day (for example, the three meals and one snack).*
▶ *Don't give drinks in beakers or bottles with a teat or valved spout.*
▶ *Always dilute fruit juices with water and only give them with meals.*
▶ *Never give sweet squashes, fruit juice drinks and fizzy drinks.*
▶ *Never give sweet food or drinks just before bedtime or during the night.*

Inadequate weight gain

As described in Chapter 1, toddlers gain weight more slowly than they did as babies and very few of them grow too slowly. One reason for poor weight gain is because a toddler is not eating enough food. This is usually because he is particularly fussy about food and mealtimes are not being managed well. Chapters 5 and 6 deal with this topic in more detail.

Poor weight gain might also indicate that your toddler has an underlying disease and your GP will be able to refer you to a paediatrician to check for this.

Toddlers who are deprived of love and attention may also not gain weight adequately. Fortunately this is a rare cause of poor weight gain.

> **Insight**
>
> Many parents worry unnecessarily that their toddler is not gaining enough weight. Toddlers should become slimmer and slimmer until they are about five years old but parents are not always aware of this.

Vitamin D deficiency and rickets

Toddlers with low vitamin D levels will have poor bone development and may go on to develop rickets, which is when the bones become soft and misshapen. This is more likely in dark-skinned toddlers of Asian, African, Afro-Caribbean and Middle Eastern origin that are living in northern Europe and America, than in white toddlers. It has begun to increase in the UK again recently as many parents do not give toddlers the recommended vitamin drops containing vitamin D (see Chapter 2, page 31).

Vitamin D is a fat-soluble vitamin that is essential for bone growth and general health. It increases the absorption of calcium from milk, cheese and yoghurt and other foods containing smaller amounts of calcium. The deposition of calcium and other minerals into bone is controlled by vitamin D. Vitamin D is also important in boosting the immune system and protecting toddlers against infections. Research now shows that it may help prevent type 1 diabetes in toddlers.

Vitamin D is sometimes called 'the sunshine vitamin', as most vitamin D is made in our skins when we are outside in daylight. Very few foods contain vitamin D – oily fish is the best source. Margarines, follow-on and growing-up formulas and one or two breakfast cereals are fortified with vitamin D. Meat and egg yolks only contain tiny amounts.

In the UK, sunlight is only strong enough to make vitamin D in skin between April and September – we need to make enough in these months to last us throughout the winter. Nowadays many people spend little time outside, particularly those with office jobs and work that keeps them indoors. People with dark skins need more sunlight to make vitamin D in their skin and those dark-skinned ethnic groups who live in northern areas of Europe and America commonly have low vitamin D levels.

Toddlers have very high requirements for vitamin D and many do not get enough vitamin D from their food, nor do they make adequate amounts in their skin. The toddlers in the UK most at risk are:

▶ *those with dark skins*
▶ *those who live in more northerly areas – the further toddlers live from the equator, the longer they need to spend outside in the sun to make enough vitamin D*
▶ *those who do not spend much time outside in summer months and whose skin is mainly covered with clothing or sunscreen when they are outside*
▶ *those who were born with low levels of vitamin D – these are toddlers whose mothers had low levels of vitamin D during pregnancy.*

About one mother in four begins her pregnancy with low vitamin D levels and if she doesn't take the vitamin D supplements that are recommended during pregnancy and breastfeeding, she will continue with low levels during pregnancy which can affect her baby's health. Mothers most likely to have low vitamin D levels during pregnancy are those who:

▶ *have dark skins*
▶ *do not spend much time outside in summer months and cover most of their skin when they are outside.*

PREVENTING LOW VITAMIN D LEVELS IN YOUR TODDLER

The Department of Health recommends that all toddlers take a vitamin supplement containing vitamin D to make sure they maintain adequate vitamin D levels. Many vitamin supplements for toddlers contain vitamin D, but ask your pharmacist for one with 7.5 micrograms of vitamin D3, which is the form of vitamin D which is more active. The NHS Healthy Start children's vitamin drops are ideal, but are only sold through some NHS health clinics. Ask your health visitor where to get them.

Does food affect behaviour?

Although there is a lot of discussion on this topic, there is very little evidence for many of the claims made.

LACK OF FOOD AND LOW BLOOD SUGAR LEVELS WILL AFFECT BEHAVIOUR

This is well-proven, because a hungry toddler will be miserable. While eating, the blood sugar level rises giving a feeling of satiety. About an hour after a meal, the blood sugar level will begin decreasing. By the next time we are due to eat, the blood sugar level will have fallen to a level where we feel hungry.

Toddlers who are miserable due to hunger and low blood sugar levels may be irritable and unco-operative. However, it does not follow that all toddlers that are miserable and unco-operative will necessarily be hungry!

Keeping to a routine of meals and planned nutritious snacks in between will keep blood sugar levels more even and keep your toddler happier and more content. However, life does not always go to plan and there will always be times when your toddler may be late for a snack or meal.

DOES EXCESS SUGAR MAKE TODDLERS HYPERACTIVE?

There is speculation that toddlers who eat very sugary food become hyperactive with high blood sugar levels. There are no scientific trials that show this. Ideally sugar should be included in small amounts at mealtimes. However, at parties or celebrations toddlers may eat more sugar at one time than they normally do. Whether their excitement is due to the extra sugar in their blood or due to the atmosphere of mixing with other toddlers at a party is not clear.

DO OMEGA 3 FATS AFFECT THE BRAIN AND BEHAVIOUR?

Although many supplement companies have promoted omega 3 fats as making children less hyperactive and better at school work, scientific trials do not support this. Normal children who are eating enough omega 3 fat will not benefit from extra omega 3 in supplements. There are some scientific studies that suggest that some children with dyslexia, dyspraxia, ADHD and autistic spectrum disorders may benefit from a supplement of EPA, which is one of the omega 3 fats. However, the studies are inconclusive so far and not all children with these conditions will benefit. It is best to talk to you child's doctor for some advice on trying a supplement, as not all supplements with omega 3 necessarily contain EPA.

DO FOOD ADDITIVES AFFECT BEHAVIOUR?

There is no definite evidence to confirm that food additives affect behaviour adversely, although it has been suspected for some time. A recent study has suggested that certain colours and one preservative may have a negative effect on children's behaviour. More studies are needed to confirm this, but at present the Food Standards Agency have advised manufacturers to remove the following additives from food, drinks and medicines.

Colours: *tartrazine E102*
        ponceau 4R E124
        sunset yellow E110
        carmoisine E122
        quinoline yellow E104
        allura red AC E129
Preservative: *sodium benzoate E211*

LACK OF IRON MAKES TODDLERS TIRED AND LISTLESS

This is discussed in the section on iron deficiency anaemia in this chapter (see page 173).

TEST YOURSELF

1 *What is the most common nutritional deficiency in toddlers in the UK?*

2 *Which foods are the best sources of iron?*

3 *Which toddlers are the most likely to become iron deficient?*

4 *Which measurement is used to check if toddlers are overweight or obese?*

5 *How do toddlers usually become obese?*

6 *How do toddlers get dental caries?*

7 *Which habit is the most damaging for toddler's teeth?*

8 *What is the first step in resolving constipation in toddlers?*

9 *In the UK which toddlers are most likely to have low vitamin D levels and be at risk of rickets?*

10 *Do certain foods or ingredients affect behaviour in children?*

10

....

Food allergies and food intolerances

In this chapter you will learn:
- *about food allergies and food intolerances*
- *what causes them and how they are diagnosed*
- *about coeliac disease and eliminating gluten from the diet*
- *how to eliminate foods completely from your toddler's diet.*

The number of toddlers and children who are allergic or intolerant to foods is rising and the reasons why are not known. Many suspect it is due to environmental factors which may include:

- ▶ *the chemicals in our environment, many of which have only been introduced in the last 50 or so years*
- ▶ *our lifestyles, including how clean we keep our homes*
- ▶ *improving public health measures that prevent a lot of contagious infections in toddlers*
- ▶ *the changes in the food we now eat – which is more likely to be processed and less likely to be fresh from a local producer.*

If you suspect your toddler reacts to one or more particular foods it is very important that you get expert medical advice rather than trying various elimination diets or following advice from unqualified practitioners. You could make your toddler ill if you cut out too many foods from his diet so that he doesn't have enough to eat or doesn't get enough of all the nutrients that are needed for growing and developing.

What is a food allergy and what is a food intolerance?

Although most people use the term 'food allergy' loosely to cover all unpleasant reactions to food, experts have now classified the different reactions to food based on how the body is responding to the food. Food hypersensitivity is the term used to cover all the different types of reaction to foods, and food allergy is part of that.

Food allergies

When a toddler is allergic to a food, a protein in that food will trigger his own immune system to respond in a variety of ways. It may be a rapid, severe response or a slower, less severe response, depending on whether or not the antibody IgE is released by the immune system. Not everyone makes IgE.

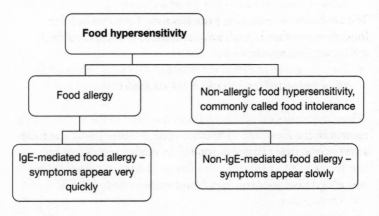

IgE-MEDIATED FOOD ALLERGY

In toddlers who do make the antibody IgE, a protein in the food reacts with the IgE and one or more of the following symptoms will appear very quickly:

- *diarrhoea*
- *asthma*
- *breathing difficulties*
- *eczema gets worse*
- *hives (blotchy red rash) or urticaria*
- *itching*
- *pallor*
- *rashes*
- *redness*
- *swelling of lips, tongue, face*
- *vomiting*
- *wheeziness*
- *anaphylaxis.*

Anaphylaxis is the most serious reaction and includes breathing problems, heart failure, and a rapid drop in blood pressure. Toddlers who suffer in this way need immediate medical attention. Parents of these toddlers will be taught how to use an Epipen and given one to carry with them at all times so that they can use it in an emergency.

The anaphylaxis campaign provides useful information for food allergy sufferers with anaphylaxis; look on their website www.anaphylaxis.org.uk.

NON-IgE-MEDIATED FOOD ALLERGY

When antibodies other than IgE are involved in the reaction to a protein in the food, the symptoms appear more slowly – usually a few hours after eating the food. The typical symptoms are:

- *abdominal pain or colic, bloating and wind*
- *constipation*
- *diarrhoea*

- *eczema*
- *reflux*
- *vomiting a few hours after the meal*
- *wheeziness.*

This table details the foods that can cause the two different types of allergic reaction in toddlers.

Food	Food allergies	
	IgE-mediated food allergy – symptoms appear rapidly	Non-IgE-mediated food allergy – symptoms appear slowly
egg	✓	rarely
fish	✓	rarely
shellfish: prawn, shrimp, crab, lobster and crayfish	✓	rarely
peanuts (also called ground nuts)	✓	rarely
tree nuts: almond, hazelnut, walnut, cashew nut, pecan nut, brazil nut, pistachio nut, macadamia nut, Queensland nut	✓	rarely
sesame	✓	rarely
milk	✓	✓
wheat	rarely	✓
soya	rarely	✓
kiwi fruit	rarely	rarely

NON-ALLERGIC FOOD HYPERSENSITIVITY OR FOOD INTOLERANCE

When a toddler has a food intolerance, the toddler's immune system does not respond to the food but an unpleasant reaction to food still occurs. The symptoms usually appear a few hours or even days after eating the food and they are rarely life-threatening. Foods which toddlers can be intolerant of include:

- **Citrus fruits** *sometimes contain high levels of benzoic acid which can cause a harmless flare reaction around the mouth.*
- **Fruits and vegetables containing salicylates or histamines** *can cause reactions similar to food allergy such as hives and skin rashes, even facial swelling in some toddlers.*
- **Foods containing biogenic amines** *can cause headache, nausea and giddiness. They include:*
  - ▷ *cheese, especially if matured*
  - ▷ *fermented foods such as blue cheese, sauerkraut, fermented soya products*
  - ▷ *yeast extracts*
  - ▷ *fish, especially if stale or pickled*
  - ▷ *microbial contaminated foods*
  - ▷ *chocolate*
  - ▷ *some fruits, especially citrus fruits, bananas and avocado pears.*
- **Monosodium glutamate** *is a flavour enhancer and some foods contain large amounts of it. In some toddlers it may cause flushing, headache and stomach aches.*
- **Milk** – *toddlers may sometimes become intolerant to milk for a short time following a bout of viral gastroenteritis. During this time they lack the enzyme lactase and consequently they are unable to digest lactose which is the sugar in milk. This can cause loose stools and wind after eating milk or milk products. It usually resolves within a few weeks.*

Additives

Whether additives in food such as artificial colours and preservatives cause reactions is currently unclear and needs further investigation. Recent research indicates that you should avoid giving toddlers any foods, drinks or medicines containing:

Colours: *tartrazine E102*
            ponceau 4R E124
            sunset yellow E110
            carmoisine E122
            quinoline yellow E104
            allura red AC E129
Preservative: *sodium benzoate E211*

How common are food allergies?

Food allergies and intolerances are very distressing for toddlers and parents, but not all of them will last throughout your toddler's life. Most toddlers grow out of it by the time they are around three years old. Only about two in 100 toddlers remain allergic to one or more foods as they get older. Ask your doctor about a suitable age to retest your toddler so that you don't continue to avoid a food long after he may have grown out of his allergy.

Insight

My son had a friend of 16 who was still checking every day with the school catering staff which dishes in the school lunch contained egg and which did not. His egg allergy had been diagnosed when he was about 12 months old and had never been rechecked. He may well have grown out of this allergy before three years of age but had been making his life and that of others more difficult for many years.

Finding out if your toddler has a food allergy or food intolerance

Toddlers may have some of the symptoms listed in this chapter, but they will not always be caused by a reaction to food. For example, less that half of toddlers with eczema have this skin condition because of a reaction to food.

Insight

Parents are usually very disappointed when they cannot resolve their child's eczema by taking foods out of the diet.

If you suspect your toddler is reacting to a food, talk to your GP or health visitor who can refer you to a paediatrician or an allergy clinic. If you just cut foods out of your toddler's diet yourself you could inadvertently be cutting out key nutrients he needs for growing and developing. Any food cut out will need to be substituted with other foods from the same food group. If the food suspected of causing a reaction is milk, an alternative milk can usually be recommended by a dietician or prescribed by your doctor.

How are food allergies and intolerances diagnosed?

IgE-MEDIATED FOOD ALLERGIES

Blood tests and a skin prick test are the only medically recognized tests that will help in diagnosing an IgE-mediated food allergy. They will suggest likely foods or non-food allergens that may be causing the problem. These tests can be organized at an allergy clinic. There are many alternative therapists that advertise other tests for diagnosing food allergies, however none of these are reliable and you should not use them for your toddler.

Once the tests at an NHS allergy clinic are completed you will need to cut out all traces of the suspected food or foods from your toddler's diet for about two weeks to see if the symptoms improve. If they do, any suspected foods can be given to your toddler again to see if the symptoms come back. A doctor will decide when a food should be reintroduced to your toddler. If the reaction is likely to be rapid and severe, this step may need to happen in a hospital where immediate treatment can be given if your toddler needs it.

You need expert advice from a dietician to cut out a suspected food completely as you may not be aware of all the foods that can contain traces of a suspected food. You must also keep a written symptom chart over the period before, during and after cutting out a food as it is easy to over- or underestimate the effect this trial exclusion diet is having if you are not carefully recording symptoms.

First, grade the severity of the symptoms you are going to record, for example:

Severity of symptoms	Diarrhoea
1	slightly loose stool
2	very loose stool
3	liquid stool

Next, record the timings of all the food and drinks your toddler has, along with the time of any symptoms and the severity grade:

Time	Food and drinks consumed	Symptoms
7:30	Small bowl Cheerios with full-fat milk and banana slices 1 cup milk	
8:30		diarrhoea – 2
10:30	4 fl oz/120 ml cup of apple juice diluted 50% with water 1 digestive biscuit	
12:00	2 tbsp pasta 1 tbsp meat sauce 3 carrot sticks 2 cauliflower florets 1 flavoured fromage frais 6 grapes 4 fl oz/120 ml cup of water	
1pm		diarrhoea – 1

Once you and your doctor or dietician have agreed that your toddler has an allergy or intolerance to a certain food, or a number of foods, the only effective management is avoiding the culprit food or foods. The extent to which the food needs to be avoided will vary from toddler to toddler. Some toddlers with IgE-mediated food allergies need to completely avoid the food – even in trace amounts. Others may be able to tolerate small amounts of the food they are allergic or intolerant to.

A doctor can prescribe an Epipen for toddlers with severe food allergies. This is an injection-pen containing adrenaline which prevents toddlers suffering from severe breathing difficulties and even collapse, which can arise if there is an anaphylactic reaction to food.

NON-IgE-MEDIATED FOOD ALLERGY AND FOOD INTOLERANCE OR NON-ALLERGIC FOOD HYPERSENSITIVITY

The only way to test whether a food is causing either of these conditions is, as discussed previously, to cut out all traces of the food from your toddler's diet for about two weeks to see if the symptoms improve. If they do, the suspected food can be given to your toddler again to see if the symptoms come back. This can usually be done in consultation with a dietician as the reaction to the food when it is reintroduced is not likely to be severe.

COELIAC DISEASE

Toddlers with this condition cannot tolerate the protein gluten which is found in the three cereals: wheat, rye and barley. All food and drinks made from these three cereals need to be eliminated from the diet. Some toddlers may also need to avoid oats if they are also sensitive to a protein in oats, which is similar to gluten. Often oats are contaminated with traces of wheat, rye or barley and so toddlers are usually advised to avoid oats along with wheat, rye and barley as a matter of course.

This disease is no longer considered a food allergy or a food intolerance but is an autoimmune disease. It is diagnosed with blood tests and a biopsy of the intestine. The treatment for the disease is a gluten-free diet and this will be necessary for the rest of your toddler's life.

Feeding a toddler with a food allergy, food intolerance or coeliac disease

It may seem daunting but it will get easier. Explain to your toddler which foods he needs to avoid and encourage him to tell others about his allergy.

You can buy clothes, stickers, t-shirts, watches and jewellery which alert people to the food allergy that your toddler has. Websites selling these are: www.kidsaware.co.uk, www.medicalert.co.uk and www.sostalisman.co.uk.

SEEK RELIABLE ADVICE TO ENSURE YOUR TODDLER CONTINUES TO GROW AND DEVELOP NORMALLY

Ask to see a registered dietician who can advise you on:

- *which foods you toddler can eat and which foods he will have to avoid*
- *which family foods to use in place of foods your toddler has to avoid*
- *how to check food labels for food ingredients you must avoid*
- *any food products you may be entitled to have prescribed for your toddler*
- *making sure your toddler gets all the nutrients he needs for growing and developing*
- *where to buy certain foods*
- *organizations that can give you extra advice and support.*

A dietician can also help you plan meals and menu plans for your family and, if necessary, will write to a nursery or school about the special diet your toddler needs.

Do not take advice from a nutritionist unless he/she is registered with the Health Professions Council or the Association for Nutrition. Anyone can call themselves a nutritionist and although some are well qualified and registered with the Nutrition Society, many have dubious qualifications and could give you advice that could harm your toddler. The training of other nutritional therapists is not recognized by the NHS as being adequate to advise on diets for food allergies.

Elimination diets for food allergies, food intolerance and coeliac disease

CUTTING OUT EGGS

Cutting out boiled, poached, fried eggs and omelettes seems obvious and will not cause nutrient deficiencies because a little more meat or fish can be eaten instead. However, many foods contain eggs as an ingredient (for example, cakes, some biscuits, some ice cream, mayonnaise, quiche, pancakes and some pasta). Often eggs are used to glaze baked goods. You will need to check labels very carefully for the following ingredients: albumin, dried egg, egg powder, egg protein, egg white and yolk, frozen egg, globulin, lecithin (E322), livetin, ovalbumin, ovoglobulin, ovomucin, ovovitellin, pasteurized egg and vitellin. Information from manufacturers and supermarkets will help you choose suitable foods.

Some toddlers may be able to eat very small quantities of egg in cooked foods such as cakes, as cooking denatures some of the protein, making it less likely to cause a reaction in some toddlers.

Four out of five toddlers with an allergy to egg will grow out of it by the time they are five years old, so make sure you have your toddler retested before he begins school.

CUTTING OUT FISH AND SHELLFISH

These foods can be replaced by having a little more egg or meat. However, fish is a very good source of omega 3 for your toddler that will not be replaced by extra meat and eggs. By using rapeseed oil for cooking and walnut oil in salad dressings you will provide extra omega 3 fats to replace those not eaten in fish. Using some ground or chopped walnuts in cooking will also provide more omega 3 fats. The following also include fish and will need to be avoided: anchovy, Worcestershire sauce, aspic, caviar.

CUTTING OUT PEANUTS AND TREE NUTS

Peanuts are from a different biological family to tree nuts and so toddlers are not usually allergic to both of them; toddlers will be allergic to either peanuts or tree nuts. However, normally you will be advised to avoid all nuts whatever the allergy, as it is very common for both tree nuts and peanuts to be processed in the same factories which can lead to cross contamination of tree nuts with traces of peanuts and vice versa.

For those allergic to peanuts, peanut oil (also known as ground nut oil and arachis oil) needs to be avoided, as do satay sauces and any foods containing nuts such as cakes, biscuits and breakfast cereals.

Cutting out nuts will not have a big impact on their diet unless your toddler is vegetarian. Eating more lentils or dhal or other pulses will provide similar nutrients to those found in nuts.

CUTTING OUT SESAME

The obvious foods to avoid are sesame seeds, sesame oil and tahini. Many foods contain these ingredients, particularly hummus, halvah and many Turkish, Greek, Chinese and Japanese foods. Sesame can also be present in bread, biscuits, salad dressings and sauces.

CUTTING OUT MILK

Along with milk you will need to cut out yoghurt, fromage frais, cheese, butter, cream and any foods containing these products. Because this involves the elimination of a whole food group, your toddler needs to have a substitute food to provide the same nutrients that milk provides.

Most toddlers who are allergic to cows' milk will also be allergic to goats' and sheep's milk, so these cannot be used as an alternative. A soya milk which is fortified with extra calcium is often the substitute milk used, but there are some hydrolysed milks that your doctor can prescribe for you if your toddler also needs to avoid soya. There are now oat milks that are also fortified with calcium. Rice milks should not be used as the milk drink for under fives.

CUTTING OUT WHEAT

Cutting out wheat is very difficult as many foods are based on wheat flour. This includes bread, pasta, couscous and almost all biscuits and cakes. Wheat flour is often used as an ingredient for thickening sauces, and wheat rusks are added to sausages and other processed meats. You will need expert advice for this diet and you will have to read all labels very carefully. Triticale, kamut and spelt wheat will also have to be avoided. Other ingredients you need to avoid are: bran, breadcrumbs, bulgar wheat, cereal filler, couscous, durum wheat, flour, rusk, semolina, starch, vegetable protein, wheatgerm and wheatgerm oil.

Eating more rice, potatoes, oats and foods based on these foods will substitute for bread, pasta and couscous. Sago, tapioca, quinoa and millet can also be used. You will also find a variety of pastas, breads and crispbread based on flour from other cereals such as maize, polenta, rye, oats, chickpeas, gram, lentil, bean, potato, rice, millet, arrowroot and buckwheat. You will need to check the label to make sure they are wheat-free, as some may contain a small percentage of wheat flour making them unsuitable – for example, rye bread may be made from 90 per cent rye flour and 10 per cent wheat flour.

CUTTING OUT WHEAT, RYE, BARLEY AND OATS TO ELIMINATE GLUTEN FOR COELIAC DISEASE

This diet is more restricted than cutting out wheat as foods containing rye, barley and oats also have to be cut out. However, because there are large numbers of the population who are coeliac and who need to follow a gluten-free diet, there are a few specialist food companies that make gluten-free bread, crispbread, cakes, biscuits and breakfast cereals and sell them via the internet. Your toddler may be entitled to some of these on prescription if he is diagnosed with coeliac disease. Most GPs are happy to prescribe them, but some are not. Supermarkets and health food stores also stock ranges of gluten-free products. Some gluten-free products may contain wheat starch which is processed to be gluten-free. If gluten is contained in food it must be marked in the ingredients list on the label.

The Coeliac UK website offers a lot of information and support: www.coeliac.co.uk.

CUTTING OUT SOYA

Soya flour is used along with wheat flour in many foods – many breads have some soya flour in them. You will therefore need to read labels carefully and avoid the following: hydrolysed vegetable protein, soya lecithin, soya sauce, miso, soya albumin, soya beans, soya flour, soya milk, soya nuts, soya oil, soya proteins, soya sprouts, tempeh, texturized vegetable protein, tofu.

CUTTING OUT KIWI FRUIT

Any other fruit may be eaten in place of kiwi fruit. Toddlers who are allergic to kiwi fruit may also be allergic to latex.

Buying food for toddlers with food allergies or intolerances

Shopping for a special diet can be a challenge at first, but you will find it gets easier with time.

Just avoiding certain foods is not adequate. You also need to avoid the food products and ingredients that are made from the food that your toddler needs to avoid. These are:

Food to avoid	Ingredients to avoid
milk	butter, casein, cheese, cows'/sheep's/goats' milk, evaporated or condensed milk, cream, curd, ghee, lactoglobulin, lactose, milk solids, whey, yoghurt, milk proteins
egg	albumin, dried egg, egg powder, egg protein, egg white and yolk, frozen egg, globulin, lecithin (E322), livetin, ovalbumin, ovoglobulin, ovomucin, ovovitellin, pasteurized egg, vitellin
wheat	bran, breadcrumbs, bulgar wheat, cereal filler, couscous, durum wheat, farina, flour, rusk, semolina, starch, vegetable protein, wheatgerm and wheatgerm oil

(Contd)

Food to avoid	Ingredients to avoid
foods containing gluten	bran, breadcrumbs, bulgar wheat, cereal filler, couscous, durum wheat, farina, flour, rusk, semolina, starch, vegetable protein, wheatgerm and wheatgerm oil, rye, barley and oats
fish	anchovy, Worcestershire sauce, aspic, caviar, fish stock and fish sauce
peanuts (also known as ground nuts)	peanuts, ground nuts, peanut oil (which could also be called arachis oil or hypogeaia), peanut flour, peanut protein (it is best to avoid all other nuts as well, as they may be contaminated with small amounts of peanuts)
other nuts (which are called tree nuts)	almond, hazelnut, walnut, cashew, pecan nut, Brazil nut, pistachio nut, macadamia nut and Queensland nut (you do *not* need to avoid coconut, nutmeg and butternut squash)
soya	hydrolysed vegetable protein, soya lecithin, soya sauce, miso, soya albumin, soya beans, soya flour, soya milk, soya nuts, soya oil, soya proteins, soya sprouts, tempeh, texturized vegetable protein, tofu
sesame	sesame seeds, sesame oil, tahini

FOOD LABELS

You need to read food labels very carefully, checking the list of ingredients for anything that you need to avoid. Always read the food label of food you are buying, even if you know the food product well. Sometimes the manufacturer may change the recipe slightly and include new ingredients. The label won't always be modified to say 'new' or 'improved'.

European legislation now requires that all pre-packed food must be clearly labelled if it contains any of the following foods:

▶ *cereals containing gluten (i.e. wheat, rye, barley, oats, spelt, kamut or their hybridized strains)*
▶ *eggs*
▶ *fish and shellfish*
▶ *peanuts or ground nuts*
▶ *soybeans*
▶ *milk and lactose*
▶ *nuts*
▶ *celery*
▶ *mustard*
▶ *sesame seeds*
▶ *sulphur dioxide and sulphites.*

These foods must be included in the ingredients list if they are included in the food.

However, foods sold loose, in small packages and bottles and catering packages are exempt from this guidance, so do not buy food in multipacks.

FREE-FROM FOODS AND LISTS

There are now special 'free-from' ranges in most supermarkets. Both supermarkets and health food shops carry a good range of specialized foods. Look out for foods such as egg-free, milk-free, wheat-free, gluten-free and nut-free foods.

Most supermarkets and manufacturers also produce 'free-from' lists on which all their own-brand products are listed, according to their suitability for various diets. Ring the supermarket or manufacturer's customer care line and they will happily send you a list of 'free-from' foods for the food allergy or intolerance that your toddler has. Continue to check the food labels when you buy the foods as they may have been changed since you received your last list.

Cooking your own food for your toddler with a food allergy or intolerance

You should be able to use your own recipes by adapting them, but you can also try out new recipes. You will find recipe books for particular food allergies in all good bookshops. Your dietician or anyone with a food allergy may be able to give you some well-tested recipes.

If you are able to cook the same food for the whole family, then you will not have problems of cross contamination in the house. However, you may be removing a food item from your toddler's diet while the rest of the family continue to eat that food. If this is the case, you need to be careful that there is no cross contamination of a food ingredient your toddler needs to avoid from one of the family foods into your toddler's food. You will need to make sure you:

▶ *wash cooking utensils thoroughly*
▶ *take special care when washing chopping boards or work surfaces*
▶ *wash your hands thoroughly before preparing special foods just for your toddler*
▶ *do not re-use oil for cooking different foods*
▶ *do not use the same spoon for dishing up different foods.*

Eating outside the home

Eating outside the home presents several challenges, especially if you toddler has an IgE-mediated allergy. It is best not to take risks and if you are not confident that you know about all the ingredients in a food then do not give the food to your toddler.

EATING WITH FRIENDS OR FAMILY

When you are going to eat at someone's home, try to give them plenty of notice of your toddler's food allergy or intolerance.

Ring well in advance and discuss the menu with whoever is preparing the food. They may be quite flexible and may be happy to modify the menu to suit your toddler. You may have to ask lots of questions about the ingredients and the method for food preparation to avoid possible cross contamination.

PICNICS AND BARBECUES

Talk to those in charge of the food in advance, so they know about your toddler's food allergy or intolerance, to ensure that suitable foods are available. However, it may be preferable to pack a picnic basket just with food for your toddler.

Take extra care with barbecue sauces, or a chef's 'special ingredients'. If there is any uncertainty about the ingredients, especially in the case of severe allergies, do not let your toddler eat the food.

BIRTHDAY PARTIES

Your heart may sink at the thought of your toddler with a food allergy going to a party that might be rather chaotic with no one taking special notice of which foods your toddler is eating. Ring the parents hosting the party to discuss your toddler's food allergy or intolerance. Some hosts may be very obliging; however, you cannot always expect all the party food to be prepared according to your toddler's needs. Parents of a toddler with an IgE-mediated food allergy might prefer to attend the party along with their toddler so they can help to choose appropriate party food. If you arrive early, you may have the opportunity to check the labels and to serve your toddler first in order to avoid any potential cross contamination from one food to another. Alternatively you may prefer to pack a special box of suitable party food for your toddler to take and eat.

RESTAURANTS AND CAFES

Restaurants can be risky, as you will not have the ingredient labels available to scrutinize. Try phoning ahead and ask to speak with the manager or chef, who can give information regarding the menu so that you can discuss safe options for your toddler to eat. Ask questions about the ingredients, the method of food preparation and possible cross contamination until you are convinced that the food will be safe to eat.

When ordering food, ask the person who is preparing the food to be aware of cross contamination and to double-check the ingredients. It is not adequate to rely on asking a waiter if a specific dish has a particular ingredient. They are not likely to be fully aware of all the ingredients, particularly as some chefs prefer to keep their recipes a secret.

In the US, it has become trendy to carry a 'chef card' that outlines the foods that the person must avoid. The card can be presented to the chef or manager and serves as a reminder of the food allergy. You could develop a chef card for your toddler:

▶ *Print the information on brightly coloured paper.*
▶ *Print several copies of the chef card so that a few extra copies are available.*
▶ *Laminate the chef card so that it does not get damaged or stained.*

Don't rely on the chef card to replace talking to the waiter and/or manager of a restaurant.

AT NURSERY

Entrusting a nursery to feed your toddler is a stressful decision if he has a food allergy, but most nurseries will have a protocol for dealing with toddlers who are on an exclusion diet. However, there is always the possibility of hidden ingredients, cross contamination between foods or your toddler trying another toddler's food when staff are not supervising as carefully as needed. This is especially important if the toddler has an IgE-mediated food allergy.

Give the staff written information about your toddler's food allergy or intolerance and discuss it with the head teacher and his class teacher. Most food service staff are educated about food allergies and intolerances, but include in your written advice what to avoid and which foods can be substituted in their place.

Give the nursery an updated list of ingredients to avoid and make staff aware that catering packs do not always list the ingredients, making it impossible to tell if the food is safe for your toddler. They should not rely on lists of 'safe' pre-packaged food because ingredients can change without warning, making such lists out of date quickly. If in any doubt, you can ask to read the labels yourself.

Finally, ask to have a look at the food service guidelines regarding food preparation, cross contamination when serving food and cleaning procedures, to make sure you are happy that they are adequate.

GOING ON HOLIDAY TO NON-ENGLISH SPEAKING COUNTRIES

When travelling abroad to foreign countries where you don't speak the local language, you will need accurate translations of the key foods and ingredients your toddler needs to avoid. Websites that provide a series of translation sheets and cards for various allergies are:

www.allergyaction.co.uk
www.allergyuk.org
www.kidsaware.co.uk
www.yellowcross.co.uk

Select a translation sheet in the language required and for the diet required and you will be able to use it when shopping and eating in cafes and restaurants.

TEST YOURSELF

1 *Why is the number of children with food allergies increasing?*

2 *Why do some symptoms of food allergy appear quickly in some people and more slowly in other people?*

3 *At about what age do most toddlers grow out of food allergies and intolerances?*

4 *About how many children remain allergic or intolerant to food throughout their lives?*

5 *Which foods do toddlers with coeliac disease need to avoid?*

6 *What are the foods toddlers are most commonly allergic to or intolerant of?*

7 *Which toddlers need to carry an Epipen?*

8 *How are food allergies and intolerances diagnosed?*

9 *At about what age should toddlers be retested to see if they have grown out of their food allergy?*

10 *What is the difference between food allergy and food intolerance?*

11

Feeding toddlers with diabetes
and other long-term diseases

In this chapter you will learn:
- *how to feed toddlers with diabetes*
- *about coeliac disease*
- *how to feed toddlers with cystic fibrosis*
- *how to feed toddlers with cancer*
- *about tube feeding toddlers via a nasogastric tube or a gastrostomy.*

It can be very traumatic to learn that your toddler has a long-term disease that will require extra treatment and care. It may be the end of a long road where you suspected something was wrong, but it took what seemed like an age to have your toddler diagnosed with a specific disease. This may bring some relief that your toddler can now be treated appropriately, but parents sometimes feel guilty particularly if the disease is genetically inherited. You may even become depressed for a time. Medical staff should understand this and give you time to come to terms with the diagnosis and the extra responsibility you will now be taking on to care for your toddler. With some diseases you may need to take extra care feeding your toddler, but each medical team should have a paediatric dietician who will be able to answer your questions and help you with advice and support to make feeding your toddler a pleasure.

The relatively common diseases that require extra care in feeding are:

▶ *diabetes*
▶ *coeliac disease*
▶ *cystic fibrosis*
▶ *cancer.*

There are many other diseases and syndromes where advice from a dietician will be necessary to help you to feed your toddler, but they are more rare and beyond the scope of this book.

Feeding a toddler with diabetes

Diabetes is an autoimmune disease in which the cells in the pancreas that produce the hormone insulin are destroyed. Without enough insulin, glucose in the blood will not pass into the body's cells to provide a source of energy. The glucose will remain in the blood and the blood glucose levels will rise very high. This is called hyperglycaemia. Toddlers with hyperglycaemia may lose weight and complain of excessive thirst. You might smell ketones in his breath, because they are released when cells break down fat to get energy. This happens when cells are not getting enough glucose. If hyperglycaemia (high blood glucose levels) is not treated, your toddler can eventually pass into a coma.

After your toddler has been diagnosed with diabetes he will be prescribed insulin. There are several options for giving the insulin and you and your doctor will discuss and agree what is the best regime for you and your toddler. Insulin cannot be given by mouth as it would not remain intact and effective after passing through the stomach and gastrointestinal system, so it needs to be administered directly into your toddler's blood. You may give the insulin doses as a few injections throughout each day. Parents will be taught how to test blood glucose levels and how and when to adjust the amount of insulin given. Alternatively you may choose for your toddler to have a small pump with a fine tube inserted under his skin. The pump will automatically release insulin via the thin tube into your toddler's blood as blood sugar levels rise.

Your diabetic toddler should be offered a healthy balanced diet as described in Chapter 3, so that he eats foods containing all the nutrients he needs. The carbohydrate that your toddler eats is broken down into sugars that are absorbed into his blood and changed to glucose. Your toddler needs to have doses of insulin corresponding to how much carbohydrate is eaten, so that his blood glucose levels remain relatively close to the normal range.

You will plan your toddler's diet with your dietician and he/she will teach you how much carbohydrate to give your toddler each day and how to count how much he has eaten. Often a list of foods each containing 10 g carbohydrate is used to help you work out how much food will provide the correct amount of carbohydrate. These food portions are called 10 g carbohydrate exchanges and examples are listed in the table below. Your dietician will help you devise a list using all the family foods you offer your toddler.

The amount of carbohydrate offered will vary from toddler to toddler, but on average toddlers are offered about 13–18 exchanges of 10 g carbohydrate each day, depending on how much food they usually eat.

10 G CARBOHYDRATE EXCHANGES

	Food items	Quantity providing 10 g carbohydrate
bread	wholemeal or white slices rolls or baps	½ large slice or 1 small slice ½ roll

(Contd)

	Food items	Quantity providing 10 g carbohydrate
breakfast cereals	porridge	7 tablespoons
	Weetabix	1 biscuit
	Cornflakes/Cheerios	5 tablespoons
rice and pasta	cooked brown or white rice	3 tablespoons
	cooked pasta shapes	3 tablespoons
	spaghetti	10 long strands
	tinned spaghetti	⅓ small tin
potatoes	boiled potatoes	1 small
	baked potatoes	1 medium
	chips	5 thick cut
beans	baked beans in tomato sauce	5 tablespoons
	dried uncooked beans	2 tablespoons
fruit	apple	1 medium
	pear	1 medium
	banana	1 medium
	grapes	10
	orange	1 medium
	satsumas/clementines	2 small
	dried fruit	1 tablespoon
yoghurt and ice cream	natural yoghurt	1 carton
	fruit sweetened yoghurt	½ carton
	ice cream	1 scoop
biscuits	oatcakes	1 large
	crackers	2
	crispbread (wholewheat or rye)	2
	digestive	1

	Food items	Quantity providing 10 g carbohydrate
drinks	milk unsweetened pure fruit juice	2 glasses of 100 ml 2 glasses of 50 ml pure juice diluted with 50 ml water

Commercial foods include the amount of carbohydrate on the label. From this you should be able to work out how much carbohydrate is in a portion of food that your toddler eats.

Sweet puddings, confectionery and other sugary foods do not have to be cut out altogether. However, only small amounts are acceptable and they should be given as part of your toddler's carbohydrate exchanges. They are better given at the end of meals rather than as snacks, as they will be less likely to make the blood glucose levels rise too high.

Do not buy special diabetic foods for your toddler as they are not necessary because you can include small amounts of normal foods that are sweetened with sugar. It is better to use reduced sugar foods where possible, such as reduced sugar jam. Special diabetic foods usually contain artificial sweeteners in place of sugar to give them a sweet taste. Sorbitol, which is a sweetener and often used in special diabetic foods, could give your toddler diarrhoea.

A routine of meals and snacks is important so that you are offering similar amounts of carbohydrate at each meal and snack. If you are giving your toddler 15 carbohydrate exchanges each day, then you might distribute them through the day like this:

Breakfast:	3
Mid-morning snack:	2
Midday meal:	3
Mid-afternoon snack:	2
Evening meal:	3
Snack before bed:	2
Total for the day:	15

A one-day menu might look like this:

Meal or snack		Number of carbohydrate exchanges	Total number of carbohydrate exchanges for each meal or snack
Breakfast	2 Weetabix	2	3
	100 ml milk	½	
	½ banana, sliced	½	
Mid-morning snack	½ apple, sliced	½	2
	1 digestive biscuit	1	
	100 ml milk to drink	½	
Midday meal	1 large slice toast with butter	2	3
	2½ tbsp baked beans	½	
	cucumber and carrot sticks		
	5 grapes	½	
Mid-afternoon snack	1½ digestive biscuits	1½	2
	1 satsuma	½	
	water to drink		
Evening meal	3 tbsp cooked pasta bolognaise sauce	1	3
	broccoli florets		
	1 carton fruit yoghurt	1	

Meal or snack		Number of carbohydrate exchanges	Total number of carbohydrate exchanges for each meal or snack
	5 strawberries 50 ml fruit juice diluted with water	½ ½	
Snack before bed	1 large slice toast with butter	2	2

WHAT IS THE GLYCAEMIC INDEX?

The glycaemic index of the meals and snacks your toddler eats is a measure of how quickly blood glucose levels rise after eating that meal or snack. Sugary foods such as sweets and confectionery have a very high glycaemic index and the blood sugar will rise high very quickly if these are eaten on their own. To keep the glycaemic index of a meal or snack low so that the blood sugar rises slowly you need to offer a balanced diet as described in Chapter 3, offering foods with fibre at each meal. For example:

▶ *include fruit with breakfast and at least one fruit and one vegetable with the other two meals*
▶ *offer a mixture of white and some wholemeal varieties of bread and cereals (for example, wholemeal bread and porridge).*

WHAT IS HYPOGLYCAEMIA?

If you toddler's blood glucose levels fall below the normal range he will be hypoglycaemic. The brain can only use glucose as an energy source to function as it cannot break down fat or protein to provide energy. During hypoglycaemia, blood glucose levels become too low for the brain to work properly.

Hypoglycaemia may occur when:

▶ *your toddler has not had enough carbohydrate to eat – he may be late for his meal or a snack or he may have refused to eat*
▶ *your toddler had extra exercise without eating extra carbohydrate or reducing his insulin dose*
▶ *too much insulin has been given – this may be a mistake or it may have been given at the wrong time*
▶ *food may not have been absorbed because your toddler has diarrhoea or has vomited.*

General symptoms of hypoglycaemia are:

▶ *pallor*
▶ *mood swings*
▶ *irritability*
▶ *headache*
▶ *hunger*
▶ *fatigue*
▶ *becoming unco-operative*
▶ *becoming confused*
▶ *finally losing consciousness and fitting.*

Of course toddlers will not usually be able to describe any of these symptoms, but you might notice him being confused or unco-operative. He might say he feels funny or has shaky or wobbly legs.

To treat hypoglycaemia, you need to give your toddler some carbohydrate that will be rapidly absorbed to restore his blood glucose levels to within the normal range. Carbohydrate that is rapidly absorbed will be glucose or sugar or a sugary food or drink. Examples are:

▶ *glucose tablets or sweets to suck*
▶ *about 50 ml of a glucose drink such as Lucozade*
▶ *2–3 teaspoons of jam or honey or syrup.*

If you toddler has become confused or unco-operative, you may need to squeeze a glucose gel into his mouth or rub it on his gums where the glucose will be absorbed rapidly to raise blood glucose levels out of the danger zone. Glucose gels are available from pharmacies and one can be prescribed for your toddler so that you can keep it handy for hypoglycaemic emergencies.

If hypoglycaemia happens frequently, then it is time to reassess the insulin regime and how much and when he is eating carbohydrate. You should discuss this with your doctor and dietician.

COPING WITH FOOD REFUSAL IN TODDLERS WITH DIABETES

Toddlers will not understand the importance of eating a certain amount of food and as with all toddlers you will encounter times when your toddler will refuse to eat the food you offer. This can cause more anxiety for parents of diabetic toddlers who are concerned about hypoglycaemia. Follow the advice given in Chapters 1 and 5 and do not make any fuss when your toddler refuses to eat certain foods. Do not coerce him to eat or be tempted to begin force-feeding him.

For some toddlers who eat well with no problems, there will be little cause for concern. However, if you are very anxious, your toddler may realize this and use food to manipulate you. If you offer sweet foods to make sure he has had enough carbohydrate, he will soon realize that by refusing savoury food, he is assured of receiving more sweet foods.

Usually as blood glucose levels fall, your toddler will become more hungry. If he eats less at one meal, just give some extra bread or crispbread at his next snack and give the snack a bit earlier than usual.

Discuss any problems you have with your diabetes team as various solutions are possible. Insulin is available in different preparations – some act very quickly while others act more slowly over a longer period of time. You may be able to give quick-acting insulin after the meal, depending on how much food your toddler has eaten.

Another solution is to keep blood glucose levels slightly on the high side to reduce the risk of hypoglycaemia when less food than usual is eaten.

Coeliac disease

This is also an autoimmune disease, which means that the body produces antibodies that attack its own tissues. For toddlers with this disease the protein gluten causes the destructive antibodies to be produced which damage the tissue of the small intestine, causing malabsorption of food. In this case your toddler might have any of the following symptoms:

- *weight loss*
- *poor growth*
- *diarrhoea*
- *nausea*
- *wind*
- *tiredness*
- *constipation*
- *anaemia*
- *mouth ulcers*
- *headaches*
- *hair loss*
- *skin problems.*

Gluten is found in the three cereals: wheat, rye and barley. All food and drinks made from these cereals need to be eliminated from the diet of a toddler with coeliac disease. Some toddlers may need to avoid oats as well, as they may be sensitive to a similar protein in oats and sometimes oats are contaminated with traces of wheat, rye or barley.

How to feed toddlers with this disease is covered in Chapter 10 on food allergies and intolerances.

There are many specialist food companies that make gluten-free food products and your GP may prescribe some of these for your toddler. Coeliac UK www.coeliac.co.uk is the charity that offers support and advice to families with coeliac disease.

Cystic fibrosis

Cystic fibrosis (CF) is a genetic disorder which is inherited from both parents. It is relatively common in white families and less so in Asian, African and Middle Eastern families. Several of the glands in the body do not function very well and this causes lung disease, malabsorption of food and very salty sweat. Cystic fibrosis is usually diagnosed by measuring the amount of salt in a child's sweat. Symptoms of the disease vary considerably between toddlers and some may have more respiratory problems, while others have more problems with malabsorption of food, particularly the fat in food.

The problems of malabsorption are due to a poor production of enzymes from the pancreas which are needed to digest foods in the small intestine so that they can be absorbed into the body. To improve the absorption of their food, toddlers with cystic fibrosis will be prescribed pancreatic enzyme supplements. These are given in capsules which can be swallowed. Your toddler will need to take these with all his meals and snacks. A vitamin and mineral supplement will also be prescribed for your toddler as the fat-soluble vitamins A, D, E and K are usually poorly absorbed by those with cystic fibrosis.

Toddlers with cystic fibrosis do not grow as well as normal toddlers. They often have a poor appetite, especially if they are often ill with respiratory illnesses. Some may have reflux which can cause pain on eating. This can also cause more stress for parents who are very keen for their toddlers to eat well to prevent more illness. Parents of toddlers with CF report more feeding problems than do parents of normal toddlers.

To make sure they grow well, these toddlers need to eat more food with a higher energy content. They are encouraged to eat more foods containing high amounts of fat and sugar, in addition to a balanced diet of foods from the four main food groups described in Chapter 3.

You will usually plan your toddler's diet with a dietician and he/she will give you advice on how many capsules of pancreatic enzymes to take with each meal and snack. You will also get some advice on increasing the calories your toddler eats in normal foods by adding extra sugar and fat to foods. You may be advised to:

▶ *sprinkle extra sugar onto breakfast cereals, puddings and other sweet foods*
▶ *stir extra cream or milk powder into milk and puddings*
▶ *fry foods rather than grilling or baking them*
▶ *add extra oil or butter to vegetables, pasta, rice, sauces and gravies.*

If your toddler does not grow well enough, you may have to give him high-calorie drinks that will be prescribed for him. If your toddler finds eating extra calories very difficult and your doctor is concerned about your toddler not growing, he may recommend some extra feeding through a tube during the night (see *Feeding toddlers via a nasogastric tube or gastrostomy*, page 231).

Insight

Cystic fibrosis affects toddlers to varying degrees. Most toddlers eat well with their medication and treatment and do not have many problems. Others tend to get more colds and flu and may find eating enough food more difficult.

Cancer

Toddlers with cancer may have a poor appetite and eat poorly. This may be due to:

▶ *pain*
▶ *repeated infections when the immune system is compromised due to chemotherapy and radiotherapy*
▶ *nausea and vomiting caused by chemotherapy and radiotherapy*

- *diarrhoea which may be caused either by antibiotics to treat infections or as a result of chemotherapy or radiotherapy*
- *changes to their taste buds making food less enjoyable.*

Toddlers eating poorly can become malnourished quite quickly, which will further lower their immune system and, in addition, they may begin to lose weight.

Making sure your toddler eats all the nutrients will help his immune system to remain strong to fight the disease. He may prefer small, frequent snack-style meals about five or six times each day, rather than three big meals. If he has a sore mouth he might prefer very soft foods. If he has nausea then he may prefer cold foods to hot foods.

As with CF you will be advised how to increase his calorie intake but using extra oil, butter and cream may not be suitable if he is feeling nauseous. It may be better to try the prescribable high-calorie/high-nutrient drinks.

Overnight tube feeding is often recommended for toddlers with cancer. It can help to maintain growth, prevent your toddler losing too much weight and help boost his immune system.

Insight

Overnight feeding is usually just needed for short periods of time when your toddler is finding eating difficult. If they begin tube feeding it does not mean they will always need it. Usually they just need feeding that way while they feel too sick to eat.

Feeding toddlers via a nasogastric tube or gastrostomy

If toddlers are not able to eat as much as they need to keep growing normally, your doctor or dietician might recommend some overnight feeding via a tube. This can be via:

- *a nasogastric tube or*
- *a tube connected to a gastrostomy button.*

A sterile liquid containing calories and a full range of nutrients is slowly pumped down the tube. This tube feed is prescribed by your child's doctor.

The amount to be pumped in each night needs to be calculated for your toddler depending on how much he is able to eat and drink during the day.

NASOGASTRIC TUBE FEEDING

This involves a tube being passed through your toddler's nose down into his stomach so that the prescribed feed can be slowly pumped into his stomach throughout the night. The tube is usually held in place by being taped to your toddler's cheek. They are easily pulled out and can be repassed quite easily if your toddler is co-operative.

GASTROSTOMY FEEDING

If tube feeding continues to be necessary, your doctor may suggest that a gastrostomy is formed. This will involve a very short surgical procedure to pass a tube directly through your toddler's skin and stomach wall, into his stomach. It is held in position with a plastic clamp or a button with a small inflatable balloon that sits inside the stomach. The feeding tube can then be connected directly to the gastrostomy without having to go via the nose. This has been successfully used for feeding adults and children for many years now. Once your toddler no longer needs this form of feeding, the gastrostomy button or tube can be removed and the small hole in the skin and stomach wall will close over and heal. A tiny scar may be the only indication that this route of feeding was ever used.

DISEASES THAT MAY REQUIRE TUBE FEEDING FOR YOUR TODDLER

Many ill toddlers are safely tube fed in hospital. If your toddler needs to be tube fed at home you will be trained to feed your toddler that way and there will be a support network set up for you so that you can call for help any time you have questions or have an emergency with the feeding.

Toddlers who may need to be tube fed for some time are those who:

- *are critically ill and require ventilation*
- *have severe developmental delay*
- *have malformations around the mouth*
- *do not have an adequate appetite and are not eating enough to maintain their growth and keep them healthy. This may be toddlers who are very ill with:*
  - *cancer*
  - *cystic fibrosis*
  - *inflammatory bowel disease*
  - *liver disease*
  - *kidney disease*
  - *heart disease*
  - *Crohn's disease*
  - *other rare diseases.*

TEST YOURSELF

1 *Why do diabetic toddlers need insulin?*

2 *How do food and prescribed insulin interact?*

3 *What is hyperglycaemia?*

4 *What is hypoglycaemia?*

5 *What are the symptoms of hypoglycaemia?*

6 *What should you do for a toddler who is hypoglycaemic?*

7 *Which foods do toddlers with coeliac disease need to avoid?*

8 *Why do toddlers with cystic fibrosis need to eat high-calorie foods?*

9 *What do toddlers with cystic fibrosis usually take with food to increase their absorption?*

10 *Which toddlers need overnight tube feeding?*

12

....

Buying food and supplements and eating out

In this chapter you will learn:
- *how to stock your kitchen*
- *how to choose a suitable milk drink*
- *when to buy fresh seasonal food*
- *how to choose vitamin and mineral supplements*
- *about food additives and sweeteners*
- *how to understand labels and ingredient lists on commercial food*
- *what to avoid when buying food*
- *about choosing nutritious food when eating out.*

The key to offering your toddler a healthy balanced diet is to plan the meals and snacks you will offer and then buy the foods and drinks in your plan.

The following list can be used to check that you keep the essentials available so that nutritious meals can be prepared in minutes.

In the cupboard	In the fridge	In the freezer
breakfast cereals fortified with iron	eggs	sliced bread
	milk	mini pitta breads
oats	cheese	peas
fresh bread		

(Contd)

In the cupboard	In the fridge	In the freezer
crispbread, crackers, rice cakes	butter or margarine	sweetcorn
pasta	selection of fresh vegetables	spinach
rice		lean minced meat
couscous	selection of fresh fruits	chicken – breasts or thighs
breadcrumbs	lemons or limes	prawns
potatoes	cold lean meat such as ham and lean salami	frozen fish fillets
onions		ice cream
garlic	meat or fish pâtés	
canned tomatoes or tomato passata	smoked mackerel fillets	
tomato purée	plain and flavoured yoghurts	
canned fruit in juice or light syrup	fromage frais	
dried fruit (sultanas, raisins, dried apricots)	fresh meat	
lentils	fresh fish	
canned chickpeas		
baked beans		
ground nuts (e.g. ground almonds)		
chopped nuts (e.g. walnuts)		
canned fish (tuna, salmon, sardines, mackerel)		

In the cupboard	In the fridge	In the freezer
cooking oil (rapeseed, soya, olive)		
salad oils (olive and walnut)		
vinegar		
flour (plain)		
sugar		
spreads for bread (low-sugar jam, honey, Marmite, peanut butter)		
selection of herbs and spices including oregano, bay leaves, cinnamon, ground ginger, ground cumin, ground coriander, saffron or turmeric		
salt and pepper		
for baking: self-raising flour, baking powder, bicarbonate of soda, vanilla extract		
vitamin supplement for toddlers containing vitamins A and D		

Choosing a milk for your toddler's milk drinks

Cows' milk is a suitable milk drink for toddlers from 12 months of age. Full-fat milk should be offered until he is at least two years old. The reason for this recommendation is that full-fat milk has more vitamin A than lower-fat milks and this vitamin is very important at this age for growth and development. From two years old you can change your toddler to semi-skimmed milk which some families find more convenient if they are already using semi-skimmed milk. However, it is not necessary to change and you can continue to give your toddler full-fat cows' milk throughout his childhood thereby ensuring he is getting extra vitamin A.

As an alternative to either full-fat or semi-skimmed cows' milk there are a range of growing-up or toddler milks that you can buy for your toddler. These are more expensive than cows' milk as they are modified cows' milk with extra nutrients added. If your toddler is eating a well-balanced diet and taking vitamin drops with vitamins A and D as recommended in Chapter 3, the extra expense of these milks is not really justified. However, if your toddler eats poorly then you might like to consider either giving him a vitamin and mineral supplement or giving him one of these formula milks rather than cows' milk. Usually you would not need to give both the vitamin and mineral supplement and the enriched formula milk as this would be adding extra vitamins and minerals to his diet twice.

The formula milks for toddlers in the UK are:

- ▶ *Aptamil Growing Up Milk*
- ▶ *Cow & Gate Growing Up Milk*
- ▶ *Hipp Organic Growing Up Milk*
- ▶ *Nannycare Goat Growing Up Milk*
- ▶ *SMA Toddler Milk.*

They are all fairly similar in their content and no one has an advantage over the others.

> **Insight**
>
> As the amount of milk your toddler drinks should be limited to three small cups a day, or less if they are eating yoghurt and cheese, the extra nutrients in these small amounts of growing-up milk formulas is minimal.

Commercial toddler foods

There is an increasing array of foods for toddlers being launched onto the market. These can make feeding a toddler more convenient; however, toddlers should be encouraged to eat the same food as the rest of the family at family meals as often as possible. If your toddler only eats the commercial toddler meals he will not become familiar with your family foods and will not have the opportunity to learn to like them. He might get stuck just eating the commercial toddler foods, making it difficult to feed him on social occasions when he goes to nursery or to eat in friends' homes.

Buying family foods for toddlers

Supermarkets now offer us a huge range of foods all year round. Although this means we have a huge choice, there are compromises in this. Many of us no longer know when foods are in season. Farmers markets in some areas with locally grown produce are now reinstating this choice. Seasonal food is generally cheaper, usually has more flavour and is higher in the vitamins that deteriorate with storage – particularly folic acid and vitamin C. Minerals and phytochemicals are less affected by longer storage times.

SEASONAL FOODS GROWN IN THE UK

Season	Months in the UK	Seasonal foods			
		Vegetables	Fruit	Wild meat	Wild fish and seafood
Spring	March April May	asparagus broccoli carrots jersey royal potatoes new potatoes purple sprouting broccoli radishes rocket sorrel spinach spring onions watercress	kiwi fruit lemons cherries and elderflowers oranges rhubarb apricots	lamb wood pigeon	cockles cod hake John Dory lemon sole mussels salmon sea trout cod crab
Summer	June July August	artichoke aubergine beetroot broad beans broccoli carrots courgettes cucumber fennel french beans garlic kohlrabi mangetout	blackberries blueberries damsons figs gooseberries greengages kiwi fruit loganberries melons nectarines peaches plums raspberries	lamb rabbit wood pigeon	Dover sole grey mullet haddock halibut herring John Dory lemon sole lobster mackerel monkfish plaice

Season	Months in the UK	Seasonal foods			
		Vegetables	Fruit	Wild meat	Wild fish and seafood
		marrow new potatoes onions peas peppers potatoes radishes rocket runner beans sorrel tomatoes turnips watercress	redcurrants strawberries		salmon sardines scallops sea bass sea trout squid turbot
Autumn	September October November	artichoke aubergine beetroot broccoli butternut squash carrots celeriac celery fennel kale kohlrabi leeks marrow onions parsnips peppers potatoes	apples blackberries chestnuts cranberries damsons elderberries figs grapes pears quince walnuts	duck goose grouse guinea fowl hare lamb partridge rabbit venison wood pigeon	brill clams cod crab Dover sole grey mullet haddock halibut herring hake John Dory lemon sole lobster mackerel monkfish mussels

(Contd)

Season	Months in the UK	Seasonal foods			
		Vegetables	Fruit	Wild meat	Wild fish and seafood
		pumpkin radishes rocket swede sweetcorn tomatoes turnips watercress wild mushrooms			oysters plaice scallops sea bass squid turbot
Winter	December January February	beetroot Brussels sprouts cauliflower celeriac celery chicory Jerusalem artichoke kale leeks parsnips potatoes pumpkin purple sprouting broccoli swede turnips	apples chestnuts clementines cranberries lemons oranges pears rhubarb satsumas tangerines walnuts	duck goose grouse guinea fowl hare lamb partridge pheasant rabbit venison wood pigeon	brill clams cockles haddock halibut hake John Dory lemon sole monkfish mussels oysters plaice scallops sea bass squid turbot

Buying ready meals and sauces

These are very convenient and save working mothers a lot of time. However, these foods are often quite low in vegetables and fruits and often high in salt and fat. Use them occasionally but try not to rely on them daily, as your toddler's intake of salt will be high. Increasingly there are brands with lower levels of salt that you can buy when you have the choice.

GM considerations

Genetical modification (GM) of foods involves changing the genetic material of the plant or animal to alter one specific trait of that food. It is usually to improve the yield of the crop and is often to make it resistant to a pest or infection that the crop is normally susceptible to. The nutritional content is not usually changed, although it can be if that is the reason for the genetic modification. In areas of Asia where vitamin A deficiency is a problem, a type of rice has been genetically modified to be a richer source of vitamin A. Strict controls are in place such that each genetically modified product is thoroughly assessed for any difference from its conventional counterpart.

Since 1996, GM soya, maize, oilseed rape and other minor crops have been eaten on a regular basis by hundreds of millions of people and animals in the United States and there has been no substantiated case of harm arising from their consumption. However, there remain concerns that we do not know enough about the science or any possible long-term effects of consuming GM foods. Unforeseen problems could still occur. In the UK most supermarkets have opted not to stock GM products because of consumer choice.

Organic versus non-organic

Organic food is produced without the use of most agrochemicals. Naturally occurring fertilisers and pesticides are allowed but all other pesticides, herbicides and genetically modified organisms which have mostly been developed in the last 40 years are banned.

Organic food has a much shorter shelf life and storage times need to be minimized. Because of this, organic foods will tend to have more folic acid and vitamin C as these two nutrients deteriorate with long storage times. Organic and non-organic food will contain similar amounts of all other nutrients.

Although each pesticide used in non-organic food production is checked for safety, the effects of ingesting combinations of different pesticide residues that a family might consume in a meal of several different foods, has not been checked. This is of more concern in toddlers who are growing and developing and could be more susceptible to cocktails of different chemicals.

Organic regulations do not allow for genetically modified ingredients to be included.

Salt and sodium

Salt contains sodium, and adults who eat too much sodium may get high blood pressure. For toddlers it is best not to encourage a preference for only salty foods but there is no need to cut out all salty foods as toddlers need a certain amount of sodium in order to grow. The foods that naturally contain medium amounts of sodium are milk and milk products, meat and bread. Nutritious foods that are preserved with salt such as cheese, bacon, salami, salted fish are also suitable for toddlers. They are important for your toddler because of the other nutrients they contain so don't cut out all foods that show sodium or salt on the label.

Salt is added to processed food to enhance flavour and to preserve it. When you have a choice of processed food and ready meals, buy those that are lower in sodium. For toddlers one to three years of age, the Food Standards Agency recommends a maximum of 2 g salt or 0.4 g sodium per day. This means that salty foods such as the following should only be given very occasionally:

- ▶ *crisps and salty snacks*
- ▶ *tinned foods with added salt or brine (such as tinned fish and vegetables)*
- ▶ *potato waffles, smiles and so on.*

Use herbs and spices in your own cooking to add flavour rather than adding a lot of salt and do not add salt to food at the table.

Insight

I find a lot of parents worry unnecessarily about salt. If toddlers do eat a lot of salty food one day they will just get more thirsty and need to drink more. They will not get ill because their kidneys can cope very well with a lot of salt. However, for their long-term health it is better not to encourage a preference only for salty foods.

Which fats are the best?

Toddlers need some fat as it is a good source of energy for them and fats are an integral part of the membrane around each cell. 70 per cent of the dry weight of the brain is fat, and toddlers' brains continue to grow as they do. Most foods contain a mixture of all types of fats – saturated, monounsaturated and polyunsaturated.

SATURATED FATS

Toddlers do not need to avoid saturated fat. It is an integral part of most foods. About half the fat in the important nutrient-rich foods such as meat, eggs, milk and cheese is saturated.

TRANS FATS

Trans fats are found naturally in milk and milk products and are not harmful, whereas trans fats produced by industrial processing are now known to raise cholesterol in the same way saturated fat does.

INDUSTRIAL SATURATED AND TRANS FATS

In processed foods, saturated fat and trans fats are formed when vegetable fats are heated to high temperatures and/or processed; for example, hydrogenated vegetable oil has most of the unsaturated fats changed to saturated fats and in the process trans fats are formed. Industrially produced trans and saturated fats should be kept to a minimum by avoiding a lot of processed food, or keeping it to a minimum and choosing processed foods with very low amounts of saturated and trans fats. Highly processed foods include:

▶ *high-fat snacks such as crisps*
▶ *processed foods containing hydrogenated vegetable oils (margarines, cakes, biscuits, puddings, ready-made sauces and meals)*
▶ *processed foods which have been fried (e.g. crumb-coated fish, chicken and meat products).*

UNSATURATED FATS

Two of the unsaturated fats – omega 3 and omega 6 fats – are essential for toddlers. They are needed for the developing brain, eyes and nerves in particular. They are most useful in their long chain form which is EPA, DHA and ALA. Babies can only make limited amounts of the long chain form but toddlers should be able to make adequate amounts of the long chain form if they have enough of the shorter chain form in their food.

BALANCING OMEGA 3 AND OMEGA 6 FATS IN TODDLERS' DIETS

Up until around 50 years ago, our diets had about equal quantities of these two essential fats, but nowadays we eat a much higher proportion of omega 6 fats and very little omega 3 fat. This change is thought to be one of the factors causing increased rates of allergy, asthma and hay fever in children. You can increase your toddler's intake of omega 3 fats by including foods naturally rich in omega 3 fats. The best source is oily fish such as salmon, mackerel, trout, fresh tuna, sardines, pilchards and eel. Other good sources are omega 3 rich oils, such as rapeseed, walnut, olive and soya oils. Pure vegetable oil is often rapeseed oil and some bottles of vegetable oil have the little yellow rapeseed flowers on the label to indicate their source.

Many foods supplemented with omega 3 fats are now appearing on supermarket shelves, for example: margarines, yoghurts, eggs, berry fruit juices, breads, milk, some breakfast cereals and biscuits. If your toddler is eating some oily fish once or twice each week then including these foods fortified with omega 3 fats is not necessary.

Tinned tuna is not a source of omega 3 fats because the tuna has had the fat removed before being tinned. Tinned sardines, in contrast, are a good source of omega 3 fats.

Sugar

Toddlers naturally prefer sweet foods but need to learn to like other tastes. It is not necessary to avoid all sugar, and a sweet pudding is an important part of the two main meals. However, an excess of sweet food should be avoided.

When buying food it is not easy to determine the amount of sugar that has been added to a food, even though the total amount of sugar must be displayed on the label. This figure will include natural sugars occurring in food as well as sugar added as an ingredient. The sugars naturally occurring in food are:

▶ *lactose – the sugar in milk*
▶ *fructose – the sugar in fruit*
▶ *maltose – the sugar that is present in small amounts in all starchy foods.*

Additional sugar is usually added to improve flavour and will be added in various forms:

▶ *sucrose*
▶ *dextrose*
▶ *glucose syrup*
▶ *corn syrup*
▶ *fructose*
▶ *golden syrup*
▶ *honey*
▶ *fruit juice concentrate.*

The ingredients on a food label are listed in descending order by the amount used in the recipe. If the added sugar is included in two or three forms – for example, dextrose, glucose and fruit juice concentrate – each of these items will be placed further down the ingredients list than if the sugar was only included in one form such as all as sucrose. In this way you might think that very little sugar had been added.

When looking for low-sugar foods (such as breakfast cereals), compare the sugar amount per 100 g food and buy the lower one. However, do not expect any foods to be sugar-free because of the natural sugars in most foods. Do remember that food must be enjoyed and a little sugar will do your toddler no harm. Small amounts of sugar in foods that are eaten in small quantities – such as tomato ketchup – do not need to be avoided.

Buying vitamin and mineral supplements for your toddler

The only vitamin supplements that are recommended for all toddlers are vitamins A and D. There are a variety of preparations of vitamin drops and chewy tablets for toddlers containing vitamins A and D available in all pharmacies and some supermarkets. They are quite expensive as they usually contain a number of other nutrients which your toddler doesn't need if he is getting his nutrients from a healthy balanced diet. The NHS Healthy Start children's vitamin drops contain vitamins A, C and D and are cheaper but are only sold in some NHS child health clinics. You need to ask your health visitor where to get them.

If your toddler eats so poorly that you and your health visitor are concerned about his nutrient intake, it may be advisable to give him a vitamin and mineral supplement containing a wide range of nutrients. Choose one containing vitamins A and D and with most of the minerals – look for zinc, iron and magnesium.

WHAT ARE RNIs AND RDAs?

▶ RDA (Recommended Daily Amount) of a nutrient is the amount which is recommended to be eaten on average every day. It applies to the whole population in general and is set by a European committee. The figure indicates a suitable amount for adults, not babies, toddlers or children.
▶ RNI (Reference Nutrient Intake) is the daily amount that is recommended for different age groups in the UK. There are

*several age group bands as children require differing amounts
of nutrients as they grow. The age group bands are quite
narrow: 0–3 months, 4–6 months, 7–9 months, 10–12 months,
1–3 years, 4–6 years, 7–10 years, 11–14 years, 15–18 years,
19–50 years, 50+ years. For each age group band there is a
compete set of RNIs for each nutrient.*

WHY ARE RDAs AND RNIs ON VITAMIN SUPPLEMENT LABELS?

All supplement labels are required to display the RDA, even
products for children for whom they have no relevance. Parents
tend to choose supplements by looking to see that there is
100 per cent of the RDA for each nutrient, not realising that
100 per cent RDA, even on a children's supplement is a suitable
amount for an adult, and for some nutrients will be a very high
dose for a baby or child. Vitamin A is an example of this.

CHOOSING A SUPPLEMENT FOR YOUR TODDLER BY CHECKING THE RNI

If you are buying a vitamin and mineral supplement, choose one
with 100 per cent or less of the RNI for your toddler's age: this will
be RNI for 1–3 years or for 4–6 years. Do not give supplements
that have 100 per cent RDA for all the nutrients in them to your
toddler. Suitable supplements will have less than 100 per cent RDA
but if they have 100 per cent RDA for vitamin D that is fine.

DO I NEED TO BUY SUPPLEMENTS WITH OMEGA 3 AND OMEGA 6 FOR MY TODDLER?

There are many preparations now sold that contain the essential
fats omega 3 and omega 6. They are advertised in many magazines
and shops where they are sold. However, your toddler does not
need extra omega 6 because there is plenty in his food. As discussed
in Chapter 2, there are less omega 3 fats in our food nowadays,
however, research has shown that toddlers who eat a balanced diet
including fish will not benefit from omega 3 supplements.

There may be some children with ADHD, dyslexia and dyspraxia who may benefit from supplements of the omega 3 fats EPA and DHA. However, the benefits are not certain, and not all children with ADHD and dyspraxia will benefit. It may be just a small percentage who may lack an enzyme needed to change the omega 3 and omega 6 essential fats into the longer chain form that is used by the cells in the body.

Food additives and sweeteners

Some additives are naturally occurring substances found in foods – for example, ascorbic acid is vitamin C and is often used to preserve food. However, there are other additives that have been manufactured and introduced into our environment quite recently and all the various different combinations of them have not been tested – we are all guinea pigs, in a way. The long-term effects of using them are not necessarily known. Growing toddlers are more vulnerable and it is preferable to keep their exposure to these additives to a minimum.

Most food additives must be included either by name or by an E number in the ingredient list. The ingredient list also tells you what job an additive does, such as adding colour or acting as a preservative.

WHAT ARE E NUMBERS?

Food additives that have passed safety tests and been approved for use throughout the European Union are assigned an E number. Some of these additives will be nutritious, such as vitamin C, while others will be synthetic chemicals. The additives assigned E numbers can be divided into the categories:

- *antioxidants*
- *preservatives*
- *colours*

- *flavour enhancers*
- *sweeteners.*

Flavourings do not have E numbers because they are controlled by different laws. They are added in much smaller amounts than the other additives and they give a particular flavour or smell. They may be extracted from food, or more usually they are copies of the chemicals in food that provide the flavour. They are considered very stable and very safe and do not have to be named on ingredient labels.

Antioxidants make foods last longer by helping to stop the fats, oils and certain vitamins from combining with oxygen in the air and becoming rancid and losing colour. If this happens it makes food taste 'off'.

Vitamin C, also called ascorbic acid or E300, is one of the most widely used antioxidants in food.

Preservatives delay food from 'going off', giving food a longer shelf life. Most food that has a long shelf life is likely to include preservatives, unless another method of preserving has been used such as freezing, canning or drying.

For example, to stop mould or bacteria growing, dried fruit is often treated with sulphur dioxide (E220); and bacon, ham, corned beef and other 'cured' meats are often treated with nitrite and nitrate (E249 to E252) during the curing process. More traditional preservatives such as sugar, salt and vinegar are also still used to preserve some foods, for example: sugar in jam and tinned fruit, salt in cheese and vinegar to pickle vegetables.

Foods containing the preservative sodium benzoate (E211) should not be given to toddlers as a recent study has shown that it may have a negative effect on behaviour.

Colours are added to food and drinks to make them look attractive. They are not necessary but are used to give a product a consistent colour. This may be to replace the natural colour lost during food processing or storage.

Colours commonly found in food include caramel (E150a), which is used in products such as gravy and soft drinks, and curcumin (E100), a yellow colour extracted from turmeric roots.

Certain combinations of the following artificial food colours may also be linked to a negative effect on children's behaviour: sunset yellow (E110), quinoline yellow (E104), carmoisine (E122), allura red (E129), tartrazine (E102) and ponceau 4R (E124).

These colours were often used in soft drinks, sweets and ice cream but manufacturers are now in the process of replacing them with alternative colourings.

Avoid any food or drinks containing the following as, recently, concerns that they may affect behaviour have been highlighted by the Food Standards Agency.

Colours: tartrazine E102
ponceau 4R E124
sunset yellow E110
carmoisine E122
quinoline yellow E104
allura red AC E129
Preservative: sodium benzoate E211

EMULSIFIERS, STABILISERS, GELLING AGENTS AND THICKENERS

Emulsifiers such as lecithins (E322), help mix together ingredients that would not normally mix easily, such as oil and water. Oil would normally just rise to the top of water.

Stabilisers, such as locust bean gum (E410) made from carob beans, help stop these ingredients from separating out again.

Emulsifiers and stabilisers also give foods a consistent texture. Most foods containing fat will contain them – for example, low-fat margarines, commercial cakes, biscuits, ice cream and sauces.

Gelling agents are used to change the consistency of food. The most common gelling agent is pectin (E440), which is used to make jam.

Thickeners help give body to food in the same way as adding flour thickens a sauce.

Flavour enhancers are used to bring out the flavour in foods. Monosodium glutamate (E621), known as MSG, is the most well known and it is added to processed foods, especially soups, sauces and sausages. Savoury snacks, ready meals and condiments also contain them.

Sweeteners are often used instead of sugar in products such as fizzy drinks, squash, yoghurt and chewing gum. 'Intense sweeteners', such as aspartame (E951), saccharin (E954) and acesulfame-K (E950) are many times sweeter than sugar and so only very small amounts are used.

It is best to keep sweeteners to a minimum in your toddler's diet. Many drinks contain sweeteners so it is preferable to give your toddler diluted pure fruit juice which does not contain any. Avoid the sweetener sorbitol (E420) as it is often included in quantities that can cause diarrhoea in toddlers.

Functional foods

These are foods with added nutrients that are not necessarily normally contained within that food. Long-standing examples include:

▶ *calcium added to bread*
▶ *vitamins A and D added to margarine.*

Both these additions were instigated in the 1940s during World War 2 to ensure adequate intake of nutrients during the time when certain foods were rationed.

It is now a growth area in the food industry due to the higher consumer interest in health and nutrition. Adding extra nutrients into foods is increasingly becoming part of the marketing strategy for the food industry. Recent examples are the addition of:

▶ *omega 3 fats to margarines, yoghurts, eggs, berry fruit juices, breads, milk, some breakfast cereals and biscuits*
▶ *vitamin D to fromage frais and yoghurt*
▶ *calcium to cereal bars*
▶ *prebiotics and probiotics to yoghurts and milk desserts.*

If you are offering your toddler the balanced diet discussed in Chapter 3, he will be having an adequate intake of nutrients and the extra cost of buying these fortified foods is not justified.

Reading a food label

Food labels can be confusing and although regulated by law, they do not always give you all the information you might like in an easy to understand format. Below is a sample food label, explained.

STRAWBERRY YOGHURT

Added ingredients: sugar, strawberry purée (7.4%), lemon juice, modified starch, flavouring

Nutrition Information

Typical Values	Per 125 g pot	Per 100 g
Energy	124 Kcal/526 KJ	100 Kcal/420 KJ
Protein	6.1 g	4.9 g
Carbohydrate	19.6 g	15.7 g
Of which sugars	19.1 g	15.3 g
Fat	2.4 g	1.9 g
Of which saturates	1.5 g	1.2 g

(Contd)

Typical Values	Per 125 g pot	Per 100 g
Fibre	0.3 g	0.2 g
Sodium	0.1 g	Trace
Calcium	199 mg	159 mg
(per cent RDA)	(24.9 per cent)	(19.9 per cent)

The ingredients are listed in descending order of the weight of each ingredient used in the recipe. In this example, yoghurt is the main ingredient but is not listed as it is included in the title. Sugar is the largest ingredient added and flavouring is the smallest. Because strawberry is mentioned in the name the percentage by weight of strawberries must be given. In this case 7.4 per cent of the weight is strawberry purée.

Information is given as per 100 g of food and also as per portion. Often these are adult portions so you will need to estimate how much your toddler will eat as a portion.

▶ *Protein is expressed in grams.*
▶ *Carbohydrate is expressed in grams and will be the total figure for starch and sugar.*
▶ *'Of which sugars' is expressed in grams and represents the sugar added, plus any natural sugars in the ingredients. In this case it includes the natural milk sugar (lactose) in the yoghurt as well as the natural fruit sugar (fructose) in the strawberry purée. The rest will be the added sugar but it is impossible from this information to work out how much sugar is actually added. It will be more than 7.4 grams as sugar appears above strawberry purée in the ingredients list.*
▶ *Fat is expressed in grams and is the total of saturated, monounsaturated and polyunsaturated. 'Of which saturates' is the amount of saturated fat also given in grams. This fat will be all the fats naturally present in the milk used to make the yoghurt as there are no other ingredients which contain fat.*
▶ *Fibre is measured in grams. It comes from cereals and fruit and vegetables. This small amount will come from the strawberry purée.*

- Sodium is measured in grams. To calculate the equivalent salt content, multiply by 2.5. This small amount is the natural sodium in milk as there is no salt added in making the yoghurt.
- Calcium is also measured in grams. The per cent RDA is the percentage of the recommended dietary allowance for an adult. Young children need less total calcium than adults, so this pot of yoghurt is actually providing 56 per cent of a one- to three-year-olds' daily calcium requirement.

Eating out

Eating out together as a family is now part of our lifestyle. Some restaurants are child friendly, offering high chairs and making families feel welcome. Unfortunately the choice on the children's menu is often disappointing. The choices are usually food that children happily eat because it is familiar food to most of them – usually food that is encased in fried breadcrumbs, such as chicken nuggets and fish fingers. It is usually accompanied by potato chips and no vegetables. Drinks offered are often a choice of fizzy soft drinks. An occasional meal like this will do no harm but if you eat out regularly then you need to find restaurants that will offer more nutritious foods for your toddler.

Restaurants will begin to offer more nutritious foods for toddlers and children if the customers demand it. So don't be reluctant to ask a restaurant:

- to make up a child's portion of choices on the adult menu
- to split a nutritious meal from the adult menu between two children.

Your toddler, who may be very wary of new foods, may eat very little in a restaurant because the foods are all unfamiliar to him. This can be quite frustrating if you are paying for a meal for him. It might be better to give your toddler a small portion of your food from your plate as he may be more likely to eat the food you are eating. He may feel most safe eating something from your plate.

FAST FOOD RESTAURANTS

Meals offered in fast food restaurants are usually not well balanced. Fruit and vegetables are provided in tiny quantities if at all and the main foods are often high in fat, sugar and salt. However, they offer very good value and you may wish to go from time to time, especially if you are with older children who have been won over by the clever marketing campaigns which these companies invest in. If you do take your toddler, make sure you offer nourishing balanced meals during the rest of the day to correct the balance of foods for the day. Offer more fruit and vegetables at those meals.

TEST YOURSELF

1 *Is it worth buying growing-up milks that are more expensive than cows' milk?*

2 *Are organic foods better nutritionally than non-organic foods?*

3 *Will a lot of salty foods make a toddler ill?*

4 *Why should toddlers include cheese, bacon, ham and bread in their food but keep crisps and other salty snack foods to small amounts occasionally?*

5 *Should toddlers avoid saturated fat?*

6 *Do toddlers need 100 per cent of the RDA for each nutrient each day?*

7 *Are E numbers all bad?*

8 *What are the naturally occurring sugars in food?*

9 *Why does a food label not tell you how much sugar has been added to a food?*

10 *How can you compensate for taking your toddler to a fast food restaurant for a meal?*

13

Food safety and hygiene

In this chapter you will learn:
- *the foods that toddlers should avoid*
- *how to prepare and store food safely.*

Toddlers and young children are particularly susceptible to food poisoning and can become very ill quite quickly. Hence it is important to take extra care when preparing and storing food that they will eat.

Foods to avoid

Foods which are more likely to cause food poisoning should not be given to toddlers and young children under about five years of age. These foods include:

▶ *shellfish which is raw or undercooked*
▶ *fish which is raw or undercooked*
▶ *meat which is raw or undercooked*
▶ *raw or undercooked eggs – cook them until the yolk is no longer runny*
▶ *unpasteurized milk, cheese and yoghurt.*

Whole nuts may cause choking or will cause distress if a toddler inhales one. They are not recommended for children under five years.

Foods to limit

Use oily fish up to about four times per week for boys. The Food Standards Agency recommends that girls should be limited to oily fish twice per week, as oily fish can contain low levels of some toxins. These toxins can build up in girls' bodies, which they may retain into their child-bearing years.

Safe preparation of food

To avoid contaminating food with bacteria while preparing it, take the following precautions.

▶ *Wash your hands thoroughly before preparing food.*
▶ *Use clean work surfaces for preparing food.*
▶ *Use separate chopping boards and knives for meat, fish and poultry. Never cut bread, vegetables, fruit or cooked food on a board that has been used for raw meat and fish.*
▶ *Carefully wash fresh fruits, vegetables and salad to make sure all traces of soils and dirt are removed.*
▶ *Make sure all meat, poultry, fish and eggs are cooked thoroughly. For meat, this is when the juices run clear when you put a knife into the thickest part of the meat.*
▶ *Wipe up spilt food straight away.*

Safe storage of food

Once the food is cooked it can be served immediately or cooled and stored in the fridge for up to 48 hours. Food can also be frozen and stored covered in the freezer. Make sure you label the food with the date of preparation so that it is only stored for the length of time recommended for your freezer. Use the following guidelines to ensure safe food storage.

- ▶ Cover foods that are to be stored. Keep dried food in sealed containers and frozen food in airtight containers.
- ▶ Keep the temperature of your fridge at 4°C/40°F and your freezer at or below −18°C/0°F.
- ▶ Hot food should be cooled before putting into your fridge so that it does not cause the temperature inside your fridge to increase.
- ▶ Always store cooked and raw food separately in the refrigerator and store cooked food above raw meat and fish so that there is no chance of raw meat and fish dripping onto cooked food.
- ▶ Don't leave foods in the freezer for too long. Use them in rotation and check the freezer manual to see how long each food can safely be frozen.

Defrosting and reheating food

- ▶ Defrost frozen meats, chicken and fish thoroughly in the fridge before cooking.
- ▶ Thaw cooked, frozen food thoroughly in a covered container in the fridge. Once thawed it can be stored for up to 48 hours in the fridge.
- ▶ Do not refreeze food which was frozen and has been partially or completely thawed.
- ▶ When reheating food, heat it to piping hot before cooling it for serving to your toddler. Stir it thoroughly to make sure it is an even temperature and check that it is cool enough before offering it to your toddler.
- ▶ Do not reheat food more than once – this is particularly important for meat, poultry and fish.

Serving food

- ▶ Wash your hands and those of your toddler before the meal as you will both be handling the food.

- *Plates, bowls, cutlery, cups and glasses do not need to be sterilized but should be scrupulously clean.*
- *Toddlers should be sitting and supervised whenever they are given food and/or drinks. If they are moving around while eating or drinking they are more likely to choke.*
- *Any leftover food that was served to your toddler must be discarded at the end of a meal. The bacteria in his saliva, which can be mixed into the food from his cutlery or fingers, would grow in stored food and could cause illness.*

Insight

Each year many toddlers are rushed to hospital having choked on foods. The most common foods are hard foods like whole nuts or soft round foods that may become easily stuck in their throat. However, eating any food while sitting down reduces the risk of choking considerably.

Commercial foods

- *Always check 'use by' dates on commercial food and never give toddlers food which is out of date.*
- *Follow instructions on the pack for storing and cooking food.*

Picnics and packed lunches

- *When transporting food outside the home, make sure it is in a cool box with an ice pack. Drinks in cartons can be frozen to form an ice pack which will slowly melt and be ready for drinking when it is time to eat.*
- *Keep cool boxes with picnics or packed lunches in the shade or a cool place until you are ready to eat or serve the food.*
- *Wash out cool boxes and food containers when you return home so that food particles do not remain for bacteria to grow on them.*

Barbecues

▶ *Have one set of utensils for raw meat and fish. Use a separate set for serving the cooked meat and fish.*
▶ *Ensure that barbecued meat and fish are well cooked all the way through.*
▶ *Do not give toddlers burnt food from a barbecue.*

Pets

▶ *Keep pets off worktops and out of the kitchen when you are preparing food.*
▶ *Never let pets eat from family plates. Keep pet bowls separately and wash them in hot soapy water after use.*
▶ *Teach your toddler to wash his hands after stroking or handling pets.*

TEST YOURSELF

1 Why are toddlers more susceptible to food poisoning than older children and adults?

2 Which foods should not be served undercooked to toddlers but are suitable for adults?

3 Should toddlers be given unpasteurized milk and cheese?

4 Why should toddlers only be served food when they are sitting?

5 For how long can you safely store thawed cooked food in the refrigerator?

6 Should you refreeze foods that were partly or completely thawed?

7 How often can you reheat food for your toddler?

8 How should you reheat food for your toddler?

9 Why should toddlers avoid whole nuts?

10 Can you offer a meal that your toddler did not finish at a subsequent meal?

14

Beginning nursery

In this chapter you will learn:
- *how your toddler's food intake may change on beginning nursery*
- *that nurseries are not required to adopt any nutritional standards*
- *how parents can influence the food served at nurseries*
- *how to pack a lunch box for nursery.*

When it is time for your toddler to begin nursery or spend time with a childminder, you will have to hand over the responsibility of feeding your toddler to others for at least part of the day. This is a positive step for your toddler to begin to learn about a wider range of foods, different ways of having it prepared and presented. He may have to take more control over feeding himself. He will also see a large peer group eating and will be able to watch and copy their behaviour.

Encountering unfamiliar food at nursery

The foods your toddler encounters at nursery may be quite different from the food you offer him at home. He may be reluctant to try the food served at nursery for some time until he has become familiar with this new environment. He may need to watch the other children eating a snack or a meal several times before he is prepared to try. Don't be alarmed in the early days if the nursery staff report that he has eaten very little. With time, as he becomes familiar with the foods served there and as he watches the other children eating the foods, he will gradually gain the confidence to try the foods and then begin to learn to like them.

Insight

It is common for toddlers who have just begun at nursery to eat very little. It will go on for a longer time with toddlers who are very fussy and faddy about food. In addition, toddlers who are unhappy at nursery may not eat well.

Toddlers who eat poorly at nursery may leave feeling tired and hungry. Offer a nutritious meal as soon as you are home. If your toddler is ready for a sleep then offer a nutritious snack and have a nutritious meal ready soon after he wakes up. You could also offer him second portions of food at meals at home to help him make up for the small amount he may be eating at nursery.

Nutritious snacks you might offer a toddler who hasn't eaten well at nursery:

▶ *slices of fruit with a small cup of milk*
▶ *ham sandwich with cherry tomatoes and a cup of water*
▶ *peanut butter and banana sandwich*
▶ *slices of apple spread with cream cheese*
▶ *pancakes spread with fruit purée and a cup of milk*
▶ *pancakes spread with chocolate spread and a cup of water*
▶ *breadsticks or crackers with cubes of cheese and celery sticks with a cup of water*
▶ *pitta bread with hummus and apple slices with a cup of water*
▶ *muffin with grapes and a small cup of milk*
▶ *crumpet spread with honey and a cup of water*
▶ *scone with butter and jam, clementine segments and a cup of milk*
▶ *yoghurt or fromage frais and fruit slices*
▶ *small piece of fruit cake and a cup of milk*
▶ *small slice of pizza and a cup of water*
▶ *small bowl of breakfast cereal with banana slices and milk*
▶ *toast with peanut butter, carrot sticks and a cup of water.*

Some toddlers eat better at nursery than at home

In contrast, some toddlers who do not eat well at home may eat much better at nursery. If a toddler has had negative experiences around eating at home, he may find he enjoys the eating environment at nursery better. Toddlers who may eat better at nursery could be an only child, may often have been fed on their own or may have experienced some of the negative actions of parents as described in Chapter 6 (for example, they may have been coerced to eat more than they wanted to).

Another reason for eating better at nursery may simply be that your toddler has the opportunity to watch a large group of other toddlers eating foods. He may be more prepared to try new foods in this setting rather than at home, where he sees very few people eating different foods.

Insight

Parents of fussy, faddy eaters often tell me that their toddler eats better at nursery than he does at home.

Nutritional standards for nurseries

There are no nutritional standards governing the food that is served to toddlers in nurseries; a nursery can serve whatever foods it chooses. This is a failing of our education system as a nutritious diet is very important for pre-school children to:

▶ *ensure they eat nutrient-rich foods to fulfil their high requirement for nutrients*
▶ *give them the opportunity to learn to like a wider range of nutritious foods*
▶ *teach them healthy eating habits.*

Some nurseries will have had expert nutritional input in planning their menus; however, others may not. Ask the nursery if you can see their food policy or guidelines on food and ask if it has been reviewed by a registered dietician or a registered nutritionist for nutritional adequacy. Most nurseries will have a food policy but if they do not, offer to help write one and enlist the local community dietician to be involved. If there is no policy in place then you could offer to be part of a working group to look into developing a policy. A working group to develop a policy should include:

▶ *the catering staff*
▶ *local community dieticians*
▶ *teaching staff*
▶ *parents*
▶ *the children (who should be asked about their likes and dislikes).*

If this is not possible, you can recommend the nursery consider using guidelines from any of the following agencies that have developed guidelines using registered dieticians.

Nutritional guidance available for nurseries

Caroline Walker Trust
www.cwt.org.uk

This charity produces nutritional guidelines and staff training packs for different population groups. Their two publications that nurseries would find helpful are:

▶ *Eating well for under-5s in childcare*
▶ *Eating well for under-5s in childcare: Training materials*

The charity also provides photographs of the sorts of food that are suitable for children aged between one and four at www.cwt-chew.org.uk

The Scottish Government
www.scotland.gov.uk/publications

In January 2006 they published:

▶ *Nutritional Guidance for Early Years: Food Choices for Children Aged 1–5 Years in Early Education and Childcare Settings*

These guidelines are very comprehensive, setting out exactly how often various nutritious foods should be offered to children in childcare settings. However, it is not compulsory for nurseries in Scotland to follow them.

National Day Nurseries Association
www.ndna.org.uk

This organization, which has over 15,000 nurseries as members, sells the following two publications that they have developed with the help of a paediatric dietician. They also offer staff training in healthy eating for toddlers.

▶ *Your Essential Guide to Nutrition, Serving Food and Oral Health*
▶ *Your Essential Guide to Cooking Healthy, Tasty Food*

Bedfordshire Health Authority
This health authority has an under-five healthy eating award scheme (www.under5healthyeatingaward.nhs.uk/) that produces a variety of leaflets for nurseries and childminders on nutrition for under-fives.

The London Borough of Bromley
This London borough has published a food and health resource pack for under-fives' settings in Bromley:

▶ *Full of Beans! Food and Nutrition in Nurseries and Pre-Schools*

It can be downloaded from the internet:

www.bromley.gov.uk/education/childcare/full_of_beans_food_and_nutrition_in_nurseries_and_pre_schools.htm

FOOD FOR CELEBRATIONS AT NURSERIES

This is usually covered within the food policy if a nursery has one.

Nurseries that celebrate festivals with some traditional foods for the meal and snacks on the day of the festival offer toddlers the opportunity to learn about the festivals that cultures other than their own celebrate.

Birthday celebrations need to be covered carefully within a food policy. If toddlers are allowed to bring in sweets and confectionery on their birthday to share with their classmates then this can become more than an occasional treat in a large nursery group. With 30 toddlers in a group there may be a birthday every week. It would be better for the nursery to ban sweets altogether and to offer another way of celebrating each toddler's birthday, for example:

▶ *allow the birthday child to bring in balloons or pencils instead*
▶ *allow candles on the pudding at lunchtime for that day for the child whose birthday it is.*

PACKED LUNCHES

If you pack food for your toddler to take to nursery, be sure to include something from each of the four main food groups so that he has a balanced nutritious meal. Follow the ideas in Chapter 4.

Case study

The pupils in a nursery in north-east London come from a wide variety of cultural backgrounds, and parents of many children made dietary specifications. Many requests were for the children not to be given certain types of meat. Some requested no meat as the family only ate halal meat. Other parents were concerned about previous food scares and preferred their children not to have red meat. Some were from vegetarian families.

(Contd)

The nursery thought they had solved the problem by deciding to have a vegetarian menu only so that all the children could eat the same food. I was asked to assess the all-vegetarian menu. The vegetarian dishes were made up from vegetables only, with cheese and eggs being included sometimes. The menu contained virtually no high-iron foods, as no dishes containing pulses or nuts had been included to provide high-iron alternative foods in place of the excluded meat and fish. Consequently the menu offered was low in iron for preschool children who have very high iron requirements.

By working with the nursery we were able to incorporate lentils and beans into many of the vegetarian dishes so that food with higher levels of iron and zinc was offered to the toddlers. Chopped and ground tree nuts were incorporated into some of the desserts so that they would also be richer in iron and zinc.

TEST YOURSELF

1 Why do toddlers sometimes not eat well when they first begin nursery?

2 Why do some toddlers eat better at nursery than at home?

3 Are there any regulations governing the food that nurseries can offer children?

4 Where can a nursery find nutritional guidelines on meals to offer their toddlers?

15

Looking ahead

In this chapter you will learn:
- *why to offer delicious food within a healthy eating plan as your child grows*
- *how to involve your child in food shopping and cooking*
- *about preventing obesity.*

As your toddler grows into a child and begins school, continue to make feeding him a pleasant experience for both of you. Pleasure is important for your child's emotional stability and you can provide this through delicious meals served in a happy atmosphere. Healthy eating can be delicious if you are prepared to plan and allow a little time for food preparation.

Keeping up healthy eating

As your toddler grows into a child, continue to combine the five food groups as described in Chapter 3. He will eat larger portions as he grows but the combination of the food groups should remain roughly the same. You will need to begin giving more fibre than you gave him as a toddler and you can use all wholegrain bread and cereals if you wish, or a larger proportion of wholegrain to white. Limit high-fat foods as he becomes older and keep the addition of oils, butter and margarine to a minimum to keep his overall intake of fat low. Continue to encourage him to have three servings of milk, cheese and yoghurt each day to maintain his calcium intake and good bone health. Many children cut back on this food group as they get older, particularly in their teenage years.

By continuing to feed him a healthy balanced diet you will be reinforcing the messages that a normal balanced diet of foods is based on food from food groups 1 to 4, along with smaller limited amounts for the fifth food group – foods high in fat and sugar. Showing him by example what healthy eating is while he is a child will instil in him this key knowledge to return to when his is older. No matter what he rejects during his rebellious teenage years, he will know what a healthy balanced diet is and can return to it when he has finished with teenage rebelling! The huge advantage to your child of having a good knowledge of healthy eating is that if he follows it as an adult, he will be reducing his risk of developing diabetes, heart disease, cancers and osteoporosis.

Food faddiness will slowly dissipate

With time he will slowly become less wary of new foods and become more adventurous in what he eats. However, he will continue to prefer familiar foods and you will need to encourage him to try new foods. Continue to make positive comments about food and talk about their origin – how and where they are grown and processed. It will be up to you to help him to try new foods and broaden his experience. Eating out in restaurants from different cultures in the UK and while on holidays abroad will help this. Eventually his peer group will have more influence on his food choices but this won't happen until he is a teenager.

Keeping up family meals

Continue to eat together as a family as often as possible. Children who eat on their own can lose sight of what a normal meal is and the amount of food that is normal to eat. Those who develop eating disorders have often not been having family meals and have lost the knowledge of what normal portion sizes are.

Keep to a regular routine of meals and snacks. Children like this and as they become more independent will look forward to the comfort of family meals and familiar foods. Without a meal routine children will resort to snacking as they become more independent about making food choices. Snack foods do not generally provide the same high-nutrient content that meals do.

Snack foods are also higher in calories and do not normally have the balance of some low-calorie foods along with the high-calorie foods. Calorie intake is usually higher for children who snack and graze on food rather than having a routine of meals and planned snacks. This higher calorie intake can lead to obesity.

Shopping

Encourage your child to help you take foods off the supermarket shelves and put them into the shopping trolley. Take him to well laid out market stalls or greengrocers and allow him to choose a fruit or a vegetable – ask the greengrocer to put his choice in a paper bag so that he can carry it home.

Teaching your child to cook

Involve him in as much meal preparation as he can manage – ask him to help with setting the table or counting out foods to go into a bowl, for example: 'Please put four bread rolls into a basket and put it on the table.'

As soon as he is able, ask him to do some of the easy tasks involved in cooking. For example, you can ask him to:

- *weigh out certain quantities of food*
- *mix some ingredients together in a bowl with a wooden spoon*
- *count a certain number of food items into a bowl*
- *carry food to the table*
- *prepare sandwiches*
- *spread a soft food like hummus onto crackers with a blunt knife*
- *choose ingredients and put them on top of a pizza.*

Coping with the preference for sweet food

Children naturally like sweet foods and energy-dense foods which are high in fat and sugar (for example, biscuits, cakes, chocolate, ice cream, pastries and puddings). Most children tend to overeat these foods if given the opportunity, so these foods need to be limited but not completely denied. If you deny your child these foods they will become more desirable as they see other people enjoying them. Include them in small quantities from time to time, especially as part of a celebratory meal. Enjoyment of food and other activities is an important part of your toddler's emotional wellbeing.

Taking care of your toddler's teeth

Keep sugary foods to a maximum of four times per day – for example, all three meals and one snack.

Sugary foods include: sweetened breakfast cereals, puddings, cakes, biscuits, fruit juice, dried fruit, sweets, chocolate and sweetened drinks. Children who have sugary foods more than four times per day are more likely to get tooth decay. Take your toddler to the dentist for regular check-ups.

Preventing obesity

With obesity levels rising in children, it is important to get into the habit of encouraging your toddler to have opportunities for active play every day. Play with your child and help him to improve his physical co-ordination by playing games with him that involve throwing and catching balls, hitting a ball with a bat or racket. This will help him develop the co-ordination he needs to enjoy sports and physical activity as he gets older. Then you will need to help him find sports and physical activities that he enjoys.

Always allow children to eat to their appetite so that they know when they have had enough and they are not overriding the feedback mechanism, when the stomach signals that it is full, so that the brain signals satiety and eating should stop.

Keep foods to mealtimes and planned snacks and don't give high-fat foods such as packets of snacks like crisps to keep him occupied or quiet. Give rewards that are not food and do not use sweets or high-fat foods as treats or as comfort. Using food as comfort can lead to overeating and subsequent obesity.

Extra weight is not just stored fat. The extra fat is metabolically active tissue that causes poor health. Stored fat affects the way insulin and other hormones function and this increases the likelihood of:

▶ *lower levels of fitness*
▶ *increased severity of asthma and other respiratory diseases*
▶ *increased risk of insulin resistance and type 2 diabetes*
▶ *higher incidence of atherosclerosis*
▶ *increased risk of cardiovascular disease*
▶ *increased risk of becoming obese as an adult.*

Most damaging of all are the psychological effects on an obese child. They are more likely to be bullied and have:

▶ *low self-esteem*
▶ *lower quality of life*
▶ *lower academic achievement.*

An overweight child is more likely to be overweight as an adult.

AVOID TALKING ABOUT WEIGHT AND DIETING TO LOSE WEIGHT

If you struggle with your own weight, try not to talk about dieting and weight loss in front of your toddler. Healthy eating and plenty of exercise will be best for you and the best example to set for your child. Children who grow up in families where a parent is continually trying to diet may grow up with a distorted idea of what normal healthy eating should be.

LIMIT CONVENIENCE FOOD

Convenience food and ready meals are usually higher in salt, fat and sugar. They contain smaller amounts of fruit and vegetables than well-planned home-cooked foods. They are now part of everyone's lives and if they are part of your family foods then you will want to use them for your children. Limit them and always serve small portions of them, making up the rest of the meal with some extra fruit and vegetables. This can be simple raw fruits and vegetables that need minimal preparation. They will serve to lower the calorie content of the meal and add extra nutrients that are likely to be low in the convenience foods.

SALT

Do not encourage your children to develop a taste for salty foods by offering them very salty foods and encouraging them to add salt to food at the table. Salt intake needs to be limited to minimize any health problems due to sodium later in life. Lower salt intakes may help prevent a rise in blood pressure as your child gets older. It is better to flavour foods with herbs and spices rather than salt.

Processed foods, which are high in sodium and salt, should be limited and salty snacks such as crisps should be given only occasionally.

FAST FOOD RESTAURANTS

Complete meals offered in fast food restaurants are not well balanced. However, with all the marketing these firms invest in them your children will ask to go there. You are best to set a limit on how often you go – once in each of the school holidays is a good guide. On the days you do go, make sure you offer nourishing balanced meals during the rest of the day to correct the balance of foods for the day. Offer some fruit and vegetables as snacks that day as meals at fast food restaurants contain minimal amounts of fruit and vegetables. Encourage your children to choose pure fruit juice rather than fizzy drinks. If you can, dilute the fruit juice with water to decrease the acid content and the damage this can do to tooth enamel.

TEST YOURSELF

1 Why are family meals so important?

2 How can you teach your children what healthy eating is?

3 Does food faddiness slowly dissipate throughout childhood or remain strongly ingrained in children who are fussy as toddlers?

4 Does sweet food encourage a sweet tooth?

5 How can parents encourage a positive attitude to food?

6 Why is it important to play with toddlers to help them develop their physical co-ordination skills such as catching balls and hitting a ball with a racket?

7 What are the most damaging effects of childhood obesity?

8 What are the physical consequences of childhood obesity?

9 Is healthy eating in childhood the same as healthy eating for toddlers?

10 Should you avoid fast food restaurants?

Taking it further

Further reading

The Big Book of Recipes for Babies, Toddlers and Children,
Bridget Wardley and Judy More, Duncan Baird Publishers, 2004

BUYING AND EATING SEASONAL FOOD

www.eattheseasons.co.uk

Nutrition information

Child nutrition www.child-nutrition.co.uk
Little People's Plates www.littlepeoplesplates.co.uk
Infant and Toddler Forum www.infantandtoddlerforum.org
Nutrition Society www.nutritionsociety.org
The Caroline Walker Trust www.cwt.org.uk
The British Dietetic Association www.bda.uk.com

Nutritional guidelines for nurseries

Caroline Walker Trust produces two helpful publications, available
via their website www.cwt.org.uk.

- ▶ *Eating well for under-5s in childcare*
- ▶ *Eating well for under-5s in childcare: Training materials*

And from their second website www.cwt-chew.org.uk

▶ *Children Eating Well: Food Photographs for Children 1–4 years*

National Day Nurseries Association produces two helpful publications, available via their website www.ndna.org.uk:

▶ *Your Essential Guide to Nutrition, Serving Food and Oral Health*
▶ *Your Essential Guide to Cooking Healthy, Tasty Food*

The Scottish government produces a helpful publication, available via their website www.scotland.gov.uk:

▶ *National Guidance for Early Years: Food Choices for Children Aged 1–5 Years in Early Education and Childcare Settings*

The NHS website contains useful information: www.under5healthyeatingaward.nhs.uk/

The Bromley local government website contains useful information: www.bromley.gov.uk/education/childcare/full_of_beans_food_and_nutrition_in_nurseries_and_pre_schools.htm

---

Food scares

The Food Standards Agency www.food.gov.uk

Twins and triplets

Twins and Multiple Births Association (TAMBA) www.tamba.org.uk

Twins Club www.twinsclub.co.uk

Coping with food allergies and food intolerances

www.allergyaction.co.uk
www.allergyuk.org
www.anaphylaxis.org.uk
www.kidsaware.co.uk
www.medicalert.co.uk
www.medi-tag.co.uk
www.medical-bracelets.co.uk
www.sostalisman.co.uk
www.specialdietsconsulting.co.uk
www.yellowcross.co.uk

Allergy-free food, Wright T., Bounty Books, 2004

Food Allergies: Enjoying life with a severe food allergy (2nd edition), Wright T., Class Publishing Ltd, 2006

Coping with coeliac disease

Coeliac UK www.coeliac.co.uk

Coping with diabetes

Diabetes UK www.diabetes.org.uk

Organic foods and farming methods

Soil Association www.soilassociation.org

Sustain: the alliance for better food and farming
www.sustainweb.org

Meat-free diet

The Vegetarian Society www.vegsoc.org

Parkdale, Dunham Road, Altrincham, Cheshire, WA14 4QG
Tel: 0161 925 2000
www.vegsource.com for vegetarian recipes

Glossary

allergen A substance that causes an immune response.

amino acids A group of compounds which proteins are made up of. Essential amino acids are those that we cannot make ourselves and therefore we must eat them in food. Non-essential amino acids are those that we can make for ourselves if our diets are adequate.

anaphylaxis Severe difficulty breathing and heart malfunction due to a fall in blood pressure, which will eventually lead to collapse. A severe attack could result in death but adrenalin can be administered to restore the body to normal.

Asperger's Syndrome One of several *autism spectrum disorders* (ASD) characterized by difficulties in social interaction and by restricted and stereotyped interests and activities.

atopic Someone who has *atopy*.

atopy A hereditary disorder marked by the tendency to develop immediate allergic reactions to substances such as pollen, food, insect venoms and dander and is manifested by hay fever, asthma, food allergies, eczema or similar allergic conditions.

autism Autistic spectrum disorders (ASD) are a spectrum of psychological conditions characterized by widespread abnormalities of social interactions and communication, as well as severely restricted interests and highly repetitive behaviour.

BMI (Body Mass Index) The ratio of body weight to height. It is calculated by dividing body weight in kilograms by the height in metres squared.

dehydration The condition that results from excessive loss of body water; this may occur due to a high temperature and excessive sweating or diarrhoea and vomiting. It may also be due to normal water losses through skin, breathing, passing water and stools, coupled with an inadequate intake of water.

gag (on food) This happens when food is not successfully swallowed and comes back into the mouth.

gastro-oesophageal reflux See *reflux*.

glucose A form of sugar. Sugar in the blood is always in the form of glucose.

gluten A protein found in wheat, rye and barley. Oats contain a very similar protein.

halal This originates from Arabic, meaning 'lawful', and relates to meat which is acceptable to Muslims. Animals must be ritually slaughtered to provide meat that is halal.

hypoglycaemia Deficiency of glucose in the blood system, meaning blood sugar levels are lower than the normal range.

hyperglycaemia Excess of glucose in the system, meaning blood sugar levels are higher than the normal range.

oesophagus The part of the digestive canal which food and drinks pass through between the throat and the stomach.

PCHR (Personal Child Health Record) In England, this is a red book in which healthcare professionals record details about your child's health, records of immunizations and any measurements of weight, length and head circumference.

pesticides Chemicals including herbicides, insecticides and fungicides used in farming to kill pests.

phenolic compounds A large group of chemicals, some of which are found naturally in foods.

phytonutrients These are substances in plants, which boost the immune system and provide long-term protection against cancer and heart disease. They include the brightly coloured pigments in fruits and vegetables and are also called flavanoids, flavanols and isoflavones.

phyto-oestrogens Plant chemicals that behave the same way in the body as the hormone oestrogen.

prebiotics Fibre that encourages the growth of good bacteria in the intestine.

probiotics Bacteria that are beneficial to the intestines; examples are bifidobacteria and lactobacilli.

protein A complex molecule consisting of a particular sequence of chains of amino acids. Proteins are essential constituents of all living things.

pulses A group of foods that include lentils, peas and starchy beans, but exclude green beans. Examples of starchy beans are chickpeas, black-eye-beans, baked beans, white and red kidney beans, flageolet beans.

red book See *PCHR*.

reflux (or gastro-oesophageal reflux) A painful process when the contents of the stomach flow backwards, up out of the stomach into the oesophagus.

retch To make an involuntary effort to vomit.

salicylates A group of chemicals that include aspirin, some preservatives, and antiseptics. They are also found naturally in certain foods.

stool Evacuated fecal matter passed through the anus, commonly called poo.

Appendix

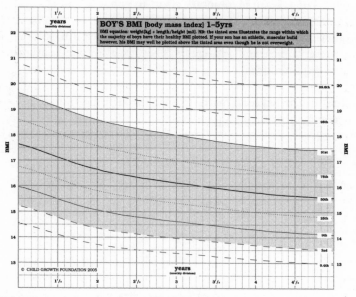

A BMI centile chart for boys. Reproduced with permission of the Royal College of Paediatrics and Child Health, London.

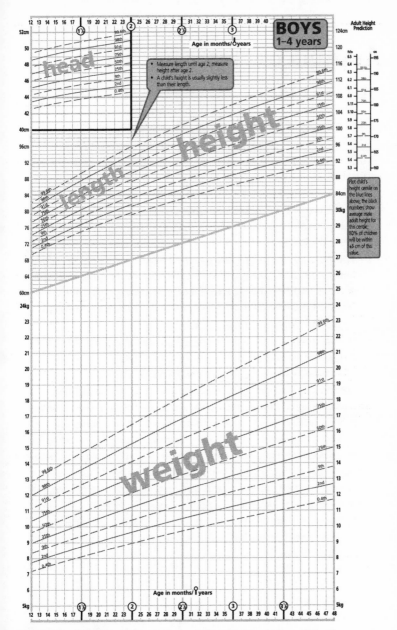

Sample head length, height and weight centile chart for boys. Reproduced with permission of the Royal College of Paediatrics and Child Health, London.

Answers to 'Test yourself' questions

Chapter 1

1 *Only about 2 kilograms per year.*
2 *A lot less than babies in their first year who gain about 6½ kilograms.*
3 *Toddlers do not need to be weighed at all if there are no concerns but if there are concerns do not weigh more frequently than once in three months as the expected weight gain is very small.*
4 *If their height and weight is increasing at the same rate as the centile lines on the growth chart.*
5 *It is a normal stage of their development.*
6 *No, some toddlers eat just about everything.*
7 *The toddler should always be allowed to decide.*
8 *He says no or cries, pushes away the food, turns his head away from the food, spits food out, vomits up food or refuses to swallow food in his mouth or tries to avoid being fed by refusing to go into his seating position or climbing out of it.*
9 *He is not hungry, is scared of eating the food offered, does not like the food offered, is too tired, is distracted or bored with eating. He may not be hungry if he is feeling unwell, is constipated, has iron deficiency anaemia or is sad, anxious or lonely.*
10 *So that he is involved in the meal, can play with the food and become familiar with it, can choose what to eat himself and can stop when he has had enough.*

Chapter 2

1 *Iron, vitamins A and D.*
2 *Yes.*
3 *Oily fish.*
4 *Red meat and liver (but liver should be limited to once per week).*
5 1 *Cleaning teeth with fluoridated toothpaste.*
   2 *Tap water if it has added fluoride or is from an area where water is naturally high in fluoride.*
6 *Food provides very, very small amounts of this vitamin – the main source is from making it in the skin when outside during the summer months when the sunshine is strong enough. Toddlers today are unlikely to spend enough time outside in the summer months to make enough vitamin D in their skin.*
7 *A lot of toddlers do not eat enough vitamin A from food.*
8 *By offering foods from all the four nutritious food groups and giving a vitamin A and D supplement each day.*
9 1 *Bread, rice, potatoes, pasta and other starchy foods.*
   2 *Fruit and vegetables.*
   3 *Milk, cheese and yoghurt.*
   4 *Meat, fish, eggs, nuts and beans.*
10 *No, because fat and/or sugar are found in most nutritious foods. Excess fat and sugar can be avoided by limiting the foods that are high in fat and/or sugar.*

Chapter 3

1 *At each meal and some snacks.*
2 *At each meal and some snacks.*
3 *Three times a day.*
4 *3–4 fl oz/100–120 ml.*
5 *From about 12 months of age, bottles of milk should be replaced with cups of milk of about 3–4 fl oz/100–120 ml.*
6 *Two to three times per day.*

7   *A little each day but these should not replace the more nutritious foods in the other food groups.*

8   *Six to eight drinks of about 3–4 fl oz/100–120 ml.*

9   *Water and milk. Fruit juices if offered should be well diluted.*

10 *Very hot, spicy food; undercooked eggs and shellfish; large fish that live for many years (swordfish, marlin and shark); whole nuts; tea; foods with banned colourings.*

Chapter 6

1   *They may be scared of eating that food, not familiar enough with the food to be confident to eat it, bored of eating that food or they may not like the taste of the food.*

2   *They usually become anxious and worry that their toddler is not eating enough.*

3   *Parents usually think their toddler will get ill and not grow properly.*

4   1   *It is up to the parent to offer nutritious meals and snacks.*
    2   *It is up to the toddler to choose what and how much he eats.*
    3   *Each meal should be a social and enjoyable occasion.*

5   *No, as the toddler may begin to reject meals if they prefer the snack or drink they are subsequently given as a meal replacement.*

6   *Their behaviour may get worse initially as they test out the limits of their parents' new behaviour.*

7   *Parents should persist with the changes.*

8   *Large drinks of sweet liquids including milk fill toddlers up and reduce their appetite for other foods at mealtimes.*

9   *When toddlers are behaving well.*

10 *Take the food away without any negative comments. Do not give any alternative food (unless it is the second planned course) until the next planned meal or snack.*

Chapter 7

1 1 *Toddlers who did not have a lot of experience at eating different textured foods when they were between 6 and 12 months.*

   2 *Toddlers who are very reluctant to accept change and move onto eating new foods.*

2 *Specialized feeding teams can help uncover the reasons why a toddler is very fussy about food and help parents decide which strategies can be used to cope with the problem and slowly resolve it.*

3 *Babies learn to like different tastes and textures of food relatively quickly between 6 and 12 months of age. Later than that the learning process takes much longer.*

4 *Sweet soft foods.*

5 *They need to be offered most of their food in the textures they can manage but should also be offered foods from the food texture group that is slightly more challenging so that in time they can learn to eat foods of that texture and become ready to move onto trying foods from the next level.*

6 *Boys.*

7 *Toddlers who do not like:*
  ▷ *getting their hands dirty and face sticky*
  ▷ *walking barefoot on textured surfaces such as sand and grass*
  ▷ *wearing certain clothes and prefer certain colours and fabric textures.*

8 *Offer messy play sessions.*

9 *These toddlers do not necessarily copy the behaviour of others and so will not copy their eating behaviour so taking much longer to learn to eat a wider variety of foods.*

10 *They are reluctant to accept change and prefer to eat just the foods with which they are familiar.*

Chapter 8

1 *Meat and poultry.*
2 *Meat, poultry and fish.*
3 *Meat, poultry, fish and eggs.*
4 *All animal products including milk and milk products.*
5 *No, because they do not provide sufficient nutrients for toddlers.*
6 *It is better to continue on formula milk until about two years old as formula milks are enriched with certain key nutrients that are likely to be low in vegetarian diets.*
7 *Iron.*
8 *To provide all the essential amino acids needed for first-class protein. Neither nuts, pulses nor starchy foods contain all the essential amino acids.*
9 *Vitamin C increases the absorption of iron from these foods.*
10 *Rapeseed oil as it is very high in omega 3 fats.*

Chapter 9

1 *Iron deficiency.*
2 *Red meat, dark poultry meat and breakfast cereals that are fortified with iron.*
3 *Toddlers who are drinking too much milk and consequently eating fewer foods containing iron.*
4 *The Body Mass Index centile that is calculated using the weight and height.*
5 *They live in a family that does not have a healthy lifestyle.*
6 *By having sugary food and drinks more than four times a day and/or frequently drinking acidic and sweet drinks such as undiluted fruit juice and other sweet drinks.*
7 *Going to bed with a bottle of a sweet drink.*
8 *Beginning laxatives.*
9 *Toddlers with dark skins whose mothers did not take vitamin D supplements during pregnancy.*
10 *There is no strong evidence to support this theory.*

Chapter 10

1 *There is no clear answer but it is probably a combination of changes in our environment, food supply and lifestyles.*
2 *Some people produce IgE, and the reaction between the protein in the food they are allergic to and the IgE produces symptoms very rapidly. Symptoms appear much more slowly in those that do not produce IgE.*
3 *Around three years old.*
4 *About two in 100.*
5 *They need to avoid foods containing gluten which is a protein found in wheat, rye and barley. Sometimes they also need to avoid oats.*
6 *Milk, eggs, fish, shellfish, peanuts, tree nuts, wheat, soya and sesame.*
7 *Only those toddlers who are likely to have an anaphylactic reaction.*
8 *By taking the suspected food out of a toddler's diet and seeing the symptoms disappear and then seeing the symptoms reappear when the food is reintroduced.*
9 *After they are three years of age but definitely before they begin school.*
10 *A food allergy is a reaction in the immune system to a protein in food whereas a food intolerance is a non-immune reaction to chemicals in food that are not proteins.*

Chapter 11

1 *To keep their blood sugar down to normal levels.*
2 *The amounts of carbohydrate in the food eaten have to balance with the insulin given to diabetic toddlers.*
3 *The blood sugar level is higher than normal.*
4 *The blood sugar level is lower than normal.*
5 *Pallor, mood swings, irritability, headache, hunger, fatigue, being unco-operative or confused, and eventually losing consciousness and fitting.*

6   Rub some glucose gel onto his gums or if he is co-operative give him a sugary drink or food.

7   Foods that contain gluten which is found in wheat, rye and barley. Some toddlers also need to avoid foods containing oats.

8   Toddlers with cystic fibrosis absorb less energy and nutrients from food than normal so need to eat more to compensate.

9   Supplements of pancreatic enzymes.

10   Toddlers who are unable to eat and drink enough of normal food and drinks. It is usually because they feel too ill to eat and drink adequately.

Chapter 12

1   No, because toddlers who are eating well will be getting all the nutrients they need from their food and their vitamin A and D supplement.

2   No, there is no difference in the nutrient content of organic compared to non-organic foods except for a possible minimal difference in vitamin C and folic acid.

3   No, but it is best not to encourage a preference for only foods flavoured with a lot of salt.

4   Cheese, bacon, ham and bread provide significant amounts of key nutrients whereas salty snack foods such as crisps do not.

5   No, saturated fat does not cause elevated cholesterol levels in toddlers.

6   No, RDA is for adults and does not apply to toddlers. RNIs for one- to three-year-olds indicate the amount of a nutrient that a toddler needs daily.

7   No, some are nutrients, such as vitamin C.

8   Lactose in milk, fructose in fruit and maltose in starchy foods.

9   Because the total amount of sugar includes the naturally occurring sugars in food – lactose, fructose and maltose.

10   Make the other meals and snacks that are offered that day extra nutritious by including more fruit and vegetables and no fried food.

Chapter 13

1 *They are more likely to become seriously ill with food poisoning.*

2 *Raw or undercooked meat, fish, shellfish and eggs.*

3 *No, they are more likely to become ill with unpasteurized milk and milk products.*

4 *They are more likely to choke on food if they are moving around while eating.*

5 *48 hours.*

6 *No.*

7 *Only once.*

8 *Heat to piping hot, stir thoroughly to make sure the temperature is even throughout and then check to make sure it has cooled to a suitable temperature for your toddler to eat.*

9 *If inhaled they cause distress and they may cause choking.*

10 *No, any food that a toddler did not eat at one meal should be discarded because the leftover food will have a higher bacterial content from the bacteria in saliva. These bacteria will multiply during storage.*

Chapter 14

1 *Toddlers take some time to begin eating unfamiliar meals.*

2 *They may be happier to eat at nursery if nursery mealtimes are more positive experiences than mealtimes at home – particularly if there is less pressure on them to eat a certain quantity or certain foods.*

3 *Currently in England, Wales, Scotland and Northern Ireland there are no regulations that must be adhered to.*

4 *These are available in some localities but nurseries can develop their own and ask a qualified dietician or nutritionist to check them for suitability.*

Chapter 15

1 *Children who eat family meals frequently tend to eat a more nutritious diet as snacking usually involves foods of lower nutritional quality.*

2 *By eating healthy balanced meals yourself and always offering them the same.*

3 *It slowly dissipates throughout childhood in the vast majority of children.*

4 *No, because children are born with a preference for sweet food and this remains throughout their lives.*

5 *Involve children in shopping and cooking and make all mealtimes pleasant occasions. Have as many family meals together as possible.*

6 *Developing physical co-ordination early in life helps toddlers enjoy sports and a more active lifestyle in later life.*

7 *The psychological effects. Overweight and obese children are more likely to be bullied, and have lower self-esteem, quality of life and academic achievement.*

8 *Lower levels of fitness, increased severity of asthma and other respiratory diseases, increased risk of diabetes, heart disease and orthopaedic problems.*

9 *It is similar in that the same combination of the five food groups forms the basis of healthy eating. The small differences are that the portion sizes will get larger as children grow and they can cope with a higher fibre diet.*

10 *Not altogether but as the meals offered are usually high in fat and low in fruit and vegetables you need to make sure the other meals offered on the same day are low in fat and high in fruit and vegetables.*

Index